1/21/10
45.00

Bloom's Literary Themes

⌒⌖⌒

Alienation
The American Dream
Civil Disobedience
Dark Humor
Death and Dying
Enslavement and Emancipation
Exploration and Colonization
The Grotesque
The Hero's Journey
Human Sexuality
The Labyrinth
Rebirth and Renewal
Sin and Redemption
The Sublime
The Taboo
The Trickster

Bloom's Literary Themes

THE SUBLIME

Bloom's Literary Themes

THE SUBLIME

Edited and with an introduction by
Harold Bloom
Sterling Professor of the Humanities
Yale University

Volume Editor
Blake Hobby

BLOOM'S
LITERARY CRITICISM
An imprint of Infobase Publishing

Bloom's Literary Themes: The Sublime

Copyright ©2010 by Infobase Publishing
Introduction ©2010 by Harold Bloom

Bloom's Literary Criticism
An imprint of Infobase Publishing
132 West 31st Street
New York NY 10001

Library of Congress Cataloging-in-Publication Data
The sublime / edited and with an introduction by Harold Bloom ; volume editor, Blake Hobby.
    p. cm.—(Bloom's literary themes)
  Includes bibliographical references and index.
  ISBN 978-1-60413-443-8 (hc : alk. paper)
  1. Sublime, The, in literature.   I. Bloom, Harold.   II. Hobby, Blake.   III. Title.
  IV. Series.
  PN56.S7416S83 2010
  801—dc22
                                                    2009053494

Bloom's Literary Criticism books are available at special discounts when purchased in bulk quantities for businesses, associations, institutions, or sales promotions. Please call our Special Sales Department in New York at (212) 967-8800 or (800) 322-8755.

You can find Bloom's Literary Criticism on the World Wide Web at
http://www.chelseahouse.com

Series design by Kerry Casey
Cover design by Takeshi Takahashi
Composition by IBT Global, Inc.
Cover printed by IBT Global, Inc., Troy NY
Book printed and bound by IBT Global, Inc., Troy NY
Date printed: February 2010
Printed in the United States of America

10 9 8 7 6 5 4 3 2 1

Contents

Series Introduction by Harold Bloom:
Themes and Metaphors

1. TOPOS AND TROPE

What we now call a theme or topic or subject initially was named a *topos*, ancient Greek for "place." Literary *topoi* are commonplaces but also arguments or assertions. A topos can be regarded as literal when opposed to a trope or turning, which is figurative and which can be a metaphor or some related departure from the literal: ironies, synecdoches (part for whole), metonymies (representations by contiguity) or hyperboles (overstatements). Themes and metaphors engender one another in all significant literary compositions.

As a theoretician of the relation between the matter and the rhetoric of high literature, I tend to define metaphor as a figure of desire rather than a figure of knowledge. We welcome literary metaphor because it enables fictions to persuade us of beautiful untrue things, as Oscar Wilde phrased it. Literary *topoi* can be regarded as places where we store information, in order to amplify the themes that interest us.

This series of volumes, *Bloom's Literary Themes*, offers students and general readers helpful essays on such perpetually crucial topics as the Hero's Journey, the Labyrinth, the Sublime, Death and Dying, the Taboo, the Trickster, and many more. These subjects are chosen for their prevalence yet also for their centrality. They express the whole concern of human existence now in the twenty-first century of the Common Era. Some of the topics would have seemed odd at another time, another land: the American Dream, Enslavement and Emancipation, Civil Disobedience.

I suspect though that our current preoccupations would have existed always and everywhere, under other names. Tropes change across the centuries: The irony of one age is rarely the irony of another. But the themes of great literature, though immensely varied, undergo transmemberment and show up barely disguised in different contexts. The power of imaginative literature relies upon three constants: aesthetic splendor, cognitive power, wisdom. These are not bound by societal constraints or resentments, and ultimately are universals, and so not culture-bound. Shakespeare, except for the world's scriptures, is the one universal author, whether he is read and played in Bulgaria or Indonesia or wherever. His supremacy at creating human beings breaks through even the barrier of language and puts everyone on his stage. This means that the matter of his work has migrated everywhere, reinforcing the common places we all inhabit in his themes.

2. CONTEST AS BOTH THEME AND TROPE

Great writing or the Sublime rarely emanates directly from themes since all authors are mediated by forerunners and by contemporary rivals. Nietzsche enhanced our awareness of the agonistic foundations of ancient Greek literature and culture, from Hesiod's contest with Homer on to the Hellenistic critic Longinus in his treatise *On the Sublime*. Even Shakespeare had to begin by overcoming Christopher Marlowe, only a few months his senior. William Faulkner stemmed from the Polish-English novelist Joseph Conrad, and our best living author of prose fiction, Philip Roth, is inconceivable without his descent from the major Jewish literary phenomenon of the twentieth century, Franz Kafka of Prague, who wrote the most lucid German since Goethe.

The contest with past achievement is the hidden theme of all major canonical literature in Western tradition. Literary influence is both an overwhelming metaphor for literature itself and a common topic for all criticism, whether or not the critic knows her immersion in the incessant flood.

Every theme in this series touches upon a contest with anteriority, whether with the presence of death, the hero's quest, the overcoming of taboos, or all of the other concerns, volume by volume. From Monteverdi through Bach to Stravinsky, or from the Italian Renaissance through the agon of Matisse and Picasso, the history of all the arts demonstrates the same patterns as literature's thematic struggle with itself. Our country's great original art, jazz, is illuminated by what the great creators called "cutting contests," from Louis Armstrong and Duke Ellington on to the emergence of Charlie Parker's bop or revisionist jazz.

A literary theme, however authentic, would come to nothing without rhetorical eloquence or mastery of metaphor. But to experience the study of the common places of invention is an apt training in the apprehension of aesthetic value in poetry and in prose.

Volume Introduction by Harold Bloom

Shelley, who is a touchstone for the lyrical Sublime, remarked that the function of the Sublime was to persuade us to abandon easier for more difficult pleasures.

The history of the critical Sublime goes from the Hellenistic Longinus to Freud and beyond, since Freud's "the Uncanny" is our modern form of the Sublime.

After nearly six decades of writing Longinian criticism, I have learned that the literary Sublime can be exemplified but not defined. Longinus memorably located the Sublime in Homer and in Sappho, but also in the Hellenistic translation of the Hebrew God commanding Creation.

Shakespeare's sublimity is the richest and most varied in all literary history. Surely its heights-of-heights are the great personalities: Falstaff, Hamlet, Rosalind, Othello, Iago, Lear, Cleopatra. They are sublime because they expand our consciousness without distorting it. To meditate upon them is to apprehend greatness—negative and positive—and so share in the potential for greatness in ourselves.

Here are some touchstones for the lyrical Sublime in modern poetry:

> The season changes. A cold wind chills the beach.
> The long lines of it grows longer, emptier,
> A darkness gathers though it does not fall
>
> And the whiteness grows less vivid on the wall.
> The man who is walking turns blankly on the sand.
> He observes how the north is always enlarging the change,

With its frigid brilliances, its blue-red sweeps
And gusts of great enkindlings, its polar green,
The color of ice and fire and solitude.

I knew that I had seen, had seen at last
That girl my unremembering nights hold fast
Or else my dreams that fly
If I should rub an eye,

And yet in flying fling into my meat
A crazy juice that makes the pulses beat
As though I had been undone
By Homer's Paragon

Who never gave the burning town a thought;
To such a pitch of folly I am brought,
Being caught between the pull
Of the dark moon and the full,

The commonness of thought and images
That have the frenzy of our western seas.

By the road to the contagious hospital
under the surge of the blue
mottled clouds driven from the
northeast—a cold wind. Beyond, the
waste of broad, muddy fields
brown with dried weeds, standing and fallen

patches of standing water
the scattering of tall trees

All along the road the reddish
purplish, forked, upstanding, twiggy
stuff of bushes and small trees
with dead, brown leaves under them
leafless vines—
Lifeless in appearance, sluggish
dazed spring approaches—

They enter the new world naked,
cold, uncertain of all
save that they enter. All about them
the cold, familiar wind—

The bell-rope that gathers God at dawn
Dispatches me as though I had dropped down the knell
Of a spent day—to wander the cathedral lawn
From pit to crucifix, feet chill on steps from hell.

Have you not heard, have you not seen that corps
Of shadows in the tower, whose shoulders sway
Antiphonal carillons launched before
The stars are caught and hived in the sun's ray?

The bells, I say, the bells break down their tower;
And swing I know not where. Their tongues engrave
Membrane through my marrow, my long-scattered score
Of broken intervals . . . And I, their sexton slave!

Oval encyclicals in canyons heaping
The impasse high with choir. Banked voices slain!
Pagodas, campaniles with reveilles outleaping—
O terraced echoes prostrate on the plain!

And so it was I entered the broken world
To trace the visionary company of love, its voice

An instant in the wind (I know not wither hurled)
But not for long to hold each desperate choice.

These passages, in sequence, are from Wallace Stevens, W. B. Yeats, William Carlos Williams, and Hart Crane. Meditate upon them deeply enough and you will apprehend the Sublime.

THE AWAKENING
(KATE CHOPIN)

"*The Awakening*: Waking Up at the End of the Line"
by Barbara Claire Freeman, in *The Feminine Sublime: Gender and Excess in Women's Fiction* (1995)

INTRODUCTION

In her chapter on Kate Chopin's *The Awakening*, Barbara Freeman first takes issue with Longinus's famous articulation of the sublime in the poetry of Sappho. Freeman does so in order to point out what she calls significant "misreadings" and to elucidate what she believes Longinus both misses and obscures: the feminine form of the sublime, which Sappho and Chopin share, one in which "going close to death" marks "the limits of the representable." For Freeman, "Sappho's lyric and Chopin's novel both describe what occurs in response to hearing a beloved voice," a "singular event that engenders shock or crisis." Both Sappho and Chopin offer ecstatic moments from which it is impossible to extract any one authentic meaning, refusing "to satisfy the wish for a single or definitive interpretation" and, in doing so, constructing a

Freeman, Barbara Claire. "*The Awakening*: Waking Up at the End of the Line." *The Feminine Sublime: Gender and Excess in Women's Fiction*. Berkeley, CA: U of California P, 1995. 13–39, 153–160.

sublime that cannot be contained in Longinus's conception of
the sublime as a unified whole.

∽෴෴

The sublime does not so properly persuade us, as it ravishes and
transports us, and produces in us a certain Admiration, mingled
with Astonishment and with Surprize, which is quite another
thing than the barely pleasing, or the barely persuading: that it
gives a noble Vigour to a Discourse, an invincible Force, which
commits a pleasing Rape upon the very Soul of the Reader.
(John Dennis, *The Grounds of Criticism in Poetry*)

You can't make a political "program" with it, but you can bear
witness to it.—And what if no one hears the testimony, etc.?
(Jean-François Lyotard, *The Differend*)

Love is lak de sea. It's uh movin' thing, but still and all, it takes its
shape from de shore it meets, and it's different with every shore.
(Zora Neale Hurston, *Their Eyes Were Watching God*)

These waters must be troubled before they can exert their virtues.
(Edmund Burke, *A Philosophical Enquiry into the
Origin of our Ideas of the Sublime and Beautiful*)

Longinus cites only one female poet in his influential *Peri Hypsous*
(On the sublime), the first-century treatise whose fame was revived by
Boileau's French translation and commentary of 1674.[1] That poet, of
course, is Sappho of Lesbos (early sixth century B.C.), and Longinus
chooses her lyric *phainetai moi* to illustrate his view that literary excellence depends upon the writer's ability to harmonize differences and
create an organic whole.[2] Anticipating the New Critic's demand that
the perfect poem, like a "well-wrought urn" or "verbal icon," achieve
the status of an autonomous unit, Longinus praises Sappho's ability
"in selecting the outstanding details and making a unity of them"
(10.1) as particularly exemplary of sublime writing. What is striking,
however, is the disparity between Sappho's poem and Longinus'
interpretation of it. Whereas the lyric describes an experience of
total fragmentation when the speaker hears her lover's "sweet voice"
(10.1), Longinus commends Sappho's skill in creating the illusion of

wholeness: according to him, she is able to join diverse parts in such a way that "they co-operate to form a unity and are linked by the bonds of harmony" (40.1).

Given this poem's crucial role in establishing Longinus' account of the sublime, it is worth examining in some detail. I cite versions of the poem as it appears in two eminent and recent translations of Longinus, the first by D. A. Russell, the second by G. M. A. Grube.[3]

> To me he seems a peer of the gods, the man who sits
> facing you and hears your sweet voice
> And lovely laughter; it flutters my heart in my breast.
> When I see you only for a moment, I cannot speak;
> My tongue is broken, a subtle fire runs under my skin;
> my eyes cannot see, my ears hum; Cold sweat pours off me;
>   shivering
>   grips me all over; I am paler than grass;
> I seem near to dying; But all must be endured ... (10.2)

The translation in Grube's edition renders the last two stanzas as follows:

> Yea, my tongue is broken, and through and through me
> 'Neath the flesh, impalpable fire runs tingling;
> Nothing see mine eyes, and a noise of roaring
> Waves in my ears sounds;
>
> Sweat runs down in rivers, a tremor seizes
> All my limbs and paler than grass in autumn,
> Caught by pains of menacing death, I falter,
> Lost in the love trance (10.2)

And here, in Russell's translation, is Longinus' commentary:

> Consider Sappho's treatment of the feelings involved in the madness of being in love. She uses the attendant circumstances and draws on real life at every point. And in what does she show her quality? In her skill in selecting the outstanding details and making a unity of them ... Do you not admire the way she brings everything together—mind and body, hearing

and tongue, eyes and skin? She seems to have lost them all, and to be looking for them as though they were external to her. She is cold and hot, mad and sane, frightened and near death, all by turns. (10.1–3)

Longinus' insistence that the poem's sublimity resides in its representation of unity, its ability to connect disparate elements and "bring everything together," is especially puzzling given that Sappho seems so little concerned with univocity. Longinus values the poem because he believes it achieves precisely the opposite of what in fact it does: despite his assumption that its excellence depends upon Sappho's skill in replacing the diverse with the singular, there is little, if any, textual evidence for his celebration of homogeneity. Sappho juxtaposes such apparent dualisms as life and death, hot and cold, or sanity and madness not, as Longinus would have it, in order to create harmony, but rather to unsettle the notion of organic form upon which his notion of the sublime depends. Rather than unify the disparate, Sappho foregrounds the activity of self-shattering. Instead of warding off fragmentation, she insists upon it. It is as if the goal of Longinus' commentary were to domesticate and neutralize the very excessiveness Sappho's text bespeaks.

My principal concern, however, is not with the strength or weakness of Longinus' literary criticism. I wish instead to examine the function Sappho's lyric plays in Longinus' treatise in order to suggest that his is a paradigmatic response to the irruption of a threatening and potentially uncontainable version of the sublime, one that appears to represent excess but does so only the better to keep it within bounds. The move Longinus makes in relation to Sappho is particularly instructive since, as we shall see, later theorists echo it time and time again. Longinus' commentary on Sappho plays a constitutive role in the sublime's theorization by shaping the ways in which the subject's encounter with excess, one of the sublime's most characteristic and enduring features, may and may not be conceptualized.[4] Neil Hertz's brilliant "Reading of Longinus," which is itself representative of late twentieth-century American theorists' commitment to a romantic (or Wordsworthian) sublime, continues this tradition by repeating the very same scenario.[5] Hertz not only recuperates an instance of difference in a literary text and reads it as forming a unified whole; perhaps more important, he constructs a theory of the sublime that perpetuates its tactic of exclusion.

This chapter's exploration of significant misreadings in the history of the sublime, along with the role and place of gender in producing that history, will let us look at ways in which the sublime might be written otherwise, were that dimension not repressed. Kate Chopin's novel *The Awakening* amplifies and elucidates precisely those elements of the sublime that Sappho foregrounds and Longinus obscures. *The Awakening*, which stands at the dawn of twentieth-century American women's fiction and brings forward some of its basic preoccupations and themes, also suggests a particular version of the feminine sublime, here understood not as a transhistorical or universal category, but rather as the attempt to articulate the subject's confrontation with excess in a mode that does not lead solely to its recuperation. At stake in Chopin's novel is the very "transport" (*ekstasis*) Sappho inscribes, a "going close to death" that marks the limits of the representable. Here the sublime is no longer a rhetorical mode or style of writing, but an encounter with the other in which the self, simultaneously disabled and empowered, testifies to what exceeds it. At issue is not only the attempt to represent excess, which by definition breaks totality and cannot be bound, but the desire for excess itself; not just the description of, but the wish for, sublimity.

I

As Chopin remarks, "The beginning of things, of a world especially, is necessarily vague, tangled, chaotic, and exceedingly disturbing."[6] We begin with a discussion of Longinus not only because, as the author of the first treatise on the sublime, he defines the set of problems that will coalesce under this name, but because his treatment of Sappho is paradigmatic of the kinds of disturbances that are at the very heart of the sublime's theorization. In order to grasp the significance of his response to Sappho, however, we need to understand Longinus' view of sublimity, the better to ask in what ways Sappho's lyric both exemplifies and undercuts it.

First and foremost, the sublime is a certain kind of linguistic event, a mode of discourse that breaks down the differences and involves a merger between speaker (or writer) and hearer (or reader). "Sublimity," according to Longinus, "is a kind of eminence or excellence of discourse" (1.3). It is not an essential property of language but rather makes itself known by the effect it produces, and that effect is one of ravishment; as Russell puts it, "whatever *knocks the reader out is sublime*" (xiii). Sublime language disrupts everyday consciousness: "great writing . . . takes the reader out of himself"; it "tears everything up like a whirlwind, and exhibits the orator's whole power at a single blow" (1.4).[7] The sublime utterance, which itself attempts to represent excess, also involves its production: it is accompanied by a threefold identification between speaker, message, and listener in which the latter comes "to believe he has created what he has only heard" (7.2). This identification displaces the identity of its participants and is characteristic of the moment of *hypsous*, that state of transport and exaltation that for Longinus is the mark of sublimity. One of the defining features of sublime discourse is its ability to blur customary differences between speaker and hearer, text and reader. As Suzanne Guerlac points out, "this paradoxical moment is presented by the text as being both the effect and the origin of the sublime, which engenders itself through 'impregnating' the soul of the listener."[8]

Unlike the listener's experience of discourse that seeks merely to please or to persuade, the effect of sublime language entails a certain loss of control. Longinus emphasizes that the sublime "produces ecstasy rather than persuasion in the hearer" and insists that this "combination of wonder and astonishment always proves superior to the merely persuasive and pleasant. This is because persuasion is on the whole something we can control, whereas amazement and wonder exert invincible power and force and get the better of every hearer" (1.4). The discourse of the sublime, then, is integrally bound up with the subject's responses to what possesses it, to the nature and effects of such a merger, and to the ways in which various forms of identification may be understood. At stake is the question of how to theorize ravishment.

Although Longinus never explicitly confronts this issue, his treatise suggests (or is most frequently read as if it suggested) that the moment of *hypsous* becomes a struggle for dominance between opposing forces, an almost Darwinian contest in which the strong flourish and the weak are overcome.[9] For the sublime not only produces an identification between speaker and audience but entails a modification in relations of power between the parties involved, and the diversity of ways in which such modifications may be conceptualized is at the heart of critical debates regarding the sublime.[10] Bloom's theory of the anxiety of influence has as its origin Longinus' precept, itself borrowed from Hesiod, that "strife is good for men" (13.4). The orator attempts to possess the auditor in much the same way that the poet wishes to transport the reader; the view of creativity as bound up with the quest for mastery and ownership shapes Longinus' view of literary production itself. Poets struggle amongst themselves to best one another: even Plato would not have attained greatness without the need to show his superiority to his rival Homer, for he could not have "put such a brilliant finish on his philosophical doctrines or so often risen to poetical subjects and poetical language, if he had not tried, and tried, wholeheartedly, to compete for the prize against Homer, like a young aspirant challenging an admired master" (13.4). Many contemporary American theorists of the sublime reinforce this claim.[11] Thomas Weiskel, for example, insists that "discourse in the *Peri Hypsous* (*on Great Writing*) is a power struggle," while according to Paul Fry, "the Longinian sublime appears in a climate of antagonism, as rivalry between authors."[12]

But if the sublime is, to borrow Fry's phrase, always "a drama of power" and "a struggle for possession," I must stress what Longinus and the majority of his critics do not: that the kind of power at stake in Sappho's lyric differs in important respects from the other examples Longinus cites as illustrative of the sublime.[13] For Sappho's ode affirms a form of possession that redefines traditional modes of domination and relations of power. By exploring the differences between Sappho's ode and Homer's—since he is the other poet Longinus chooses to exemplify "excellence in selection and organization" (10.1)—we will see that Sappho's lyric offers an alternative to Longinus's belief that the sublime entails a struggle for domination in which one party submits to another, and that his misreading of Sappho has significant consequences for the sublime's theorization.

For Longinus, who believes that "sublimity will be achieved if we consistently select the most important of those inherent features and learn to organize them as a unity by combining one with another" (10.1), the ability "to select and organize material" is one of the factors that "can make our writing sublime" (10.1). Comparing Sappho's skillful description of "the feelings involved in the madness of being in love" (10.1) with Homer's talent for portraying storms, he especially praises the latter's skill in depicting "the most terrifying aspects" (10.3). And both poems provide impressive examples of realistic description. Sappho conveys precisely what "lovers experience"

(10.3); "she uses the attendant circumstances and draws on real life
at every point" (10.1); the result of her art is "that we see in her not
a single emotion, but a complex of emotions . . ." (10.3). Indeed, their
similar gift for accurate representation prompts Longinus' comparison
of the two poets. Like Sappho, Homer is a genius because he is able
to choose the details that will convey the essence of an experience.
Longinus cites a passage in which Homer likens Hector to a storm at
sea as exemplary:

> He [Hector] fell upon them [the Greeks] as upon a swift
>   ship falls a wave,
> Huge, wind-reared by the clouds. The ship
> Is curtained in foam, a hideous blast of wind
> Roars in the sail. The sailors shudder in terror:
> They being carried away from under death, but only just.
>   (10.5)

Sappho and Homer share the ability to select and combine the
most disparate elements of an awesome event in order to present a
complete, unified portrait of it. But Longinus implies that the two
poets have more in common than rhetorical or stylistic facility: he
also suggests that each poet is concerned to describe a version of the
same experience, as if the terror of almost dying at sea were the same
as almost dying of love. This assumption, however, conflates two very
different kinds of near-death experiences and ignores a crucial distinction between the kind of death, or perhaps more important, the kind
of ecstasy, at stake. Sappho's and Homer's lyrics may be alike in that
both depict the speaker's encounter with death, but they do not exhibit
the same concern with self-preservation. While Homer writes about
escaping death, Sappho describes the process of going toward it. And
whereas the Homeric hero either wins or loses, lives or dies, Sappho's
protagonist can only "win" by losing and "death" becomes one name
for a moment of *hypsous* whose articulation eludes any literal description. Sappho, unlike Homer, is not concerned with strife or combat,
nor does her poem support the notion that the sublime entails the
defeat of death. Moreover, the kinds of power relations about which
she writes do not involve dominance, in which one identity subjugates
another, but a merger in which usually separate identities conjoin. Such
a junction displaces the ordinary meaning of "possession" wherein one

either owns or is owned, and instead suggests that the poet/lover can possess that by which she is also possessed.

Sappho's lyric thus articulates a version of sublimity that differs radically from the Longinian sublime of power and rivalry. In so doing, it foregrounds what Longinus and subsequent theorists ignore: the deployment of agency to intensify and underscore the wish for dispossession, and to recognize in the scene of self-dispersal a site of self-empowerment. What is particularly striking about the poem, to echo Chopin's phrase, is Sappho's affirmation of the need for "the unlimited in which to lose herself" (29). But whereas Sappho's poem refuses any binary formulation of life and death, Longinus' commentary, like Homer's lyric, reinforces their separation, and we shall see that Longinus' repression of a certain heterogeneous and irreconcilable desire has far-reaching consequences in the history of the sublime's theorization.[14]

[...]

III

Words at their most sublime have the force and feel of water. The ocean is *The Awakening*'s central character, the axis around which the narrative turns. From the beginning it is represented as a linguistic presence, possessing a voice that speaks to Edna's soul. What it says simultaneously resists and impels symbolization. Unlike the green and yellow parrot whose voice inaugurates the novel by mechanically repeating the same unintelligible phrase and who, Chopin tells us, speaks "a language which nobody understood" (3), the sea speaks the language of the unsayable.[15] Its voice, "seductive, never ceasing, whispering, clamoring, murmuring, inviting the soul to wander for a spell in abysses of solitude; to lose itself in mazes of inward contemplation" (15), necessarily partakes of many tongues and reaches Edna "like a loving but imperative entreaty" (14). Perhaps because the ocean possesses a multitude of voices, the command it proscribes is never reducible to any single precept or act.

The sound of the ocean haunts the novel. Like a lover's half-forgotten touch, it betokens absence; indeed, it is a carrier of absence, giving Edna—or whoever hears it—access to a certain kind of knowledge. Hearing it, for example, implies the ability to hear the sound of "wake" within "awakening" and thus to recognize that the same word can signify both life and death, for "wake" simultaneously denotes consciousness of life and a funeral rite, a collective ritual for the dead. (There is a wake within *The Awakening*, but it takes place before Edna's death, at a feast she gives as a gift to herself.) That the same word has contradictory meanings, or means contradiction, points to the irreconcilable coexistence of opposites without the possibility of resolution. Signs of life are equally signs of death, and hearing the ocean's voice impels knowledge of their proximity.

Chopin consistently refuses a dualistic formulation of the relation between life and death, sleeping and waking, or pleasure and pain, and in so doing radically alters a Homeric (or romantic) view of the sublime in which the protagonist's encounter with a potentially overwhelming obstacle leads to heightened powers and a resurgence of life. Displacing the notion that the sublime attests to a polarization of opposites is the novel's insistence upon their co-implication. The voice of the sea indicates polarities only to combine them. Although, for example, Edna perceives the sea's touch as "sensuous, enfolding the body in its soft, close embrace" (15), its waves also "sway," "lash," and "beat upon her splendid body" (27). Chopin thus implies that what lulls may just as easily lash, that what soothes also inflames, and that nursery songs can kill.

Sappho's lyric and Chopin's novel both describe what occurs in response to hearing a beloved voice. In *The Awakening*, as in *phainetai moi*, hearing the other's voice makes something happen: it is a singular event that engenders shock or crisis. The novel's beginning thus reproduces Longinus' description of the unique relation between orator and auditor at play in the sublime, in which the hearer's (or reader's) identification with the speaker (or text) allows the latter to imagine that he "has created what he has merely heard" (1.4). The rapport between Edna and the ocean's voice replicates not only that between orator and auditor in the Longinian sublime, but that between lover and the beloved in Sappho's poem: hearing its address inaugurates a desire where previously there was none. In this case the reader hears through Edna's ears, and what she hears is the ocean.

Chopin's representation of the ocean continually emphasizes its independence from the domain of vision. It is significant, for example, that Edna hears it for the first time in total darkness. Wakened after midnight by the return of her husband, Léonce, Edna sits alone on the porch and suddenly hears "the everlasting voice of the sea, that was not uplifted at that soft hour," a voice that breaks "like a mournful lullaby upon the night" (8). Absence of light allows awareness of a kind of presence one does not need eyes to discern: the sea's "mournful voice" breaks like a lullaby, a song sung by mothers to comfort their children and send them to sleep, as if its capacity to offer solace suggests a relation between the representation of absence and a distinctly aural register.

Throughout the history of the sublime the sea has often served as its most appropriate, if not exemplary, metaphor; and it is worth recalling some traditional representations of this relation the better to understand just how dramatically Chopin's construction of the oceanic sublime differs from them. In both Longinus and Burke, the sea is a major source of sublime sentiment. For Longinus the ocean's majesty is self-evident: he holds that "a natural inclination . . . leads us to admire not the little streams, however pellucid and however useful, but the Nile, the Danube, the Rhine, and above all, the Ocean" (42, Russell). For Burke the ocean is so appropriate a symbol of sublimity that he chooses it to illustrate the precept that "whatever therefore is terrible, with regard to sight, is sublime too" (53). Our differing responses to the sight of "a level plain of a vast extent on land" and to the "prospect of the ocean" show that the latter "is an object of no small terror" in a way that the plain, despite its vastness, is not: the ocean's capacity to arouse terror is the source of both its power and its sublimity (53–54). In Schopenhauer the ocean actually outranks all other forms of natural display. Transfixed and uplifted by its sight, the "undismayed beholder" watches "mountainous waves rise and fall, dash themselves furiously up against steep cliffs, and toss their spray high into the air; the storm howls, the sea boils, the lightning flashes from black clouds, and the peals of thunder drown the voice of the storm and sea." Indeed, Schopenhauer holds that such oceanic immensity yields "the most complete impression of the sublime."[16] In each case, however, the ocean's sublimity is bound up with vision: the sea is something a detached observer looks at, usually from afar. That Edna is transfixed by the ocean's sound rather than its sight is important because here Chopin revises typical constructions of the oceanic sublime. Edna transgresses Kant's injunction that "we must be able to view (it) as poets do, merely in terms of what manifests itself to the eye [*was der Augenschein zeigt*]—e.g., if we observe it while it is calm, as a clear mirror of water bounded only by the sky; or, if it is turbulent, as being like an abyss threatening to engulf everything."[17] Edna's relation to the ocean would, according to Kant, be neither poetically nor philosophically correct: merely looking at the sea holds no particular interest for her. She has a natural, if untutored, aptitude for painting and "a serious susceptibility to beauty" (15), yet only the ocean's voice and touch affect her. Chopin's oceanic sublime is not something "we must regard as the poets do, merely by what the eye reveals," but rather functions as a mode of address.[18] As in Sappho, sublime encounters are occasioned by something heard.

Edna's first encounter with the sublime is marked by an identification with what she hears. The sound of the ocean's "everlasting voice," which disrupts the everyday world she has taken for granted, speaks a language radically different from any she has previously heard and it leaves a mark: "an indescribable oppression, which seemed to generate in some unfamiliar part of her consciousness, filled her whole being with a vague anguish. It was like a shadow, like a mist passing across her soul's summer day" (8). Sound tears and Edna has been torn. Thus begins her awakening.

Learning to swim is merely its continuation. Although hearing the ocean's voice awakens her desire, Edna does not venture into it until she has been touched by another kind of sound, namely, by one of Chopin's preludes. Listening to music composed by the artist whose name replicates the author's own is a prelude to immersion in that which she has heard. Passion comes in waves that sway the soul, but sound also gives rise to waves and hearing them precedes Edna's awakening.

Toward the end of a festive midsummer soirée, Robert Lebrun arranges for Mademoiselle Reisz, a renowned but eccentric pianist, to play for the assembly. Hearing the prelude has a dramatic effect on Edna: usually music "had a way of evoking pictures in her mind" (26), but now she sees nothing; what she hears possesses and overcomes her. That Edna's most profound encounters are occasioned by what she hears suggests that hearing may entail entanglement in a way that seeing does not. For hearing, as Gerald C. Bruns reminds us, is not the spectator's mode:

> The ear is exposed and vulnerable, at risk, whereas the eye tries
> to keep itself at a distance and frequently from view (the private
> eye). The eye appropriates what it sees, but the ear is always
> expropriated, always being taken over by another ('lend me your

ears'). The ear gives the other access to us, allows it to enter us, occupy and obsess us ... hearing means the loss of subjectivity and self-possession ... [and] puts us in the mode of being summoned, of being answerable and having to appear.[19]

Bruns's gloss on Heidegger's *On The Way To Language* also applies to Edna's response to Chopin: "the very first chords which Mademoiselle Reisz struck upon the piano sent out a keen tremor down Mrs. Pontellier's spinal column ... she waited for the material pictures which she thought would gather and blaze before her imagination. She waited in vain. She saw no pictures of solitude, of hope, of longing, or of despair" (27).

How to say something that cannot be said, that confronts us with the inability to present it? The problem that has occasioned the discourse and theory of the sublime is the same as that posed by *The Awakening*: the difficulty of symbolizing an excess that resists visual or linguistic formulation but is there nonetheless. Edna's experience of what Hertz would call "blockage"—her inability to translate sense-impressions into images—calls for a radically different mode of perception, but one that does not lead to an enhanced sense of self. Adorno's conviction that music's value resides in its ability to call "for change through the cryptic language of suffering" is enacted by the prelude's effect on Edna: she trembles, chokes, is blinded by tears, and then, as if to seek deeper knowledge of the "cryptic language" she has heard, she learns to swim.[20] The figurative parallel between the prelude, whose notes arouse passion in her soul, and the ocean, whose waves like music beat upon her body, is established just before Edna, with the other guests, walks down to the ocean and swims for the first time.

Edna's first swim is neither an attempt to appropriate the ocean's power nor a submission to it. It does not represent a struggle for dominance over a force that, as in Homer, has the power to engulf her, but rather, as in Sappho, allows a relation to "the unlimited" in which she seeks "to lose herself" (29). Swimming offers a way of entering awareness; finding her "self" is, paradoxically, a matter of entering the water of the Gulf of Mexico and learning how to lose that which she has found:

> That night she was like the little tottering, stumbling, clutching child, who all of a sudden realizes its power, and walks for the

first time alone, boldly and with over-confidence. She could
have shouted for joy. She did shout for joy, as with a sweeping
stroke or two she lifted her body to the surface of the water ...
she turned her face seaward to gather in an impression of space
and solitude, which the vast expanse of water, meeting and
melting with the moonlit sky, conveyed to her excited fancy. As
she swam she seemed to be reaching out from the unlimited in
which to lose herself. (28–29)

Learning to swim also entails awareness that the ocean can be lethal.
Swimming too great a distance from the shore and at the limits of
her strength, Edna experiences a "flash of terror"; "a quick vision of
death" smites Edna's soul but she manages to regain the land.[21] She
perceives her experience as an "encounter with death" (29) yet makes
no mention of it.

Nor do most of Chopin's critics. For although, as Sandra Gilbert
and Susan Gubar point out, "in the past few decades *The Awakening*
has become one of the most persistently analyzed American novels,"[22]
surprisingly few critics have discussed the role of the ocean and its
voice, an omission made all the more startling given Chopin's insistence upon it.[23] Dale Bauer, Sandra Gilbert, Susan Gubar, and Patricia
Yaeger discuss the ways in which the sea functions as a metaphor for
Edna's awakening, yet none of these critics recognize that it is also
a metaphor for language itself. Nor are they attuned to the ways in
which Edna's newly awakened desire must also be understood as a
desire for the sublime.

[...]

IV

Critics of *The Awakening* continue to be perplexed by the nature of
Edna's desire. As Walter Benn Michaels argues convincingly, what is
most confusing about the novel is not that Edna's desires are frustrated,
but rather that so many of them are fulfilled: as he points out, the narrative "is marked by Edna's inability ... to reshape her own ability to get
what she wants."[24] And Edna's wishes do appear to be granted without
apparent effort on her part. She wants to become an artist and quickly
finds a market for her work; longs for freedom from her husband,
children, and domestic routine and soon has personal and financial

independence; desires sexual adventures and has them; indeed, the only thing Edna wants and does not get is Robert's love, but the reader suspects that had he not left her she would have left him, that frustration rather than fulfillment conditions her desire. The view of Edna as suffering somewhat narcissistically from the "problem" of getting nearly everything and everyone she wants draws support from her own assessment of her capacity to desire: "there was no one thing in the world that she desired. There was no human being whom she wanted near her except Robert; and she even realized that the day would come when he, too, and the thought of him would melt out of her existence, leaving her alone" (113). Edna's world seems simultaneously to offer her nothing she can want at the same time that it satisfies her every whim, and Michaels's assessment of the novel's conclusion, in which he holds that Edna's suicide "may best be understood neither as the repudiation of a society in which one can't have all the things one wants nor as an escape from a society in which one can't want all the things one can have but as an encounter with wanting itself" (498), would appear irrefutable. I argue, however, that understanding Edna's desire within the context of the sublime offers an alternative to this interpretation.

What does "an encounter with wanting itself" entail? On the one hand, Michaels implies that such an encounter signals the death of desire. Getting what you want means no longer being able to want it, for desire's satisfaction implies its annihilation. Seen in this light, Edna's desire can be understood only as an addiction to the unavailable, as a never-ending quest for something new to want. But Michaels also suggests another interpretation of such an encounter, "in which the failure of one's desire for things and people need not be understood as exhausting all desire's possibilities" (498). Basing his second account upon Edna's remark to Dr. Mandelet that "I don't want anything but my own way," he implies that Edna's desire "can survive both the presence and the absence of any desirable things" (498) but is nonetheless doomed to failure because it is separated from the realm of subjects and objects. Seen in this light, Edna's problem is not her inability to desire, but her "submersion in it and idealization of it, an idealization that immortalizes desire by divorcing it both from the subject (which dies) and the object (which is death) that it seems to require" (498–99). In either case, for Michaels "an encounter with wanting itself" entails an encounter with death. The specificity of Edna's desire, however, redefines both of Michaels's accounts; Edna's "encounter with wanting itself" is unintelligible unless we explore what Michaels ignores: her wish for "the unlimited in which to lose herself." For although, as Michaels points out, "no body in Chopin can embody the infinite" (499), Edna desires precisely what she cannot embody.

What, or perhaps more important, how does Edna want? In *The Awakening* fulfillment entails not satisfaction but prolongation; it is neither a matter of getting what one wants (independence, money, sexual freedom, etc.) nor of removing desire from the realm of contingency. Rather, it involves a certain relation to excess, one that requires the representation or "embodiment" of that which one cannot possess. What Michaels fails to notice is that Edna's encounter with desire is simultaneously an encounter with language, here embodied by the ocean's voice, and that she wants the ocean's "everlasting voice" because it alone signifies that which is in excess of any boundary or limit. Like the bluegrass meadow that "she traversed as a child, believing that it had no beginning or end" (114), the ocean offers itself as sustaining a relation to that which she cannot represent. Given the choices available to her, the "fulfillment" of Edna's desire can only be merger, and presumably death, in the element that first awakened it. And although Edna wants to maintain a relation to what the ocean represents, her world offers nothing beyond the satisfaction of her demands. In this case, then, "desire gives birth to its own death" (496) because death within the force that awakened desire is all that remains for Edna to want. By the end of the novel there remains "no one thing in the world that she desired" (113)—a situation that comes about not because she is now incapable of wanting nor because she wants too much. The "object" of Edna's desire is neither a person nor a thing but a sustained relation to the ocean and everything it signifies.

To make what is unnameable appear in language itself—the desire at stake in the sublime is akin to Edna's desire for the ocean's voice: both defy the subject's representational capacities and can be signified only by that which, to borrow Lyotard's formulation, "puts forward the unpresentable in presentation itself," seeking "new presentations not in order to enjoy them but to impart a stronger sense of the unpresentable."[25] At issue is not a mastery of the ineffable, as in Hertz's and Weiskel's account of the romantic sublime, but rather an attestation to the unspeakable and uncontainable elements within language itself. This version of the sublime contests what Weiskel contends is the "essential claim of the romantic sublime: that man can, in feeling and speech, transcend the human" (3). Indeed, Edna wants the opposite: to find in "the unlimited" not a site of self-transcendence but rather a means of self-loss.

Edna's final swim—her going (and coming) "close to death"—must be understood both within the context of her initial encounter with the ocean and as the consequence of having awakened to desire in a social and political milieu that, as Gilbert and Gubar so rightly suggest, offers no means of articulating and sustaining her capacity for desire.[26] When, at the end of the novel, Edna tells Doctor Mandelet "perhaps it is better to wake up after all even to suffer, rather than to remain a dupe to illusions all one's life" (110), nowhere does her culture allow a means of representing her connection to the voice by which she has been called. In this context Edna's love for Robert bears no relation to his availability but rather results from his ability to manifest and facilitate her connection to the other. He is the only character attuned to Edna's need for the unlimited and until his departure for Mexico he is central to her intensifying relationship with it. Edna wants Robert because he sustains rather than satisfies her desire.

If Sappho's lyric ends by representing a merger that conflates the difference between any two sets of terms without at the same time annihilating their difference, so the end of *The Awakening* underscores the proximity and irreconcilability of opposites. Offering disparate accounts of Edna's walk into the ocean, Chopin first compares Edna to a crippled bird whose disabled wings make flying, or, in this case, living, impossible. Standing at the edge of the Gulf, Edna sees that "a bird with a broken wing was beating the air above, reeling, fluttering, circling disabled down, down to the water" (113), images that lead us to interpret Edna's last swim as a sign of her failure to survive in an oppressive world. But Chopin proceeds to suggest just the opposite. Before going into the sea, Edna removes her old bathing suit: she casts "the unpleasant, pricking garments from her, and for the first time in her life she stood naked in the open air, at the mercy of the sun, the breeze that beat upon her, and the waves that invited her" (113). Standing naked under the sky Edna feels "like some new-born creature, opening its eyes in a familiar world that it had never known," reversing the earlier connotation in which she saw that "all along the white beach, up and down, there was no living thing in sight" (113). As in Sappho's lyric, Chopin maintains the residue within language that is unhearable at the same time that she finds a new idiom for presenting its voice. But Edna's last walk into the ocean does not institute "a new idiom" in the sense that it puts speech in the place of silence (thus upholding the view that language is merely a vehicle of communication). Rather her response bears witness to the incommensurable voice she has heard. This is a "going close to death" that cannot simply be rendered by a phrase but to which phrases can testify nevertheless. Chopin's construction of the ocean's voice and the woman's response presents itself as one example of such an idiom: as a figure for the sublime, the ocean is also a figure for the unfigurable.

The novel's final paragraph, which describes Edna's last moments of consciousness, continues to foreground contradiction:

> She looked into the distance, and the old terror flamed up for an instant, then sank again. Edna heard her father's voice and her sister Margaret's. She heard the barking of an old dog that was chained to the sycamore tree. The spurs of the cavalry officer clanged as he walked across the porch. There was the hum of bees, and the musky odor of pinks filled the air. (114)

Chopin insists upon the disparate. Images of triumph—looking into the distance, vanquishing "the old terror"—coincide with symbols of authority and oppression, and then give way to sensory impressions that can be construed in neither context: the "hum of bees, and the musky odor of pinks." As Jane P. Tompkins remarks:

> Contradictory signs are everywhere.... The sight of an injured bird implies defeat, but Edna's shedding of her bathing suit signals rebirth. The act of swimming out so far seems both calculated and almost unconsciously performed. Edna's final vision, as she goes under, is sensual and promising, Whitmanesque, but qualified by images of a chain and spurs.[27]

But whereas Tompkins chastises Chopin for leaving the reader at sea in ambiguity, Chopin's conclusion foregrounds the very incommensurability Edna desires but cannot represent. Concluding the novel by placing images that apparently exclude one another in a relation of mutual interdependence, Chopin refuses to satisfy the wish for a single or definitive interpretation of Edna's last act, and in so doing constructs a sublime in which there is no end of the line.

NOTES

1. For a brief discussion of the text's authorship and history see *"Longinus" on Sublimity*, trans. D. A. Russell (Oxford: Clarendon, 1965), x–xii. See also the introduction and notes accompanying Russell's edition of the Greek text *"Longinus" on the Sublime* (Oxford: Clarendon, 1964). Following Neil Hertz, I have also consulted another recent translation, G. M. A. Grube's *Longinus on Great Writing* (New York: Bobbs-Merrill, 1957). Unless otherwise noted all further references to Longinus are to Russell's translation and occur in the text.
2. Sappho's famous ode is preserved only through inclusion in Longinus' treatise. For a discussion of Longinus' and Boileau's treatment of the poem, see Joan Dejean, *Fictions of Sappho: 1546–1937* (Chicago: University of Chicago Press, 1989), 84–87.
3. The reader may wish to read Sappho's ode in the original Greek and then compare Julia Dubnoff's literal translation of it with those provided by Russell and Grube:

> That man to me seems equal to the gods,
> the man who sits opposite you
> and close by listens
> to your sweet voice
>
> and your enticing laughter—
> that indeed has stirred up the heart in my breast.
> For whenever I look at you even briefly
> I can no longer say a single thing,
>
> but my tongue is frozen in silence;
> instantly a delicate flame runs beneath my skin;
> with my eyes I see nothing;
> my ears make a whirring noise.
>
> A cold sweat covers me,
> trembling seizes my body,
> and I am greener than grass.
> Lacking but little of death do I seem.
>
> But all must be endured since . . .

I have relied upon the versions of Sappho that appear in Russell and Grube primarily because these are the translations Neil Hertz cites, and it is his particular reading of Sappho's lyric that is the object of this critique.

4. Peter De Bolla interestingly defines sublime discourse as discourse that produces the very excessiveness it purports to describe (*The Discourse of the Sublime: Readings in History, Aesthetics, and the Subject* [New York: Basil Blackwell, 1989], 12): "the discourse of the sublime . . . is a discourse which produces, from within itself, what is habitually termed the category of the sublime and in doing so it becomes a self-transforming discourse. The only way in which it is possible to identify this newly mutated discursive form is via its propensity to produce to excess. . . . Hence the discourse on the sublime, in its function as an analytic discourse or excessive experience, became increasingly preoccupied with the discursive production of the excess."

5. Neil Hertz, *The End of the Line: Essays on Psychoanalysis and the Sublime* (New York: Columbia University Press, 1985), 1–20. Subsequent references are to this edition and occur in the text.

6. Kate Chopin, *The Awakening*, ed. Margaret Culley (New York: Norton, 1976), 15. Subsequent references are to this edition and occur in the text.

7. Grube, *Longinus on Great Writing*, 4.

8. Suzanne Guerlac, *The Impersonal Sublime: Hugo, Baudelaire, Lautréamont* (Stanford: Stanford University Press, 1990), 3. Guerlac emphasizes that the Longinian sublime is not "merely rhetorical" but "occurs as a force of enunciation determined neither by subjective intention nor by mimetic effect" (11). Thus, she argues, "the Longinian emphasis on the act of enunciation, and, in particular, the call for the dissimulation of figurative language, is incompatible with the mimetic structure of metaphor that is at the basis of the analyses of the romantic sublime" (194). Unlike Weiskel, for whom the sublime functions as a transcendent turn, Guerlac finds in the sublime "the site within the metaphysical tradition, and within the tradition of aesthetics, of resistance to mimesis, to metaphorical recuperation or 'resolution' and to aesthetics" (194–95); see 182–93 for Guerlac's discussion of Weiskel's *Romantic Sublime* (which I cite in note 12).

9. Ronald Paulson ("Versions of a Human Sublime," *New Literary History* 16, no. 2 [Winter 1985]: 427) points out that while "studies of the sublime, from Burke to Monk and Hipple, used to focus on the enumeration of qualities in the sublime object or, more precisely, as they are reflected in the mind of the spectator . . . in the last decade, mediated by Nietzsche and Freud, by Harold Bloom and Thomas Weiskel, the focus has shifted to the agon between subject and object. The former is both/either a participant within a sublime confrontation and/or a spectator without."

10. Longinus' assumption that the sublime entails a transformation of conventional power relations anticipates Burke's famous dictum: "I know of nothing sublime which is not some modification of power" (Edmund Burke, *A Philosophical Enquiry into the Origin of our Ideas of the Sublime and Beautiful*, ed. Adam Phillips [Oxford: Oxford University Press, 1990], 59).

11. See in particular Harold Bloom, *The Anxiety of Influence* (New York: Oxford University Press, 1973). For Bloom the poet achieves sublimity only through overcoming the threat represented by the work of a "strong" precursor poet. In addition to Neil Hertz and Thomas Weiskel, recent proponents of this view include Marc W. Redfield who, in a provocative analysis of Fredric Jameson's notion of a postmodern sublime ("Pynchon's Postmodern Sublime," *PMLA* 104, no. 2. [March 1989]: 152), argues that the sublime moves "from a threatening diffusion of signs toward a more structured conflict, which enables a self to prop itself up, so to speak, on its own anxiety, reading the confirmation of its existence in the image of its threatened destruction." In the same issue of the *PMLA*, R. Jahan Ramazani reaffirms the view that the sublime entails confrontation and/or struggle between opposing forces ("Yeats: Tragic Joy and the Sublime," *PMLA* 104, no. 2 [March 1989]: 164). Drawing upon the accounts of Hertz and Weiskel, he interprets the sublime "as a staged confrontation with death" in which "the anticipation of death gives rise to a counterassertion of life." For Ramazani "death precipitates the emotional turning called the sublime, although theorists of the sublime often refer to death by other names, or by what Kenneth Burke terms 'deflections': nothingness, castration, physical destruction,

semiotic collapse, defeat by a precursor, and annihilation of the
ego. Death is the recurrent obsession for these theorists, from
Longinus to Heidegger and Bloom."

12. Thomas Weiskel, *The Romantic Sublime: Studies in the Structure
    and Psychology of Transcendence* (Baltimore: Johns Hopkins
    University Press, 1976), 5; Paul H. Fry, "The Possession of the
    Sublime," *Studies in Romanticism* 26, no. 2 (Summer 1987):
    188.

13. Fry, "Possession of the Sublime," 189–90. See also Fry's
    discussion of Longinus' treatment of Sappho in "Longinus
    at Colonus," in *The Reach of Criticism: Method and Perception
    in Literary Theory* (New Haven: Yale University Press, 1983),
    47–86.

14. A discussion regarding Longinus' commentary on Sappho
    occurs between Suzanne Guerlac and Frances Ferguson in *New
    Literary History* 16, no. 2 (Winter 1985), the issue entitled "The
    Sublime and the Beautiful: Reconsiderations." Although their
    dispute does not directly engage Sappho's portrait of desire or
    Longinus' reaction to it, it does address a closely related topic:
    the status of the subject and the kind of subjectivity at stake
    in the Longinian sublime. Does the sublime as represented by
    Longinus threaten or uphold the "unified self-identity of the
    subject" (275)? Guerlac and Ferguson propose very different
    answers, but both explore the question by examining Longinus'
    reading of Sappho.

    In the article "Longinus and the Subject of the Sublime,"
    Guerlac argues that theorists who emphasize pure "force
    of feeling" and who read Longinus from an exclusively
    phenomenological point of view "obscure a more radical force
    at work in the Longinian sublime, one which threatens the
    very notion of the subjectivity, or the unified self-identity of
    the subject" (275). Guerlac proposes to read *On the Sublime*
    "in terms of a 'rhetoric' of enunciation, instead of expression"
    in order to show that in the Longinian sublime "the subject
    of feeling, or the 'aesthetic' subject, is disrupted as well as
    the subject of certainty or the theoretical subject" (275). The
    success of Guerlac's argument depends upon her discussion
    of Longinus' treatment of Sappho. She argues that what

Longinus appreciates in the poem of Sappho "is clearly not a representation of unity, or of a unified body. The body is portrayed as broken, fragmented" (282). Rather, Longinus appreciates "the force of enunciation" through which Sappho is able to portray, and ultimately unify, the fragmented body. In Guerlac's view it is this "force of enunciation which unifies these fragments, combin[ing] them into a single whole; embodying the text and the body—which now serves as a figure for the unity of composition of the text" (282). Although Guerlac appears to challenge the notion that the sublime implies (or helps construct) a unified subject, she does not question the prevailing view that the Longinian sublime entails the achievement of textual unity or dispute his reading of Sappho's lyric. Like Longinus', Guerlac's reading represses Sappho's emphasis on semiotic and erotic transport and reiterates the view that the sublime text functions as an antidote to division. Guerlac's "force of enunciation" repairs, not underscores, fragmentation and helps to maintain textual unity, if it is not indeed equivalent to it. For if the effect of figurative language is to give the semblance of unity, how can it follow that "there is no stable ground or truth or sincerity in the event of sublimity, which, through a force of enunciation, disrupts the stable identity of the subject" (285)? Unity remains the master trope whether the "force of enunciation" or the subject produces it; Guerlac now ascribes to it the unity and power previously ascribed to the subject.

Guerlac fails to notice precisely what Ferguson remarks in her elegant article, "A Commentary on Suzanne Guerlac's 'Longinus and the Subject of the Sublime'": "the capacity of rhetoric to produce what we might call 'a subjectivity effect'" (292). Ferguson argues that although Guerlac substitutes rhetoric for subjectivity and ascribes to the former the function previously reserved for the latter, nothing has really changed. What difference, Ferguson asks, does it make if the *subject* is divided when *language* is not? "Figurativity thus comes in aid of the notion of unity, in substituting for the shattered bodily unity a figurative wholeness. What is thus disconnected in one register is unified in another" (293).

While it would be extremely interesting to know Guerlac's response to Ferguson's remarks, particularly noteworthy in this context is that their debate centers on Longinus' reading of Sappho.

15. The phrase "language of the unsayable" derives from the title of the book edited by Sanford Budick and Wolfgang Iser, *Languages of the Unsayable: The Play of Negativity in Literature and Literary Theory* (New York: Columbia University Press, 1989).

16. "Selections from *The World As Will and Idea*," Book 111, section 39, in *Philosophies of Art and Beauty: Selected Readings in Aesthetics from Plato to Heidegger*, ed. Albert Hofstadter and Richard Kuhns (New York: The Modern Library, 1964), 464.

17. Immanuel Kant, *Critique of Judgment*, section 29, trans. Werner S. Pluhar (Indianapolis: Hackett, 1987), 130. Subsequent references are to this edition and will appear in the text, along with German terms from the original (*Kritik der Urteilkraft*, ed. Wilhelm Weischedel [Frankfurt: Suhrkamp, 1974]) that I add to show that Kant talks about sacrifice and uses concepts of power and subordination to explain the function of the imagination. For an intriguing discussion of this passage, see Paul de Man, "Phenomenality and Materiality in Kant," in *Hermeneutics: Questions and Prospects*, ed. Gary Shapiro and Alan Sica (Amherst: University of Massachusetts Press, 1984), 132–35.

18. For an insightful discussion of the oceanic sublime, see Steven Z. Levine, "Seascapes of The Sublime: Vernet, Monet, and the Oceanic Feeling," *New Literary History* 16, no. 2 (Winter 1985): 377–400.

19. Gerald L. Bruns, "Disappeared: Heidegger and the Emancipation of Language," in *Languages of the Unsayable: The Play of Negativity in Literature and Literary Theory*, ed. Sanford Budick and Wolfgang Iser (New York: Columbia University Press, 1989), 127–28.

20. Theodore W. Adorno, cited in Bruns, "Disappeared," 144.

21. Edna's "flash of terror" of course recalls Burke's dictum that "terror is in all cases whatsoever either more openly or latently the ruling principle of the sublime" (*Enquiry*, 54). [...]

22. Sandra M. Gilbert and Susan Gubar, *Sex Changes*, vol. 2 of *No Man's Land: The Place of the Woman Writer in the Twentieth Century* (New Haven: Yale University Press, 1989), 98. Subsequent references are to this edition and occur in the text.

23. Some of the influential readings of *The Awakening* that do not discuss the ocean's role or "voice" include Margaret Culley, "Edna Pontellier: 'A Solitary Soul,'" in her edition of *The Awakening*, 224–28; Anne Goodwin Jones, "Kate Chopin: The Life Behind the Mask," in *Tomorrow is Another Day: The Woman Writer in the South, 1859–1936* (Baton Rouge: Louisiana State University Press, 1981), 135–82; Susan J. Rosowski, "The Novel of Awakening," *Genre* 12 (Fall 1979): 313–32; George M. Spangler, "Kate Chopin's *The Awakening*: A Partial Dissent," *Novel* 3, no. 3 (Spring 1970): 249–55; Margit Stange, "Personal Property: Exchange Value and the Female Self in *The Awakening*," *Genders*, no. 5 (July 1989): 106–119: Ruth Sullivan and Stewart Smith, "Narrative Stances in Kate Chopin's *The Awakening*," *Studies in American Fiction* 1, no. 1 (1973): 62–75; Lawrence Thornton, "*The Awakening*: A Political Romance," *American Literature* 52, no. 1 (March 1980): 50–66; Paula A. Treichler, "The Construction of Ambiguity in *The Awakening*: A Linguistic Analysis," in *Women And Language in Literature and Society*, ed. Sally McConnell-Ginet, Ruth Borker, Nelly Furman (New York: Praeger, 1980), 239–57; Otis B. Wheeler, "The Five Awakenings of Edna Pontellier," *Southern Review* 11, no. 1 (1975): 118–128; and Cynthia Griffin Wolff, "Thanatos and Eros," in Culley's edition of *The Awakening*, 206–18. For a reading that considers Chopin's treatment of Whitman, see Elizabeth Balken House, "*The Awakening*: Kate Chopin's 'Endlessly Rocking' Cycle," *Ball State University Forum* 20, no. 2 (Spring 1979): 53–58. For an overview of critical responses to *The Awakening* prior to 1977, see Priscilla Allen, "Old Critics and New: The Treatment of Chopin's *The Awakening*," in *The Authority of Experience: Essays in Feminist Criticism*, ed. Arlyn Diamond and Lee R. Edwards (Amherst: University of Massachusetts Press, 1977), 24–38.

24. Walter Benn Michaels, "The Contracted Heart," *New Literary History* 21, no. 3 (Spring 1990): 498. Subsequent references will be in the text.

25. Lyotard, *The Postmodern Condition*, [trans. Regis Durand (Minneapolis: University of Minnesota Press, 1984)] 81.

26. Gilbert and Gubar, *No Man's Land*, 97.

27. Jane P. Tompkins, "*The Awakening*: An Evaluation," *Feminist Studies* 3, nos. 3–4 (Spring–Summer 1976): 24.

DUINO ELEGIES
(RAINER MARIA RILKE)

"*Stimmen, Stimmen:* The Chorus of the Sublime in Rilke's *Duino Elegies*"
by David Brendan Hopes, University of North Carolina at Asheville

---

One assumes all questions in a poem to be rhetorical. Questions, petulant or serene, lyrical or despairing, are the irritants around which poetry grows like a pearl. Whitman allows the child to inquire, "What is grass?" that he may answer with a truth known before the question was asked, that it is the scented remembrancer of the Lord, "designedly dropt." This is the rhetorical query triumphant, wherein the question or series of questions build before an inevitable crescendo of affirmation. God speaking out of the whirlwind in the book of Job is perhaps the most profound example of this mode, which is, finally, meant to overwhelm. The probable answer to Prufrock's barrage of questions about peaches and white flannel trousers and other critical issues is likewise known before the query is expressed. Others, like Shelley's "if winter comes, can spring be far behind?" are more wistful; perhaps "defiant" is the word, the bloodied poet-hero shaking his fist from the ruins. A more complicated species of poetical question presents a proposition to be explored or debated through the poetic text. While the investigation may seem to indicate an authentic rather than a rhetorical question, one feels that the poet at least hoped he knew what the answer was—or was pretty sure that no answer existed—and wound his way through the mazes of thought and imagery until he arrived at the anticipated place. A lighthearted example is contained in Shakespeare's brief song, "Where, oh, where is fancy bred / In the heart or in the head?" from the casket scene in *The Merchant of Venice.* The answer is not finally known—Shakespeare knew that when he asked—though all the romantic activity of the play revolves around the answering of it.

The poetic question serving as the proposition of an internal debate is a mode that dominates the twentieth century. One thinks particularly of Yeats's great line from "Easter 1916"—"and what if excess of love bewildered them until they died?" This question is the foundation of Yeats's political vision—the grinding interface of love, sacrifice, valor, and brutality—and the answering of it leaves us no closer to any serviceable mode of action. The poet clearly believes that excess of love *did* in fact bewilder them until they died, but what then to do with that perception? Refuse to love? Pity those who do? Try to balance the emotions so to love just enough—in which case no Rising and no Ireland? The question is directed outward; the poet seeks to understand people and phenomena around him, in history, in Dublin, in the world, assuming himself to *be* a self, capable of observing exterior things with some measure of perceptual confidence and integrity.

I invoke Yeats in order to establish a counterpoint for Rainer Maria Rilke, whose continuing appeal is based partially upon the fact that he does not automatically assume himself to *be* a self, but, as in the *Duino Elegies*, oftentimes a chorus of not necessarily harmonious voices. The voices of the poem have several quite definite tasks to perform: They must glean fragments and remembrances of a shattered self from the ruins of the world, and they must, largely through memory, partly through the most wistful and exquisite expressions of faith, seek to forge them back into an entity fit to call itself a man. External worldly matters are considered in the "Sonnets to Orpheus" and the exquisite French lyrics, but the *Duino Elegies*—Rilke's masterpiece and one of the great works of the century—are the cry of an annihilated soul striving to gather itself out of the wind. The voices do occasionally whine—the Elegies can be trying if you are not in the proper mood—but they can also thunder and then are sublime past almost anything else one finds in the last century that has largely rejected the sublime as an object or mode of poetic expression.

Yeats and Rilke are contemporaries with certain interesting parallels—an artistic bent that threatened in their youths to decline into dilettantism, passionate love choices which did not or could not lead to marriage, an obsession with the aristocracy—and yet possessing such different perspectives, such varied sources of inspiration, that they might have inhabited different cultures in different millennia, rather than the war-threatened western Europe that they shared. Rilke's *Duino Elegies* were being composed—beyond the first burst of inspiration at the Princess's chateau at Duino, which flowered into the first two elegies before completion at Chateau Muzot—when Yeats wrote "Easter 1916." Yeats waited three years to publish his poem, though he seems to have written it quickly, with a sureness that comes from confidence in one's own perceptions. Rilke writes the *Duino Elegies* over a period of 10 years. Rilke shoulders his way through miasmas of depression. Rilke is interrupted and delayed by the events of the world. The *Duino Elegies* cannot thrive in the midst of events because they are not about events. They are about internal *sturm und drang*, about suffering and confusion and longing that no external observer could fully verify. Yeats—or for that matter, Eliot in "Prufrock"—begins in a world we recognize and can almost immediately evaluate. Rilke arises from deep in his own head, amid the chorus of his yet unintroduced voices, and opens with one of most impressive rhetorical queries of all poetry:

> Who, if I cried out, would hear me among the Angelic
>   orders?

What a welter of conditionals! *If!* The poet is not even sure he is going to cry out. Some translations do render the "wenn" in Rilke's German as "though" or "when," instead of "if," but I think these do not wish to face the full exhaustion of the spiritual moment. The poet is not sure he is going to cry, and if he does, he is not sure to whom. The Angelic orders are multiform and nonspecific, and invoking them is like praying to a star, hoping that one in the myriad is inclining its ear at the crucial moment. One is humble. One expects to pass beneath the notice of the angels. But one is also proud and cautious, holding off from uttering a name—such as Raphael, who is alluded to in the Second Elegy, but not named—lest one appear to be a fool in an age of secularity, indeed of mockery. One may reference an angelic being, but calling upon him from the heart of one's heart takes more power.

And what if one does not cry out? Having demonstrated the inability to re-establish integrity, having demonstrated helplessness before the task of assembling a life from the chaos of incident, one, like Blake's Albion, falls into meaner and meaner versions of the self. An unexpected truth examined by the turbulent twentieth century is that one does not make a life out of memories. There must be an integral self, some permanent personal definition, for memories to arrange themselves within. Otherwise, thought might be a chorus of interesting voices, but there will be no unison, no sublime *fortissimo*, the voices growing more discrete and isolated until they are random chirpings in a dark landscape, pretty enough but without significance.

In the Fourth Elegy, Rilke acknowledges the full potential of the human mind for misdirection, how it is capable of great things but for some reason usually shrugs its way without struggle to the grave:

> Who can show a child as he really is;
> set him starlike in his proper firmament
> and place the rod of distant measure
> in his hand?
> Who bakes the grey bread of his death
> and leaves it hardening, sharp as a
> sweet apple's inedible core,
> in his rounded mouth? . . . Murderers
> are easy enough to understand.
> But to hold death,
> the whole of death,
> even before life is fairly begun—
> to contain it gently
> and without complaint—
> that defies understanding.

The rhetorical question which begins this passage—"Who can show a child"—is immediately answerable in context and with two answers: the poet, and the angel, but the poet only when he becomes the angel. And becoming the angel, forging together a sufficient number of the fragments to build again the shattered single Voice, is the work Rilke lays out for the *Duino Elegies*. Sublimity is not exterior; it is a state of being that was once the whole of being but is now no more than a rather grander voice among the voices. The poet remembers too much and dares too little. He must stop listening, find a voice, and cry.

> Part of the enduring hesitancy, of course, is fear:
> And even if one were to suddenly
> take me to its heart, I would vanish into its
> stronger existence. For beauty is nothing but
> the beginning of terror, that we are still able to bear,
> and we revere it so, because it calmly disdains
> to destroy us. Every Angel is terror.

Why is every angel terror? Because of the fullness of personality, of assertion, the blazing yang to the self-immolating yin of the poet. No, that is not correct: Yin is the complement of yang, not the absence of it. The angel is the full possession of all that we long for and fear to pursue. He is as discomfiting as "yes" in a room of "maybes." Finally, the angel is terror because he is an identity that our own timidity has cast aside. He is us, the way we were, perhaps, but assuredly the way we could be. He is terrible, because if we do attain him, we will no longer recognize ourselves. Again to reference Yeats, we will be the terrible beauty that disturbs us and frightens us in our ordinary state. Our whole self is terrible to our present fragment. From the Fourth Elegy:

> . . . am I not right to sit here,
> staring at the puppet stage,
> if only to gaze so steadily
> that an angel must arise,
> obedient to balance,
> to startle the stuffed skins
> into living action.
> Angel with marionettes!
> Actual theater at last!

One might wish to be the angel or resign oneself to being a marionette with, at least, the glory of being manipulated by an angel. Significantly, the poet here is neither but an onlooker, still wholly outside every aspect of the performance. That is the worst place of all. It preserves judgment but denies any possibility of action.

The *Duino Elegies*'s contact with the sublime occurs most dramatically in the opening lines, and though sublimity in theme and language reappears, those occasions are clearly echoes of this, like some imperial music that was once heard up close receding and receding until it is all but inaudible. The fact that the first elegy is the most fully achieved (by and large) is what the poem is essentially about. One observes there is something Wordsworthian in a very long poem about the perfection of first brief moments, but Rilke takes more responsibility than Wordsworth, is far more interesting in despair and far less resigned—not resigned at all—to the darkness. The *Duino Elegies* are designed to seduce Sublimity into returning, into ravishing him back into his former home in the heart. The first cry is the loudest and then subsides, as if the crier were afraid of the power and pathos of his own voice, as if he were afraid of what would become of him if the quest were achieved.

A number of people who acted as rescuing angels in Rilke's life may be cited, people with restful chateaux and a certain cushion of means, and those who look for biographical clues to the identity of the angel will not be frustrated. But the angel is Rilke himself in fullness of spirit, a lost identity persistently (if sometimes timidly) invoked and lyrically longed for; that the poetry of the *Duino Elegies* is the means by which a fragmented soul seeks reunification with a former, or perhaps potential, empyreal condition. The Angel, as heavenly spokesman, as reconciler, as awakener, as revealer of truth, possesses all the powers one attributed to poets in more poetic ages. Rilke wants that for himself, recognizes that as his true inheritance, but is all but powerless to ask for it. Of all the post-Romantic train, Rilke is the one who most closely equates sublimity and terror, and what is more terrifying than the photo of oneself as a football hero or a young lover, or the poem one wrote years past in heroic ecstasy? One may begin to assume there is only one character in the *Duino Elegies*, and that character is the poet speaking in the multiple voices of his fall, ranging from the cowering lover of the Third Elegy, who fears to reveal the "hidden, guilty river-god" of the blood, to the angel himself, the uninvited yet longed-for visitor, who, again like Blake's Albion, is the self in sublimity.

In the Third Elegy, the potential father murmurs to the potential mother:

> O my love, consider the child
> we would fain conceive was never

an individual, but a multitude,
the personification of the fathers
lying in our depths like mountains
leveled to the lowest summits . . .

What a task Rilke sets for himself! Not only is the soul a multiple, a conglomeration of competing voices struggling, but they are minimalized "like mountains leveled to the lowest summits." The voices the poet makes manifest are doomed within their own historical context, minions of old orders, upholders of exhausted societies about to enter the flames—or withered and gone in the flames—of World War I. The dedication of the poem reads: "The Property of Princess Marie von Thurn und Taxis-Hohenlohe." Whatever the princess's personal qualities, she is a representative—a remnant, one might say—of an age whose power is drained. The refinement and salons and sunny spas and hopeful decadence of the milieu from which the poem, or at least the poet, springs, are not efficacious in forming an integral identity. They are memories of lovely things gone. Those who build their lives on memory are halted there, dead-stopped in a moment in time, by the failure of the imagination.

It would come close to minimalizing this great poem to observe too closely its historical context, the inference that it can be read in one sense as a decadent age's elegy to itself. Contemporary—which is to say, twenty-first century—readers may lack sympathy for the isolation of the voices in these elegies. We have the world at our fingertips in a spectrum of gratifications that are immediate, if not always very profound. Let me suggest that the *Duino Elegies* is prophetic, as was Jeremiah, in that it portrays an age at the brink of hell brought on by its own inclinations, by its own bad habits. The twenty-first century is, so far, the enemy of introspection, partially because so much of the twentieth was glutted with it, intellectually castrated by it. Rilke can no more escape the net of inwardness than can the rest of Europe in his time, but he is at least prepared to cry out for help, or annihilation. Ninety years later, inwardness is indeed conquered, not by sublime personal integrity and restoration, but by an even vaster chorus of voices, comprising nearly all the voices of the world, in which one can lose oneself so thoroughly there is no further need for *self* at all. The angel who actually answered the poet's intended cry in history was not the one he anticipated at all. This is why this poem must still be read: The true redeemer yet approaches.

In the Sixth Elegy, Rilke addresses the fig tree:

> Fig tree, I've long found it significant
> that you omit, almost entirely, to flower,
> but, early in the season, urge unheralded,
> your purest secret into resolute fruition.
> Like the jet of a fountain, your arched bough
> drives the sap downward, then up: and it leaps from its sleep
> barely waking, into the bliss of its sweetest achievement.
> See: like the god into the swan
> We, though, linger,
> ah, all our pride is in flowering, and, already betrayed,
> we reach the late core of our final fruit.

The flower comes without the fruit. There is no age coming after his and born out of its achievement.

In an astonishing passage in the Ninth Elegy, Rilke begins to turn, begins to consider that he may be, at least, of the same tribe as the angel, an entity capable of giving as well as crying out for a gift:

> Praise the world to the Angel, not the unsayable: you
> can't impress him with glories of feeling: in the universe,
> where he feels more deeply, you are a novice. So show
> him a simple thing, fashioned in age after age,
> that lives close to hand and in sight.
> Tell him things. He'll be more amazed: as you were,
> beside the rope-maker in Rome, or the potter beside the Nile.
> Show him how happy things can be, how guiltless and ours,
> how even the cry of grief decides on pure form,
> serves as a thing, or dies into a thing: transient,
> they look to us for deliverance, we, the most transient of all.
> Will us to change them completely, in our invisible hearts,
> into—oh, endlessly, into us! Whoever, in the end, we are.

Done with crying out, perhaps embarrassed by it by now, the poet—by long labor, or by one of those dazzling bolts of insight, often completely unrelated to the thing asked, which are the true gifts of such angels as

there are—recognizes that all the while, in the very act of lamentation, he was in possession of the necessary, integrated voice: the voice
of the poet. Tell the angel about the rope maker in Rome, show him
how happy things can be, and what might he give in return? He might
hold up a mirror, in which you see yourself doing the necessary thing,
a face transfigured by joy, the way you always could have been had
you not allowed the abyss of introspection to open. The Tenth Elegy
begins in the same vein:

> Some day, in emergence from this fierce insight,
> let me sing jubilation and praise to assenting Angels.
> Let not a single one of the cleanly-struck hammers of my
>   heart
> deny me, through a slack, or a doubtful, or
> a broken string. Let my streaming face
> make me more radiant: let my secret weeping
> bear flower. O, how dear you will be to me, then, Nights
> of anguish. Inconsolable sisters, why did I not
> kneel more to greet you, lose myself more
> in your loosened hair? We, squanderers of pain.
> How we gaze beyond them into duration's sadness,
> to see if they have an end. Though they are nothing but
> our winter-suffering foliage, our dark evergreen,
> *one* of the seasons of our inner year—not only
> season—: but place, settlement, camp, soil, dwelling.

We had been given the elements of sublime celebration from the start.
The traditional sublime moment—one thinks of Coleridge's Ancient
Mariner blessing the water snakes unawares—is the moment when
our gaze leaves ourselves and settles on the other, on Mont Blanc, the
grass, sunrise in the Vale of Chamouni. Yet, in the *Duino Elegies*, our
inward gaze creates a radiant end, sublimity.

EMMA
(JANE AUSTEN)

"'Hurrying into the Shrubbery': The Sublime, Transcendence, and the Garden Scene in *Emma*" by David C. MacWilliams, in *Persuasions: The Jane Austen Journal* (2001)

INTRODUCTION

While David C. MacWilliams observes the way Jane Austen "responded to the cult of the sublime with humor and irony," MacWilliams argues "that Austen did not always disparage the cult of the sublime, and in fact, could use it seriously and positively in narrating the sense of joy her protagonists experience in climactic scenes." Supporting his argument with a close analysis of one specific scene—the garden exchange between Knightley and Emma—MacWilliams concludes that, while Austen always enjoyed poking fun at "the cult of the sublime," she "has written a sublime passage of a thoroughly sublime event."

In her novels, Jane Austen frequently responded to the cult of the sublime with humor and irony. You will recall a few of the most

MacWilliams, David C. "'Hurrying into the Shrubbery': The Sublime, Transcendence, and the Garden Scene in *Emma*." *Persuasions: The Jane Austen Journal*, Vol. 23 (2001): 133–138.

memorable moments; for example, any of Catherine's imaginary
gothic horrors in *Northanger Abbey* will suffice, and Marianne's "transporting sensations" (88) over dead leaves in *Sense and Sensibility* will
raise a chuckle, and so will Sir Edward's literary blustering in *Sanditon*
(396). These examples remind us that Austen's attitude towards the
sublime was often rather leery.[1] I argue, however, that Austen did
not always disparage the cult of the sublime, and in fact, could use it
seriously and positively in narrating the sense of joy her protagonists
experience in climactic scenes.

I wish to examine one such scene specifically, the garden encounter
between Knightley and Emma in *Emma* (Volume III, Chapter XIII).
Here Austen employs a tone and terminology that derive from the late
eighteenth-century cult of the sublime. Emma and Knightley undergo
a sublime transcendence in the garden, both of them going from very
apprehensive emotional states, to sudden shock, to a heightened joy,
to a kind of bliss.

Austen's indebtedness to the eighteenth-century rhetorician Hugh
Blair has been well documented,[2] and a discussion of the sublime
is a major theme in his *Lectures on Rhetoric and Belles Lettres*. The
sublime, he explains, "produces a sort of internal elevation and expansion; it raises the mind much above its ordinary state, and fills it with
a degree of wonder and astonishment, which it cannot well express.
The emotion is certainly delightful; but it is altogether of the serious
kind" (69). We can apply Blair's description of the emotion to that
which Emma and Knightley experience in the garden when Knightley
suddenly proposes (and Emma less suddenly accepts). Austen has,
of course, her unique interpretation of the emotional moment; the
awfulness is not quite so stirring, but the delight is felt by both characters and wonderfully expressed in her narrative—though not so well
expressed by the characters themselves!

In her narration of the garden scene, Austen uses five conventions
of the sublime aesthetic that were widely associated with the notion
in her day. Two of them are conditions that must be met before the
sublime can be experienced: the individuals must be morally good,
and the location of the event must be out of doors. The event itself
progresses in three stages. First, there is the fear or anxiety which
precedes the transcendence; next, there is the sudden, unexpected
striking of the sublime sensation; and finally, the individuals experience

a transformation, if even momentarily, from common emotions to a sense of magnificence.

Knightley and Emma both satisfy the first precondition, that of being morally good. In his *Lectures*, Blair describes "the moral, or sentimental Sublime," something discovered mainly "under the name of Magnanimity or Heroism." He explains that "high virtue is the most natural and fertile source of this moral Sublimity" (66–68). Emma demonstrates such virtue at the end of chapter twelve. She is walking about her room, ruing her poor conduct to Jane Fairfax, the possibility that Harriet and Knightley would marry, and worse, that the marriage would be the result of her own doing. But she finds consolation, we remember, "in the resolution of her own better conduct, and the hope that, however inferior in spirit and gaiety might be the following and every future winter of her life to the past, it would yet find her more rational, more acquainted with herself, and leave her less to regret when it were gone" (423). Having made this resolution, Emma has reconfirmed the nobility of her character by humbling herself and choosing what is morally correct. She is prepared for the sublime experience in chapter thirteen. Knightley, meanwhile, has been going through his own trials down in London, worrying about the love he imagined Emma had felt for Frank Churchill. He arrives at Hartfield greatly perturbed, expecting to find Emma heartbroken and irrevocably beyond his reach. Nevertheless, as her friend he is willing to help her in her sadness, and he offers sympathy and his usual sound, mature advice, "'Time, my dearest Emma, time will heal the wound'" (426). Knightley reconfirms his nobility of character by doing what is morally correct: sacrificing his own desires, as Emma has done, and helping his friend despite the pain he might feel.

The second precondition that must be met is that the scene take place outdoors, and of course, Knightley proposes in the garden not long after stormy weather has passed. The tempest Austen describes in chapter twelve and in the first several lines of thirteen is a typical motif of an approaching sublime event. According to Blair, storms and foul weather are often harbingers of the sublime. "In general we may observe," he writes, "that great power and strength exerted, always raise sublime ideas: . . . Hence the grandeur . . . of tempests of wind; of thunder and lightning; and all the uncommon violence of the elements" (61). The clearing weather in chapter thirteen coincides with the moral decision Emma makes at the end of chapter twelve to better her conduct and to be "more rational, more acquainted with herself" (243). Also, as the weather goes from cloudy, lonely, and melancholy in the morning to softer and brighter in the afternoon, it foreshadows the transition that is to come in Emma's fortunes. Summer returns. Emma goes outdoors and begins to feel the relief which the transition in nature and in her behavior provide: "Never had the exquisite sight, smell, sensation of nature, tranquil, warm, and brilliant after a storm, been more attractive to her" (424). Her spirits are somewhat heightened and revived as she hurries into the shrubbery, but her slight peace is demolished with the sudden arrival of Knightley.

The sublime experience is building. The protagonists' moral goodness is confirmed and they are outdoors and the storm is past. Austen now employs the first of the three stages of the sublime event, fear and anxiety. Austen's narrative assumes a hurried, anxious pace as Knightley approaches:

> [S]he had taken a few turns, when she saw Mr. Knightley passing through the garden door, and coming towards her.—It was the first intimation of his being returned from London. She had been thinking of him the moment before, as unquestionably sixteen miles distant.—There was time only for the quickest arrangement of mind. She must be collected and calm. In half a minute they were together. (424)

At Knightley's arrival we see the second stage of the sublime event: surprise.

Mr. Knightley's arrival unsettles Emma. The narrative of the greeting ritual mirrors that unsettled feeling. "The 'How d'ye do's,' were quiet and constrained on each side." The moment begins with an uneasy constraint creating a tension that continues rising by Austen's use of third person where the first is required and by her blend of dialogue and narration. She confuses the reader's expectations and mirrors the confusion felt by the characters as they make small talk. Emma "asked after their mutual friends; they were all well.—When had he left them?—Only that morning. He must have had a wet ride.—Yes.—He meant to walk with her, she found. 'He had just looked into the dining-room, and as he was not wanted there, preferred being out of doors'" (424). The juxtaposition between indirect and direct speech and the use of the third person where the first is logically required, as well as the unusual switch in narrative point of view between dialogue and narrative are all techniques typical of Austen, but in this case they leave the reader with a sense of foreboding, one heightened by the vocabulary, "fears, pained, silent, dread, unnatural," that Austen uses.

As Knightley and Emma talk and clarify matters inadvertently, they experience a series of emotional shocks. Nothing is planned; they are at the mercy of their own anxieties. Knightley stumbles, hesitates, and propels himself into the proposal, speaking alternately to himself, then Emma:

> "As a friend!"—repeated Mr. Knightley.—"Emma, that I fear is a word—No, I have no wish—Stay, yes, why should I hesitate?—I have gone too far already for concealment.— Emma, I accept your offer—Extraordinary as it may seem, I accept it, and refer myself to you as a friend.—Tell me, then, have I no chance of ever succeeding?" (429–30)

Austen's narration here captures the turbulence of mind the characters experience through the hesitancy expressed in both narrative and dialogue—the stopping, the starting, the dashes and pauses. In describing what makes writing sublime, Blair is succinct: "Wherever ... a very magnanimous and exalted affection of human mind is displayed; thence, if you can catch the impression strongly, and exhibit it warm and glowing, you may draw the Sublime" (94). Drawing the sublime is exactly what Austen is doing in this exchange.

This point is the third stage of the sublime event, the transcendence. A full understanding, a kind of ecstasy, strikes the individual. Emma, "almost ready to sink under the agitation of this moment" is shocked, and afraid "of being awakened" (430). Shock, sudden surprise, a strike like lightning—it's how her original audience would expect a sublime event to occur. "While he spoke, Emma's mind was most busy, and, with all the wonderful velocity of thought, had been able—and yet without losing a word—to catch and comprehend the exact truth of the whole" (430). As Emma's mind races over Harriet's misfortune, the vocabulary recalls words used in the earlier part of the chapter, the pre-proposal part, with items like "groundless, mistake, delusion, nothing, agitation, doubts, reluctance, discouragement." For Emma's good fortune, we have words such as "glow, happiness, rejoice," and of course, "sublimity"—though Austen is having fun with this last term. While capturing the sublimity of the event, Austen still enjoys her irony. We recall that Emma does not avail herself of the "simple sublimity" of refusing Knightley's proposal for Harriet's sake, not for a moment.

Yet as the scene winds down and each character reviews what has occurred—the fear, astonishment, and possibilities—we read of the transcendence which has taken place in terms very usual in discussions of the sublime. Knightley can hardly believe his sudden transformation. "Within half an hour, he had passed from a thoroughly distressed state of mind, to something so like perfect happiness, that it could bear no other name" (432). Emma can hardly believe her transformation, either. The moment where she discovers his love, and Knightley discovers himself professing his love, is a sublime moment: at first one full of foreboding; then, astonishment where everything is understood suddenly; then, an uplifting of spirits and a sense of perfect happiness. Austen's description of the garden scene owes much to Blair's definition of what sublime writing should be both in the technique of narration and in the object of narration. Blair wrote that the object must not only, in itself, be sublime, but it must be "set before us in such a light as is most proper to give us a clear and full impression of it; it must be described with strength, with conciseness, and simplicity" (76). Austen always enjoyed poking fun at Blair's rhetoric and the cult of the sublime, but, with "strength, with conciseness, and simplicity," she has written a sublime passage of a thoroughly sublime event.

NOTES

1. See Lorrie Clark, "Transfiguring the Romantic Sublime in *Persuasion*," in Juliet McMaster and Bruce Stoval eds., *Jane Austen's Business: Her World and Her Profession* (New York: St. Martin's, 1996) 30–41. In her analysis of Louisa Musgrove's fall on the Cobb at Lyme, Clark discusses Austen's objections to the cult of the sublime, the main two being the safe risk of death and the aesthetic enjoyment of such a scene.

2. See especially Elaine Bander, "Blair's *Rhetoric* and the Art of *Persuasion*," *Persuasions* 15 (1993) 124–30.

WORKS CITED

Austen, Jane. *The Novels of Jane Austen*. Ed. R. W. Chapman. 3rd ed. Oxford: Oxford UP, 1933.

Blair, Hugh. *Lectures on Rhetoric and Belles Lettres*. New York: Garland Publishing, 1970.

"The Fall of the House of Usher"
(Edgar Allan Poe)

"The Sublime in Edgar Allan Poe's 'The Fall of the House of Usher'"
by Blake Hobby, University of
North Carolina at Asheville

Since its publication in *Burton's Gentlemen's Magazine* on September 18, 1839, and its subsequent inclusion in *Tales of the Grotesque and Arabesque* (1840), Edgar Allan Poe's short story "The Fall of the House of Usher" has been seen, for the most part, as a classic horror story, a diversion that quells the sort of boredom (*ennui*) that we associate with nineteenth-century readers (who, without video games and television and Web surfing, had to seek solace in books). From this perspective, Poe's story entertains, providing a needed step away from the world. But there is more to Poe than pulp fiction and Gothic horror. At the center of Poe's works lies the experience of a radical form of the sublime, one in which the horror of our mortality is represented in symbolic form. As it is in "Usher," where a gloomy house in a foreboding landscape is an embodiment of the mortal self, Poe's sublime provides a critical response to other notions of sublimity.

In *The Supernatural Sublime*, Jack G. Voller traces the aesthetic of the sublime from numerous eighteenth-century aesthetes to nineteenth-century Gothic writers. Voller contends that Gothic writers like Poe drew upon an established tradition while veering from the "conventional sublime" to the "radical supernatural sublime," finding absence instead of the sort of vision of plentitude we might associate with Romantic poets like Coleridge. For Coleridge, the imagination was of primary importance in both the perceiving and rendering of reality, a sign of divinity. If, according to Coleridge, the imagination is "the living Power and prime Agent of all human perception ... a repetition in the finite mind of the eternal act of creation in the infinite I AM," then the experience of the sublime shares in divinity via the imagination of the poet. Thus, we can see, in Coleridge's "Kubla Kahn," for example, how a fulfilling epiphany that comes in a dream is approximated in sublime language. Here the sublime functions as a kind of corrective, one that makes us aware of the eternal forever at play beyond human reach. As we will see, however, Poe is a Gothic writer we now wed with a dark Romantic sublime that subverts such a vision of plentitude.

For Voller, "the radical supernatural sublime finds in the space of suspension the key to its subversive power":

> The conventional sublime creates, out of the failure that occurs in these moments of arrest and expansion, a sense of transcendent achievement and metaphysical plentitude. The project of the radical supernatural sublime is to seize the moment, foreground it, and by close scrutiny reveal it to be a moment of absence, a revelation enabled by the supernatural sublime's inversion of the traditional understanding of infinity as evidence of an omnipotent divine present. In is radical mode, Gothic fiction unmasks the dissimulation of transcendence, and that gesture of unmasking, that recognition of helplessness and unfulfillment *as such* is the revelation of the decaying corpse in the place of God. (29–30)

As a tale that exemplifies the dark side of our sublime existence, "The Fall of the House of Usher" places the reader and narrator in close proximity, both witnesses to the splendor and horror that lie in a condition without cure, life, which, no matter what experience edifies it, is ultimately overshadowed by the awe-filled and terrifying specter of death.

As a form of the sublime that subverts expectations for sublimity, Poe's sublime is deeply ironic, an experience of anticipation never fulfilled, a powerful grotesque tale that borders on the unbelievable. As something that negates as it forms, Poe's aesthetic contains the sort of extreme irony Philip Shaw equates with the sublime:

In a very real sense, the sublime does indeed verge on the ridiculous; it encourages us to believe that we can scale the highest mountains, reach the stars and become infinite when all the time it is drawing us closer to our actual material limits: the desire to outstrip earthly bonds leads instead to the encounter with the lack, an encounter that is painful, cruel, and some would say comic. The sublime, somewhat ironically, given its overtly metaphysical ambitions, turns out to be a form of materialism after all. Perhaps the sublime is irony at its purest and most effective: a promise of transcendence leading to the edge of an abyss. (10)

Such an ironic conception of the sublime is helpful when considering Poe, especially in a later grotesquerie called "The Premature Burial" (1844), in which Poe lampoons stories about grotesque resurrections that occur after being buried alive. There, and also in "Usher," we see Poe capitalize on the nineteenth-century obsession with death and morbidity. Of course, by this I do not mean to indicate that Poe created a burlesque with "Usher" as he did with the latter buried-alive story. On the contrary, "The Fall of the House of Usher," from its first epigram, which frames the story, makes it clear that Poe is engaging not only the ideas of eighteenth- and nineteenth-century aestheticians but also that Poe is dealing with an earnest subject. By tracing sublime elements in the story, we can appreciate Poe's artistry and also his critical awareness of the sacred sublimity of the self, an entity attuned to the world and all of its suffering. But we can also see Poe providing an ironic commentary upon the nature of the sublime as he creates a sublime experience in "Usher."

Poe quotes two lines of De Béranger that serve as the story's epigraph and provide two dominant images: heart and lute. This opening quotation, "His heart is a hanging lute; / As soon as it is touched it resonates" (my translation of "Son cœur est un luth suspendu; / Sitôt qu'on le touche il résonne"), focuses the story on interiority, the way the inner self, as embodied by a blood-pumping organ, responds to the external world. The image of the heart is paradoxical: As its beating is the source of life for human beings—life both in terms of physical and spiritual well-being—so does its atrophy signal the end of life. Interestingly, the harp reverberates like the imagination of the poet does in Coleridge's "Aeolian Harp" and in "Dejection: An Ode."

In this sense, "Usher" responds to a Romantic notion of the sublime, one in which the poet's imagination serves as a conduit to the divine. In addition to this image, the De Béranger quote contains a lute. Orpheus, in Greek mythology, represents the good shepherd who plays on his lute to charm wild beasts. Orpheus' lute thus may signal mastery of conflict or restoration of harmony, not only the mastery of an external conflict but self-knowledge and mastery of the self. With the images of heart and lute, the epigram establishes a framework for the tale, one in which the sublimity of mortality appears as an experience that the self must undergo.

As Poe begins the tale, he creates a first paragraph inundated with reflective, dreamlike language. Under an oppressively darkened sky that resembles the darkness of the subconscious mind, an unnamed narrator describes his arrival in a dreamy twilight landscape. Poe paints a surreal picture in the tale's opening that looks like a dream or nightmare:

> During the whole of a dull, dark, and soundless day in the autumn of the year, when the clouds hung oppressively low in the heavens, I had been passing alone, on horseback, through a singularly dreary tract of country; and at length found myself, as the shades of evening drew on, within the view of the melancholy House of Usher. (532)

Many carefully chosen images coalesce in the opening lines that indicate the narrator is having a vision. The "dull, dark, and soundless day" with its alliteration mirrors the strange and uncharted areas of the narrator's subconscious mind (532). The narrator recounts his first glimpse of the house of Usher, remembering how "a sense of insufferable gloom pervaded my spirit" (532). As the narrator looks at the house, his heart resonates. From the tale's beginning, Poe establishes a significant relationship between the house and the narrator. The narrator is an observer intimately connected with and strongly affected by the sight of the house. The narrator describes the house as "insufferable" and beyond any feeling that "the sternest natural images of the desolate and terrible" have ever created in him (532). As he gazes at the "vacant and eye-like windows" of the house, windows that seem to peer at him, he describes feeling an "utter depression of the soul." He can only compare this depressive response to the aftermath of an opium dream, such as Coleridge experienced before composing "Kubla Kahn." This dream, or depressed state, presents "a mystery all insoluble" in which "shadowy fancies" lead him to wonder. The narrator, brought to an intense level of feeling and introspection, dismounts his horse. Looking down into a "black and lurid tarn" that lies just before the ghostly Usher manor, he sees "inverted images, . . . ghastly tree-stems," and the house's "vacant and eye-like windows" (533). Gazing down into the dark and reflective tarn, the narrator appears as Narcissus alone before his pool of blue. However, instead of a blue pool, the narrator sees dark visions that hang ominously before him. Here we have an image of the Romantic, inward-turned poet encountering the sublime in his own reflection, whether that poet be Coleridge, Wordsworth, or Byron.

The second paragraph describes the narrator's rationale for making his journey as well as his relationship with the house's proprietor, Roderick Usher, who "had been one of [his] boon companions in boyhood" (533). At present, Roderick suffers from an "acute body illness," which renders him dysfunctional, cheerless, and depressed (533). This illness may represent the depressive state that mandates the narrator's trip to the house, a metaphor for his interior world. Roderick's call compels the narrator to respond with "no room for hesitation" (533). The intensity and power of Roderick's request comes because, as the narrator says: "His heart went with the request" (533). As the narrator reflects before the tarnished pool of Narcissus, he says of his childhood with Roderick: "Although, as boys, we had been even intimate associates, yet I really knew little of my friend" (533). The narrator's references to his childhood with Roderick allude to a lost inner connection. He likens his gaze into the blackened pool to a "childish experiment," one that has produced "the consciousness of the rapid increase of (his) superstition" (534). As the narrator lifts his eyes to the house from his downward contemplation of the pool, he describes a fancy that overcomes him and oppresses him (534). This fancy works so powerfully on the narrator that he sees the whole house cloaked in a "dull, sluggish, faintly-discernible, and leaden-hued" aura (534). In the next paragraph a servant leads the narrator through a "Gothic archway of the hall, . . . through many dark and intricate passages" and up various staircases and passageways (535). Metaphorically, as the narrator journeys within himself, he confronts the "anomalous species of terror" that binds Roderick Usher to the

house as a slave (537). On his interior quest the narrator takes on the
condition of the "intolerable agitation of the soul" that haunts Usher.
The narrator faces that greatest demon, which has both fatally laid
hold of Roderick and simultaneously is Roderick: "FEAR" (537).

Madeline, Roderick's phantom-like sister, mirrors the inner state
of the narrator in a similar fashion. The narrator describes Madeline:
"Her figure, her air, her features—all in the very minutest development
were those— . . . of the Roderick Usher who sat beside me" (537).
Later, as Roderick and the narrator entomb her, the narrator describes
the strange symbiosis between brother and sister:

> The exact similitude between the brother and sister here
> again startled and confounded me. Usher, divining, perhaps,
> my thought, murmured out some few words from which I
> learned that the deceased and himself had been twins, and that
> sympathies of a scarcely intelligible nature had always existed
> between them. (542)

Roderick and the narrator pass time reading, painting, imagining,
and dreaming together. The time the narrator spends with Roderick
profoundly affects him. He states that he feels he is admitted "unre-
servedly into the recesses of [Roderick's] spirit" (538). Looking into
Roderick's world, the narrator enters a strange land, which, like the
human psyche and the sublime, defies explanation. He states:

> I shall ever bear about me, as Moslemin their shrouds at Mecca,
> a memory of the many solemn hours I thus spent alone with the
> master of the House of Usher. Yet I should fail in any attempt
> to convey an idea of the exact character of the studies, or of the
> occupations, in which he involved me, or led the way. (538)

As the narrator describes, "pure abstractions" produce an "intensity
of intolerable awe, no shadow of which" he has ever felt before (538).
He reminisces about the memory of time spent with Roderick and
compares it to a religious journey.

The narrator is especially affected by the "wild fantasias" or
improvisations that Roderick renders while madly playing the guitar
(538). One of these wild improvisations affects the narrator so deeply
that he at once commits it to memory: It at once becomes part of

him. This improvisation in poetic form, "The Haunted Palace," not only contains the action of the story but also mirrors the emotional experience that the House of Usher, the Usher brother and sister, and the narrator share. In the poem's distant past, wholeness, happiness, and blessedness existed as a kind of prelapsarian state. The poem describes the distant palace as "Snow-White" with the "monarch Thought" ruling it (539). These images not only coincide with the childhood spent with Roderick, but also they remind the reader of the state before a sublime experience.

In stanza three, the poem describes "two luminous windows" in which "Spirits (move) musically, / To a lute's well-tuned law" (540). This stanza connects the epigraph's lute image with two luminous windows. The poem describes a "happy Valley" before a "sovereign" from whose palace door "came flowing, flowing, flowing / And sparkling evermore, ... In voices of surpassing beauty, / The wit and wisdom" of a blessed king (540). The king (metaphorically the narrator and also the poet) described in the poem has ruled a harmonious kingdom through the wit and wisdom of his well-tuned mind until "evil things, in robes of sorrow, / Assailed the monarch's estate" (540). The poem ends describing the present state of Roderick, the narrator, and the house in which "travelers" "Through the encrimsoned windows see / Vast forms that move fantastically / To a discordant melody, / While, like a rapid ghastly river, / Through the pale door / A hideous throng rush out forever / And laugh—but smile no more" (540). The narrator, who journeys within as does the poet, and those who journey through this tale (readers), see the maddened and discordant movement that dwells within the house.

After describing Roderick's poetic fantasy, the narrator recounts Roderick's philosophy of "the sentience of all vegetable things" (541). According to Roderick's philosophy, all things are connected. The "gray stones of the house" render a connection with his "forefathers" (541). The fungi, decayed trees, and general decay of the house are connected with his illness and the curse of the house. But, perhaps more importantly to Poe's conception of the sublime, the external, empirical world is rendered as diseased. This world is not the realm of nature so lauded by English Romantic poets and Goethe.

After describing Roderick's philosophy, the narrator tells of the last moments he spends with Roderick. During this time, the narrator reads passages aloud from a novel, *The Mad Trist* of Sir Launcelot

Canning. As he reads, things happen both outside and inside the house. Metaphorically, as the narrator looks within, changes begin to occur. Ghosts buried deep within rise, as does the sleeping Madeline. As Madeline comes to the chamber where the narrator sits reading aloud to Roderick, Roderick screams "MADMAN!" (547), a scream that signals the narrator's addressing of his own inner darkness. Madeline comes forward and unites with Roderick. The two die as the narrator confronts his greatest fears in this moment that opens unto the story's sublime final scene.

As the narrator runs out of the house he is bathed in the radiance of a blood-red moon. During this scene, the narrator/poet figure witnesses, on the one hand, something awe-filled and terrifying, while, on the other hand, he confronts pleasure from something that threatens to hurt or destroy him. As the house falls and crumbles, the narrator/poet attempts to capture this ineffable experience:

> Suddenly there shot along the path a wild light, and I turned to see whence a gleam so unusual could have issued; for the vast house and its shadows were alone behind me. The radiance was that of the full, setting, and blood-red moon, which now shone vividly through that once barely-discernible fissure, of which I have before spoken as extending from the roof of the building, in a zigzag direction, to the base. While I gazed, this fissure rapidly widened—there came a fierce breath of the whirlwind—the entire orb of the satellite burst at once upon my sight—my brain reeled as I saw the mighty walls rushing asunder—there was a tumultuous shooting sound like the voice of a thousand waters—and the deep and dank tarn at my feet closed sullenly and silently over the fragments of the *House of Usher*. (548)

This final scene provides a disturbing enlightenment experience for the narrator/poet, one that can be compared with Young Goodman Brown's nighttime forest vision (Hawthorne 1043–1044), with Paul's blinding lightning blast and fall from his horse (Acts 9: 1–19), and with the vision of the sun experienced by Plato's cave dweller in *The Republic* (169–70). The fragments of the House of Usher that stand beneath the narrator's feet are remnants of a dark, sublime experience. Above the ashes of the house, the narrator stands alone, while the

"dank tarn at [his] feet [closes] sullenly and silently over the fragments of the *House of Usher*" (548). Here we have a representation of
Poe's sublime aesthetic, one that, rather than exalting transcendence,
renders the sublime epiphany as a recognition of valuelessness. For,
if the value under scrutiny in the story is mortality itself, then here
we literally find death void of meaning, the perfect subject to exploit
Poe's dislike of the didactic in art—the meaningful, purpose-oriented
aesthetic that seeks to instruct. In this sense, Poe's tale comments
upon the terror of the supernatural, the very subject of the Romantic
aesthetic. Thus, the tale both supplements and supplants the conventional notion of the sublime, revealing Poe's vision of sublimity. In the
end, this vision exemplifies Poe's subversive sublime, an ironic, Gothic
moment of awareness that simultaneously creates sublimity while
mocking the idealism of the conventional sublime. Here Poe seems
to have a modern understanding of sublimity, an awareness of the
investment of moral and spiritual value other Romantic poets have
woven into their notions of the sublime. Such a modern, skeptical, yet
ironically playful view of the sublime mirrors the contemporary critic
James Kirwan's description of the concept:

> The sublime is of no more ethical or cognitive significance than
> the clotting of the blood. It appears at times intimately tied up
> with our values only because we make use of these values as
> material from which to produce that peculiar kind of intensely
> pleasurable, circumscribed egotism we call sublimity. Like the
> aesthetic in general, the sublime is a matter of delusion, but it
> is in no sense pathological, any more than love or any of the
> other feelings that make life worth living are pathological. (It
> is, indeed, the absence of such nonrational feelings as partiality
> for one's own children that strikes us as aberrant.) The sublime
> is a matter of the non-rational, not the irrational. However, to
> discuss it as if it were an intuition of profound truth, a matter
> of the cognitive or ethical, is to court irrationality. You may,
> indeed must, feel the aesthetic as an intuition—but you cannot
> assert that it is an intuition and expect to talk sense.

In this story, which is emblematic of Poe's dark Romantic sublime,
the sublime is an empty and emptying experience afforded by art that
brings us to dwell on the paradox of our mortality. For, we, like Poe,

Roderick, and Madeline, are invested with creative powers but are not able to escape the confines of our fate. Led step by step into a Gothic manse where a premature burial takes place, we confront primal fears. Regardless of how we try to distance ourselves, reading this story means delving into the self, that strange region we cannot touch but whose awe, terror, and emptiness we know. As a tale that creates an uncanny sense of being homelike and at once inexplicably foreign, "The Fall of the House of Usher" enshrines the self as a sublime creation, one that yearns to transcend its limits but fails trying, never grasping the true horror of its finitude.

WORKS CITED

Bieganowski, Ronald. "The Self-Consuming Narrator in Poe's 'Ligeia' and 'Usher.'" *American Literature* 60, no. 2 (May 1988): 175–187. Reprinted in *Edgar Allan Poe: A Study of the Short Fiction*, Charles E. May, ed. Boston: Twayne Publishers, 1991. 170–172.

Mabbott, T. O. Notes. *Selected Poetry and Prose of Edgar Allan Poe*. By Edgar Allan Poe. New York: Random House, 1951. 418–419.

Poe, Edgar Allan. *The Unabridged Edgar Allan Poe*. Philadelphia, Penn: Running Press, 1983. 532–548.

Shaw, Philip. *The Sublime*. New York: Routledge, 2006.

Thompson, G. R. *Poe's Fiction: Romantic Irony in the Gothic Tales*. Madison, Wisconsin: The University of Wisconsin Press, 1973. 87–97.

Voller, Jack G. "The Power of Terror: Burke and Kant in the House of Usher." *Poe Studies* 21.3 (December 1988): 27–35.

———. *The Supernatural Sublime*. DeKalb, Illinois: Northern Illinois UP, 1994.

THE FOUR ZOAS
(WILLIAM BLAKE)

"Urizen and the Fragmentary Experience of the Sublime in *The Four Zoas*"
by Blake Hobby, University of
North Carolina at Asheville

To anyone who has spent time studying William Blake's unfinished prophetic book, *The Four Zoas*, and reading commentaries by Blake scholars, themselves some of the world's finest literary critics—Harold Bloom, Northrop Frye, David Erdman and Donald Ault—it is clear that this complex poem demands interpretive feats. Filled with a host of characters, symbols, and pictorial representations that call into question any one definitive reading, *The Four Zoas* tempts readers to reason their way to an overarching interpretation. Yet the text, through the figure of Urizen ("your reason"), who tries in vain to gain mastery over the sublimity of creation, parodies any attempt to gain access to the sublime through Blake's text. Fuddled before a sublime enigma that resembles *The Four Zoas* itself, Urizen struggles for interpretive mastery. Blake's Urizen resembles and alludes to other literary and mythological characters such as Satan in Milton's *Paradise Lost* and the Hebrew God, Jehovah, or "The Ancient of Days," as he is depicted in the illustrations accompanying the poem. Urizen holds great significance in Blake's mythology: His depiction in *The Book of Urizen* is integral to our understanding of his character as it appears in *The Four Zoas*. Additionally, the metaphors describing the process by which he creates are not only found in *The Book of Urizen* but also in

Blake's "The Tyger" from his *Songs of Innocence and Experience*. As a kind of palimpsest, a figure written over an existing Blake myth, Urizen is not simply a character in Blake's works. In many ways, Urizen parallels the reader of the *Four Zoas*, who wrestles with a text that mythologizes both the horrible and beautiful aspects of creation. In the end, readers confront, through Blake's interpreter/creator, Urizen, the external and internal worlds with all of their sublime contradictions.

As "Night the Fifth" ends, the text creates sympathy for Urizen, allowing the objective distance between the reader and Urizen to collapse. Although Urizen has created a wondrous world, a divine fiction, in "Night the Second," his world is now torn asunder. Los, a Zoa who Urizen thinks to be under his control, now works to bind Orc. Orc's howls of terror fill Urizen's creation, where Urizen appears as a Babylonian exile in his own homeland:

> Ah how shall Urizen the King submit to this dark mansion
> Ah how is this! Once on the heights I stretched my throne
>   sublime
> The mountains of Urizen once of silver where the sons of
>   wisdom dwelt
> And on whose tops the Virgins sang are rocks of Desolation
> My fountains once the haunt of Swans now breed the scaly
>   tortoise
> The houses of my harpers are become a haunt of crows
> The gardens of wisdom are become a field of horrid graves
> And on the bones I drop my tears and water them in vain
> (63. 24–30)

Urizen's creation does not grant him power but pulls him into a dark, solipsistic world. Instead of creating dominion, it brings introspection and sorrow. Looking around at the world he has created, Urizen is filled with remorse; his "songs are turned to cries of lamentation" (64. 9).

Urizen is a palimpsest of some of the ideas Blake presents in *The Songs of Innocence and Experience*. "The Tyger" addresses many of Blake's obsessions, including the relationship between good and evil and our image of God. Blake is fascinated with how our perception of a creating God, a transcendent being that has ordered the world, limits the human experience. The poem conflates the *imago Dei* with the process of fiction-making. The speaker questions how a loving

God could create evil. The speaker ironizes the image of God by asking the Tyger what kind of creator might bring evil into being. But there is more at play in the poem. For "The Tyger" addresses explicitly the process of fiction-making and the desire of the artist to harness mystery in a work of art. Thus, Urizen parallels the artistic God of "The Tyger." The speaker of Blake's "Tyger" depicts the need or desire, whether in a world of presence or absence, a world of order or disorder, to frame and delimit. The poem forms a commentary on the process of making meaning and the act of reading. Not only does the poem concern itself with the image of the Creator who is God and poet but also with the Dionysian figure of the ironic interpreter, the one who, in the destruction of his own interpretive signs, spins the reader into a dizzying world. Thus, the poem, from a cultural perspective, parodies Enlightenment thought. For Blake's Tyger, meaning-making remains a burning desire within the forest of language, whether the forest be a forest of symbols, myths, religious images, theology, or philosophy. Ultimately the poem's only challenge, and the self-reflexive anxiety under which Blake suffers in the construction of the poem, is that "The Tyger," and by implication all poetry, should not mean but be, quoting the end of Archibald MacLeish's "Ars Poetica" (629). To create a thing that should not mean but be necessitates that the poet enter the labyrinthine maze of language and meaning-making, which creates great anxiety. Yet paradoxically, the anxiety of doing what is philosophically impossible within a bounded language is what brings the poem into being. Thus Blake's Tyger is not an animal bound within a cage, prevented from expressing what lies within by a thousand external bars, as in Rainer Marie Rilke's "Panther," but is a wild animal burning bright in the forest of the night, a mysterious entity that fuels the speaker's desire to name the unnamable, a creator who parallels the one described ironically by Blake in "The Tyger." Urizen's own self-chastisement parallels the interrogations of the speaker in "The Tyger," interrogations that question the idea and significance of creating a framework: "What immortal hand or eye? Could not [or Dare] frame they fearful symmetry" (*Songs* 42. 2–4). Thus, as Shaviro points out, Blake's poem deals with framing in two major senses: 1) framing as constructing or building, thus the fascination with the builder, the creator, the poet; 2) framing as contextualizing or delimiting, thus the concern with the frame, the context itself (Shaviro 238). Los, working under Urizen's

command to establish a frame for Urizen's work of art, now robs the
work of its life. He represses the initial energy of creation in order to
be able to create a narrative framework. As in "The Tyger," Blake uses
the twisting of sinews and the hammering of the refiner as metaphors
for the framing process in artistic creation. Los endeavors, as does
the creator described in "The Tyger," to create a work of art and then
place it within a frame. In fact, not only does Urizen himself attempt
to create a frame for his creation, but Blake also creates a frame for
the character of Urizen, dividing the text of the Zoas in subsections,
sections framed, limited, and at the same time ironized by Blake's
pictorial representations. Urizen is portrayed as the "Ancient of Days,"
a parody of the all-powerful God of Genesis 1 with which Blake plays
in *The Book of Urizen*. At the end of the *Book of Urizen*, several questions remain unanswered, questions that are taken up again in *The Four
Zoas*: Is Eden lost or (re)gained, or is it just an existential state within
the human breast? Will Urizen integrate? Will the sacred energies
return? Or will we all just have to wait for a later installment/develop-
ment in the Blakean mythos to know that delicious Gospel of Thomas
truth: "He who will drink from my mouth will become as I am: I
myself shall become he, and the things that are hidden will be revealed
to him" or, as in the "Proverbs" from Blake's *Marriage of Heaven and
Hell*, "Thus men forgot that All deities reside in the human breast"
(Plate II. 13)? Although *The Book of Urizen* raises these issues and
"Night the Fifth" and "Night the Sixth" reiterate them, "Night the
Ninth" provides Blake's fantastic answer.

As "Night the Sixth" opens, Urizen stands with a spear, a symbol of
Dionysus. His spear, the Dionysian *thyrsus*, is a symbol of the god who
creates and destroys, a god who in his own self-destructing creation
is a kind of ironic interpreter, one who creates unstable worlds with
words. Urizen is, on one level, a poetic representation of an increasing
awareness that begins in the early 1800s, especially with the German
scholarship of the Bible, of the act of interpreting. Urizen is a poet who
is filled with interpretation anxiety, a poet who is consumed not only by
his own anxieties but also by his own linguistic play. While beholding
"the terrors of the Abyss" he has created, Urizen stares at the world he
has created, his fiction (70. 5). The beings he has created, his own characters, "Sacrd at the sound of their won sigh" wander about "their heart
a Sun a Dreary moon" as "A Universe of fiery constellation" explodes in
their brains (70. 7, 9). To his creation, the world is incomprehensible,

a place of waters, winds, and pestilent plagues that are "beyond the bounds of their own self," a world "their own senses cannot penetrate" (70. 12). He desires to control how his characters interpret the world, yet his "voice to them [is] but an inarticulate thunder for their ears" (70.39). Staring into this world, horrified at his own inability to control the world he has fashioned, he falls.

In "Night the Eighth," all of the nights are revealed to be a dream, a "Vision of All Beulah hovering over the Sleeper" Albion (99. 10). Urizen is an aspect of the sleeper or at least an aspect of the Sleeper's dream. If the Sleeper's dream is a grand mimesis of the waking world, then Blake's poem presents reality as fuzzy fiction, a narrative loosely constructed from perspectives in which a constant war for narrative sequence, logic, meaning, and order is waged.

Four feuding figures in varying emanations fight for Albion's perception of reality. The greatest warrior is Urizen, simultaneously a parody of a dualistic god à la the Ancient of Days that Blake sketched to accompany the text and a parody of the dialectic tradition within Western philosophy. Urizen is a philosopher who generates his own myth; he is an assembler of "a mobile army of metaphors" (Nietzsche 46). He is a parodic representation of dualism inherent in the Western philosophic tradition beginning with Plato. Urizen is the creator of a slave and master theology that mirrors the kind of morality Nietzsche describes in *On the Genealogy of Morals*. But Urizen also becomes the victim of his own ironic game of interpretation, a victim of the unstable system of metaphors he employs. Urizen is the representation of one aspect of Albion and by analogy one aspect of all human beings: the aspect that seeks to understand from a linguistic context, the human faculty that seeks to define being from language itself, creating worlds in words that are then worshipped as false gods.

As "Night the Ninth" opens, Urizen appears as Rahab, the dragon of the Bible. Rahab is referenced in the first line of Genesis 1; she is the goddess of the deep over whom the creative word is spoken. She is also a favorite figure for Deutero-Isaiah whose writings date from the same period as Genesis 1. Deutero-Isaiah uses Rahab, a goddess found in the Babylonian creation myth, to assert his own theology of the word. She is the one whom Yahweh, the one who creates world with words, disperses. She is the Babylonian goddess whom the priestly writers and prophets of exile rail against while the Hebrews are held captive in Babylon from 596 to 536 B.C. Just as Genesis 1 portrays Rahab as a false god, one who creates by sexual union and reigns by force, so does Blake portray Urizen as a false creator, a usurper. To help create this image of Urizen, Blake writes Rahab over the character of Urizen. Just as Yahweh splits Rahab, speaking creative words over her abyss-like form, so does Orc break apart Urizen's Tree of Mystery, his elaborately constructed system of signification:

> The tree of Mystery went up in folding flames
> Blood issud (sic) out in mighty volumes pouring in whirlpools
>   fierce
> From out the flood gates of the Sky The Gates are burst down
>   pour
> The torrents black upon the Earth the blood pours down
>   incessant (119. 4–7)

As "the books of Urizen unroll," Orc consumes the Tree of Mystery (117. 8). Orc, himself once under Urizen's command, now pulls Urizen's creation apart. But while Rahab is destroyed by Yahweh in the Hebrew version of which "Night the Ninth" is a palimpsest, Urizen is not destroyed in Blake's poem. Here Urizen is defeated by Orc (his own creation and also a symbol for creative, passionate rebellion in the human psyche) only to be redeemed. This movement mirrors both Kant's and Burke's description of the sublime aesthetic experience: By reason—measurement—the mind grasps the infinite, but rationality is overthrown by fear, by a recognition of finitude. This defeat of reason, in the end, elevates the mind; it's a transcendental reflection that gives birth to the ethical world. Thus, for Blake, Reason creates Desire/Passion/Rebellion, is overwhelmed by it, and is redeemed. The dialectic of the sublime and of Blake's poem are analogous.

Urizen, weary from his attempts to control signification, longs to be a part of the world he has created. As he comes to awareness, he desires to be a part of the text he has fabricated; he desires to be a character in the world, one who does not analyze, control, and interpret, but one who participates in life, one who is human. Expressing the need to "reassume the human," Urizen laments:

> Saying O that I had never drank the wine nor eat the bread
> Of dark mortality nor cast my view into futurity nor turnd
> My back darkning the present clouding with a cloud

And building arches high and cities turrets & towers &
    domes
Whose smoke destroyd the pleasant gardens & whose
    running Kennels
Chokd the bright rivers burdning with my Ships the angry
    deep
Thro Chaos seeking for delight & in spaces remote
Seeking the Eternal which is always present to the wise
Seeking for pleasure which unsought falls round the infants
    path
And on the fleeces of mild flocks who neither care nor labour
But I the labourer of ages whose unwearied hands
Are thus deformd with hardness with the sword & with the
    spear
And with the Chisel & the mallet I whose labours vast
Order the nations separating family by family
Ungratified give all my joy unto this Luvah & Vala
then Go O dark futurity I will cast thee forth from these
Heavens of my brain nor will I look upon futurity more
I cast futurity away & turn my back upon that void
Which I have made for lo futurity is in this moment
    (121. 3–22)

Urizen releases his desire to control signification. Instead of living to
see how the text he has written will be read, anxious for every reader to
conform to his interpretive will, he gives up his war of words to experience those things that are beyond description, the sublime and incongruous reality to which all language alludes but which no narrative can
harness. He releases the world he has created. As Urizen abandons any
possibility of interpretation, Eternal man asks: "Where shall we take
our stand to view the infinite & unbounded?" (122. 24).

What follows Urizen's acceptance is a massive harvest, a regenera-
tion that involves the acceptance of oppositions, an acceptance that
all perspectives are provisional and limited. In this active moment,
Urizen's thyrsus becomes a sickle, a symbol of the end of time and a
symbol of the end of narrative:

Then Urizen arose and took his Sickle in his hand
There is a brazen sickle & scythe of iron hid

Deep in the South guarded by a few solitary stars
This sickle Urizen took the scythe his sons embracd
And went forth & began to reap & all his joyful sons
Reapd the wide Universe & bound in Sheaves a wondrous
    harvest
They took them into the wide barns with loud rejoicings &
    triumph
Of flute & harp & drum & trumpet horn & clarion.
    (132. 1–8)

Urizen now appears as the god of the harvest, the god who in his own self-discovery enters the world he has created as both human person and god. As the poem ends, the process of narrating and interpreting is portrayed in a dark, comic light. Human beings bound to contraries will always in their "inmost brain" feel "the crushing Wheels they rise [and] they write the bitter words / Of Stern Philosophy & knead the bread of knowledge with tears & groans" (138. 14–15). In other words, human beings will always use words to describe themselves, to know themselves, and to create the world, always grasping for sublimity, always retreating empty-handed (though ennobled by the effort).

In this, the poem's final tableaux, the expanding eyes of the new-born man (Albion), Urizen, and the reader see a life that lies beyond words and interpretation: the world of the sublime. The expanding eyes see that a world contained in language and confined in thought is a projection, an abstraction that no matter how seemingly real and how necessary is not life itself. Thus the intellectual battle began by Urizen in "Night the Sixth" ends with reconciliation. Intellectual strife dissipates, the dark religions depart in a moment where narrative and story end: an apocalypse beyond the word. In this fantastic moment, Urizen, the usurping god and the Rahab figure, moves beyond the god who destroyed him. Words, his creative tools and also the things responsible for his splitting apart, now appear before his eyes as comic elements of a fictive play beyond which "seeds of life" grow (139. 2). *The Four Zoas* provides no sense of certainty, no tangible belief. Rather, it is a grand emptying that describes the numinous realm of the sublime. As the Eternal man at the poem's close asks, "where shall we take our stand to view the infinite and unbounded?" similar questions remain for us. While the narrator places the reader in the position of Urizen, the one seduced by his own aesthetic, the text's self-reflexive, ironic stance, permits a distance that keeps the reader from becoming its victim. In fact, it is more likely that the reader, pulled between the individual and universal, the inner and the outer, the private and the public, remains at a desirable point of instability afforded by the aesthetic experience, a dizzying perspective from which all perspectives can be imagined but from which none can be authenticated—a sublime position from which the inner and outer worlds can be traversed at will.

While *The Four Zoas* parodies *Paradise Lost* and the whole tradition of biblical interpretation, the poem also supplements and supplants a story told for thousands of years, a story whose form exists in Eastern and Western traditions with differing cultural contexts and interpretive implications. Urizen, himself a palimpsest of all mythical stories of creation, brings the reader to reassess, to reread the story's other textual forms as well as *Paradise Lost*, which is itself a colossal palimpsest. *The Four Zoas*, far from simply satirizing Milton's appropriation of the garden story, seduces the reader into interpreting the poem's relationship to the other Urizen textualities. In doing so, Blake presents the seductive manner with which not only narrative but also notions of self and other, individual and society, and private and public are elicited and formed. Thus *The Four Zoas* renders the sublime. Just as Urizen creates by measurement and logic, so must Blake's readers come to terms with a fragmented text, one that tempts us to create a narrative structure out of disparate allusions and symbolism. Urizen is an ironic interpreter consumed by the game in which he engages. Blake frames Urizen as an aspect of the human psyche that transacts in isolation with great effort and infinite destructive power. *The Four Zoas* parodies this interpretive transaction, one that fails to connect to the necessary dimensions of human life, none of which can be contained in narrative. For life, art, and the self are, for William Blake, sublime creations incapable of being bound by the fetters of reason.

Works Cited

Ackroyd, Peter. *Blake: A Biography*. New York: Knopf, 1996.

Altizer, Thomas J. J. *The New Apocalypse: The Radical Christian Vision of William Blake*. East Lansing, MI: Michigan State UP, 1967.

Ault, Donald. *Narrative Unbound: Re-Visioning William Blake's* The Four Zoas. Barrytown, NY: Station Hill, 1987.

Baudelaire, Charles. "The Thyrsus: To Franz Liszt." *Baudelaire, Rimbaud, Verlaine: Selected Verse and Prose Poems*. Secaucus, NJ: Citadel, 1947.

Bidlake, Steven. "Blake, the Sacred, and the French Revolution: 18th-Century Ideology and the Problem of Violence." *European Romantic Review* 3 (Summer 1992): 1–20.

Blake, William. *The Complete Poetry and Prose of William Blake*. Ed. David V. Erdman. Commentary by Harold Bloom. New York: Doubleday, 1988.

Bloom, Harold. *Blake's Apocalypse: A Study in Poetic Argument*. New York: Doubleday, 1963.

————. *The Anxiety of Influence: A Theory of Poetry*. New York: OUP, 1973.

Burke, Edmund. *A Philosophical Enquiry into the Origins of our Ideas of the Sublime and the Beautiful*. London: Routledge, 1958.

Damrosch, Leopold, Jr. *Symbol and Truth in Blake's Myth*. Princeton: Princeton UP, 1980.

Frye, Northrop. *Fearful Symmetry: A Study of William Blake*. Princeton UP, 1947, 1969.

Haigney, Catherine. "Vala's Garden in Night the Ninth: Paradise Regained or Woman Bound?" *Blake: An Illustrated Quarterly* 20, no. 4 (Spring 1987).

Kant, Immanuel. *Critique of the Power of Judgment*. 1790. Trans. Paul Guyer. Cambridge: Cambridge UP, 2000.

Lincoln, Andrew. *Spiritual History: A Reading of William Blake's* Vala *or* The Four Zoas. Oxford: Clarendeon, 1995.

Loudon, Michael Douglas. "The Story of William Blake's *The Four Zoas*: A Guide to the Events of the Epic." Diss. University of New York at Buffalo, 1983.

MacLeish, Archibald. "Ars Poetica." *Literature: Reading, Reacting, Writing*. Ed. Laurie G. Kirszner and Stephen R. Mandell. New York: HBJ, 1997.

Rosso, George Anthony, Jr. *Blake's Prophetic Workshop: A Study of* The Four Zoas. London: Associated UP, 1993.

————. "Blake's Prophetic Workshop: Narrative, History, Apocalypse in *The Four Zoas*." Diss. University of Maryland, 1987.

Shaviro, Stephen. "'Striving with Systems': Blake and the Politics of Difference" *Boundary* 2 (10, no. 3) 1982.

Yogev, Michael. "Covenant of the Word: The Bible in William Blake's Late Prophetic Poems." Diss. U of Washington, 1991.

FRANKENSTEIN
(MARY SHELLEY)

"*Frankenstein*: Creation as Catastrophe"
by Paul Sherwin, in *PMLA* (1981)

INTRODUCTION

In "Creation as Catastrophe," Paul Sherwin takes a psycho-analytic approach to Shelley's novel, with the Creature arising from a kind of primal-scene trauma and seeking wholeness. In his restless pursuit of an impossible desire, the Creature resembles a sublime artwork, one that simultaneously repre-sents and eclipses its creator. Thus, for Sherwin, the uncanny experience of bringing things back to life—whether they be the repressed trauma of the analysand or the reanimation of the Creature, mirrors the genesis of any sublime artwork.

As *Frankenstein* gets under way, we are lured by the promise of a new beginning: Walton's pathbreaking journey to the North Pole. Bound for Archangel to assemble a crew, Walton is inspired by the cold northern wind to envision a perpetually warm and radiant paradise at the summit of the globe. To be there would be to capture the heavens in a glance, to tap earth's central power source, and to stand within the magic circle of the poets he once sought to emulate

---

Sherwin, Paul. "*Frankenstein*: Creation as Catastrophe." *PMLA* 96.5 (October 1981): 883–903.

but whose sublimity he could not match. Such extravagance is easier
to credit if we keep in mind the uneasiness it is intended to dispel:
"There is something at work in my soul, which I do not understand"
(p. 21).[1] Perhaps for his own good, and certainly at the dramatically
right moment, the quest founders somewhere in the frozen wastes
between Archangel and the Pole, just where Walton is waylaid by
Frankenstein, who is feverishly pursuing the path of the Creature's
departure. It may be more accurate to say that the quest is deflected.
For although Walton is relegated to the periphery of the fiction,
ushering in and out a wondrous tale that preempts his own, he is
profoundly implicated as well. The tale, of course, is a monitory
example meant for him, but it is also a riddle of fate that means him:
the mystery that he is and that becomes his by virtue of his fascinated
participation in Frankenstein's story. In short, Walton is in the critical
position, and nowhere is his situation better evidenced than at the end
of the novel. Frankenstein, burdened by his tale's monstrous residue,
concludes his narrative by enjoining Walton to slay the Creature after
his death. Yet the climactic encounter with the Creature unsettles
everything even more and leaves Walton powerless to act. The final
word and deed belong to the Creature, who vows to undo the scene
of his creation once he bounds from the ship: "I shall ... seek the
most northern extremity of the globe; I shall collect my funeral pile,
and consume to ashes this miserable frame, that its remains may
afford no light ... my ashes will be swept into the sea by the winds"
(pp. 222–23). To Walton, however, belongs the burden of the mystery
as he watches this self-destroying artifact vanish into darkness and
distance and contemplates a catastrophe at the Pole.

I.

Mary Shelley might well have titled her novel *One Catastrophe after
Another*. For Frankenstein, who is dubiously in love with his own poly-
morphously disastrous history, the fateful event to which every other
catastrophe is prelude or postscript is the creation. According to the
archaic model implicit in his narrative, transcendence is equivalent to
transgression, and his presumptuous deed is invested with the aura of
a primal sin against nature that somehow justifies the ensuing retribu-
tive bother. Condemned by nature's gods to limitless suffering, the

aspiring hero learns his properly limited human place. *Frankenstein*, however, knows differently. A reading alert to the anti-Gothic novel Mary Shelley inscribes within her Gothic tale will discover that nothing is simple or single. *The* critical event is impossible to localize, terms such as "justice" and "injustice" do not so much mean as undergo vicissitudes of meaning, and all the narrators are dispossessed of their authority over the text. As the central misreader, Frankenstein is the chief victim of the text's irony, the humor becoming particularly cruel whenever he thinks he is addressing the supernatural powers that oversee his destiny, for his invocatory ravings never fail to conjure up his own Creature. Indeed, the evacuation of spiritual presence from the world of the novel suggests that *Frankenstein* is more a house in ruins than the house divided that its best recent critics have shown it to be. The specter of deconstruction rises: doubtless future interpreters will describe a text that compulsively subverts its own performance and that substitutes for its missing center the senseless power play of a catastrophic Gothic machine. Yet the Gothic is always already demystified, the ruin of an anterior world of large spiritual forces and transcendent desires that the most relentless of demystifiers cannot will away. *Frankenstein*, although arguably a Gothic fiction, remains a living novel because it is a haunted house, ensouled by the anxious spirit that perturbs all belated romances.

While the unconsummated spirit raised by *Frankenstein* cannot be put to rest, one might suppose that *das Unheimliche* can be contained within the spacious edifice of Freudian psychoanalysis. Freud's antithetical system provides an interpretive context for many of the anomalies disclosed by an ironic reading: the dissonance of overt and implicit meanings, the obscure sense of having trespassed on sacred ground, the appalling secret that craves expression yet must be protected as though it were a holy thing. In addition, the novel's catastrophic model functions in a way strikingly similar to the Freudian psychic apparatus. Instead of hubris, there is the drive's excess; instead of a downcast hero assaulted by phantasmagoria, there is the boundless anxiety occasioned by the proliferation of repressed desire; and instead of the restrictive gods, there is the exalted secondary process, intended to keep the apparatus stable by binding or incarcerating mobile energy. More telling, the catastrophic model is an almost exact duplicate of the oedipal scenario, the most privileged psychoanalytic thematic and the dynamic source of Freud's mature topography of the psyche. The way is opened for a recentering of the novel's unresolved intellectual and emotional turmoil.

[...]

II.

Writing on the occasion of *Frankenstein*'s canonization, its inclusion in a "standard novels" series, Mary Shelley begins the Introduction as if discharging a grim obligation to a text that should long ago have been consigned to her buried past. She is roused again, however, when she returns to the moment of the novel's origin, her waking dream of Frankenstein's emergence as a creator. Focusing on the creator's terror, she evokes the disturbing thrill of being there, in the midst of the traumatic scene, her prose mounting in intensity and shifting to the present tense as she recounts the successive stages of her vision: the powerful engine stirring to life the "hideous phantom"; Frankenstein's hysterical flight; the "horrid thing" opening the bed curtains and fixing its eyes on him, an experience of ultimate dread that shatters the vision, leaving her breathless on her "midnight pillow" (pp. 9–10). What does it mean to be there, in the midst? It is to be swept up into a sublime dimension and to be faced by a dizzying void, to be at once an excited witness, the terrified artist, and the aroused form of chaos that gazes back at both creator and dreamer. Invention, Mary Shelley reflects, consists in creating "out of chaos" (p. 8). Once her imagination asserts itself, presenting her with the dream vision, we may associate the engine (*ingenium, genius*) with the usurping imagination, the animated Creature with the scene itself, and the chaotic mass to be set in motion with the writer's own chaos, the panic at the center of her authorial consciousness. Creator, creation, and creative agency are varying manifestations of the same anxiety that elaborates itself to compose the scene of authorship.

The novel's monstrous heart of darkness is the creation, and the creative self that inaugurates the drama resembles the "self-closd, allrepelling ... Demon" encountered at the opening of *The Book of Urizen*. Frankenstein's founding gesture, like that of Blake's fearful demiurge, is a stepping aside, but while Urizen secedes from Eternity, Frankenstein absents himself from our world of ordinary awareness and relatedness, which recedes from him in much the manner that a dream fades at the instant of awakening. Severing all contact with his family, other beings, and familiar nature, he is intent on hollowing out a zone in reality where he can be utterly alone. This ingressive movement is attended by self-loss, a radical shrinkage of his empirical self, and self-aggrandizement, a heightening of his isolate selfhood to daemonic status. He becomes a force instead of a person as all the energy of his being concentrates on his grand project: "My mind was filled with one thought, one conception, one purpose" (p. 48); "a resistless, and almost frantic, impulse urged me forward; I seemed to have lost all soul or sensation but for this one pursuit" (p. 54). The animation project, like the object intended by the Freudian libido, is a secondary affair. What matters is that it enkindles in the projector a lust for self-presence so intense that it drives out of consciousness everything except itself. Reality must yield if the self is to appear, and Frankenstein's primary creative act is to originate his own creative self.

The vertiginous upward fall that founds the creative self coincides with a rupture between daemonic mind and all that is not mind. What may loosely be termed consciousness (of self, an extravagantly augmented self so full of itself as to allow neither time nor space for self-awareness) and unconsciousness (of the normative world from which the self has detached itself) are twin-born, factoring out as discrete loci that mark the decisiveness of Frankenstein's psychic dislocation. Only in the catastrophic nature of this birth is there any significant point of contact with the repressive process that institutes ego and id as opposing agencies in the Freudian economy. Narcissism and, probably closer, psychosis are the appropriate psychoanalytic analogues, though the usefulness of these nosological entities here is questionable. I see no need, for example, to posit a specific libidinal stage or fixation point to which Frankenstein is regressing. But everything would resolve itself into a structural conflict anyway: Frankenstein's oedipal trouble impels his defensive "episode," which signals a victory of the forces of repression; and with the creation he spills back into the domain of assured analytic knowledge, the Creature amounting to a bizarre symptomatic return of the repressed that can be interpreted in the same way as the dream of a neurotic. For the psychoanalyst, then, the Creature is a figure that redoubles Frankenstein's literal unconscious complex, which is already present as an a priori with a determinate constitution; in fact, however, he is an autonomous agent, not a psychic agency, and Frankenstein's supposed unconscious is a figurative device, a critic's overhasty recourse designed to mediate or neutralize a puzzling discontinuity.

By what name shall we invoke discontinuity? For Milton in *Paradise Lost* it is Hell, a space carved out in the universe to receive the daemonic selfhood of Satan, for whom everything is a universe of death. The depth of one's particular hell is an index of how far one has fallen away from what might be perceived or known. The unconscious, in other words, is a modality of subjective experience whose meaning is estrangement. What Frankenstein creates, in order to create, is distance between his daemonized self and a newly alienated reality, and it scarcely matters whether we conceive this space as interior or exterior since it is a fantastic medial zone where the boundaries between self and world are impossible to distinguish. Within this void, between two created "nothings," self-consciousness appears. It is the place into which the baffled residue of Frankenstein's ordinary self has been cast. From its vantage, somewhere in the corner of Frankenstein's mind, it takes notes, watching with horrified fascination the extravagant career of a stranger that is also an uncanny variation of the self.

Out of this phantom place, in addition, the Creature emerges, as Blake's Enitharmon emanates from Los once Los 'closes' with the death image of Urizen, thus embracing the world view of the solipsistically withdrawn creating mind. The ungraspable Enitharmon, Los's loss and shadowed gain, embodies the suddenly exterior, objectified space that has opened up between Los and Eternity, or Los's alienated potential. The Creature is similarly a token of loss, a complex representation of the estranged universe Frankenstein has summoned into being by pushing away reality. Yet does the Creature, strictly speaking, represent Frankenstein's alienated potential? I suppose he can be read as the responsive, sympathetic imagination Frankenstein suppresses in order to create. From the psychoanalytic perspective, such repression would be very odd: imagine the id repressing the sublimated ego. The repression hypothesis must be rejected in any event because the Creature is something radically new and different, no more a double or a part of Frankenstein than Enitharmon is of Los. Instead, these emanative beings "stand for" their creators in the sense that they are interpolations, "transitional objects" (Winnicott) or texts, intended to rectify a catastrophic disalignment of self and world.

The creation is at once a new departure for Frankenstein and the climax of a developmental process that, as Wordsworth says, "hath no beginning." Frankenstein's narrative begins with an idyll of domestic bliss: in the protected enclave of his household all are incomparably virtuous and lovable; affections go deep, and yet everyone lives on the surface. Of course, it is all a lie, but the reader should be troubled by this absurdity no more than by the newborn Creature's walking off with Frankenstein's coat as protection against the cold. Just as anyone who wishes can discover the source of an individual's troubles in the past, since so much happened "there," readers inclined to locate the cause of Frankenstein's aberration in his youth will see what they expect to see in his narrative or will find that what they seek is all the more confirmed by its absence from the account. His fall may have been occasioned by Elizabeth's admission into the family circle, by William's birth, by the sinister 'silken cord' (p. 34) of parental constriction, or by a repressed primal-scene trauma. It doesn't matter: any psychotrauma is as true or as false as any other. Like all of us, Frankenstein begins fallen—or, better, falling. The brief idyll of his youth gives him something to fall away from; and the more remotely idealized the starting point, the more absolute or self-defining is his point of departure. Frankenstein simply announces that, as far back as he can remember, "the world was to me a secret which I desired to divine" (p. 36). That is, the fall from the wholeness of origins is rooted in his lust to overtake a hidden, receding presence, or a tantalizing absence, that lies behind appearances and disturbs his contact with things. This dualizing consciousness is a given of his temperament, the destiny-assigned identity theme that he lives out in the sphere of science but that he could have expressed as well in exploration or authorship. Can we improve on Frankenstein's version, or on Coleridge's characterization of Iago as "a motiveless malignity"? The aptly named Iago is the ego principle, the sublimely arbitrary human will that originates everything, including all myths of a catastrophic or transcendental point of spiritual origination, and motive hunting no more explains his willfulness than it does Desdemona's love for Othello.

Motivation, like sequential logic, is a falsification the mind cannot do without. The signal importance Frankenstein ascribes to the death of his mother suggests that the reanimation project is a deferred reaction to this event, which he terms "the first misfortune of my life . . . an omen . . . of my future misery" (p. 42). He dwells on the "irreparable evil" brought about by the rending of ties and on the "void" created by death, which he raises to quasi-supernatural status as "the spoiler" (p. 43). Presumably her death reactivates an original anxiety of deprivation associated with the departure of the maternal body, and the irrevocable loss of the mother, the primary focus of the child's reality bondings, could help to explain the intensification of Frankenstein's temperamental dualism. But while psychoanalytic theory is suggestive here, it is too restrictively bound to a particular mythic version of the past, too fetishistically centered on one of many possible mythic representations of loss. Like the oak-shattering bolt, the death of the mother is preeminently a narcissistic insult for Frankenstein. Confronted by the fact of death, he is overtaken by a primordial anxiety, not an anxiety-provoking repressed wish; and although such anxiety is apt to recoil from any number of fancied antagonists, its proper object is the most inclusive and irreducible of forces: life, our human life, in relation to which death is not an external agency but an internal component. Yet, as Kierkegaard knew, consciousness of this radical fault in existence need not, or need not only, paralyze the spirit. Dread, and perhaps even the fear of being delivered over to it, can be a sublime energizer, arousing the infinite spirit that longs for a house as large as itself.

Seeking to undo the consequences of sexuality, the sin of being born of woman, Frankenstein engages in a pursuit at once regressive and projective, mobilizing old energies in an attempt to discover a new meaning for himself. Adrift for a time after his mother's death, he is eager, once he leaves for the university, to cast off his dependence and put his talents to work. All that remains is for Waldman's sermon, perhaps more the sheer power of his voice than his overt message, to render an occasion for Frankenstein's restless drive for autonomy:

> Such were the professor's words—rather let me say such the words of fate. . . . As he went on, I felt as if my soul were grappling with a palpable enemy; one by one the various keys were touched which formed the mechanism of my being. . . . So much has been done, exclaimed the soul of Frankenstein— more, far more, will I achieve . . . I will pioneer a new way, explore unknown powers, and unfold to the world the deepest mysteries of creation. (p. 48)

This powerfully charged moment of conversion, or reconversion, founds Frankenstein as an artist. From the struggle of his second birth he emerges as a force of destiny, genius in a human form, first pronouncing the fateful name of the modern Prometheus: *franken Stein*, the free rock, the free-unfree man.

After two years of reviewing the current state of scientific knowledge, Frankenstein is abruptly halted by an audacious, yet for him inevitable, question: "Whence ... did the principle of life proceed?" (p. 51). The way is opened for his first descent into the world of the tomb: "I beheld the corruption of death succeed to the blooming cheek of life; I saw how the worm inherited the wonders of the eye and brain." At this stage Frankenstein presents himself as a detached observer of death's work, and nature offers little resistance to his inquiries. "A sudden light" breaks "from the midst of this darkness" (p. 52), whereupon he is dazzled to discover himself the first of mortals capable of disentangling life from death. Modern criticism, generally empowered by demystifying reversals, has tended both to devalue Frankenstein's discovery, regarding his life principle as a type of natural energy rather than as a genuine first, and to view his enthusiasm as a mechanical operation of the spirit. Although the great Romantic faith in the omnipotence of thought is unquestionably allied to the scientist's baleful drive for manipulative control, they remain very distinct forms of the Cartesian legacy. To the extent that the artist in Frankenstein collapses into the technician he is a loser. But now, as he stands at the source, Frankenstein is a sublime quester who has found his muse, an answering subject to inspire and direct the quest, and his delight is that of a man who has come to recognize the glory of his own inner source, his originative *I am*.

Once Frankenstein begins to describe the lengthy creation process his hitherto sequential narrative becomes curiously perturbed. The style is spasmodic, juxtapositive, and repetitive, obscuring temporal relations yet underscoring how radically divided the creator is. We hear from a practical Frankenstein, who reasons that even an imperfect effort will lay the ground for future successes; a secretly selfish utopian idealist, who dreams of a new species blessing him "as its creator and source" (p. 54); and a domestic Frankenstein, who procrastinates "all that related to my feelings of affection until the great object, which swallowed up every habit of my nature, should be completed" (p. 55). Being swallowed up is the principal terror of the narrative consciousness dominating these pages, a depersonalized, though suffering, observer of the wreck Frankenstein is becoming. Little is heard from the daemonized Frankenstein, in part because his experience of sublime uplift is wordless and in part because this "hurricane" (p. 54) has no time for words, though for the troubled eye of the storm time is agonizingly slow. Complicating matters is the superimposition of the narrative present on an episode that the fallen Frankenstein can be relied on to misconstrue, so that the complex web of the account becomes virtually impossible to unweave. Then, we may surmise, a dialectic of the following sort was at work: driving out and driven in, the creative self is agonistic, aggressively excluding otherness, and hence agonized, defensively immuring itself in resistance to any foreign body that would encroach on its sublime solitude; the barrier keeps breaking, however, leading to disabling bouts of self-consciousness, which in turn provoke even more audacious sublime rushes that threaten to overwhelm the ordinary self, that residual under-consciousness which clings ever more desperately to its bewildered identity. How one interprets the meaning of the entire experience—whether from the point of view of the daemonic self or from that of the ordinary self—probably tells more about the interpreter than about the experience itself, just as the Abyssinian maid of "Kubla Khan" emerges as the muse of paradise or the voice of the abyss depending on whether one stands inside or outside the magic circle of the conclusion.

The breathlessly eager self that is in, or is, the enthusiasm soars above the body that is taking shape. Frankenstein's workshop is located "in a solitary chamber, or rather cell, at the top of the house, and separated from all the other apartments" (p. 55). This is a masterful emblem of the mind that is its own place. [2] The windows are barred, at least for the enthusiast, whose eyes remain "insensible to the charms of nature" (p. 55). Those "charms" are an interpolation of Frankenstein the notetaker or narrator; the creator is an innerness—pure, unconditioned spirit—seeking innerness—the life or light in, but not of, things. Things themselves do not exist for him except as "lifeless matter" (p. 52) to be animated, the *fort* to his *da* (*sein*),[3] and the more they are leveled to a deadening continuity the more discontinuous is the fiery spirit that would stamp its image on a world rendered pliable to its projects and projections.

The problem is that if the sublime artist is to "pour a torrent of light into our dark world" (p. 54) of mortal life, he must take a detour through reality. To wrest the spirit from things he must, for a second time, penetrate into the center of the earth, and to prepare a frame for the reception of life he must now not only see and know but also touch the body of death. Undertaking a shamanistic descent into chaos, a place of "filthy creation" (p. 55) where life and death conspire to breed monstrous shapes, Frankenstein is flooded with nausea: "Who shall conceive the horrors of my secret toil, as I dabbled among the unhallowed damps of the grave, or tortured the living animal to animate the lifeless clay?" (p. 54). Is Frankenstein speaking of vivisection, or is the tortured living body his own? His aggression, whether directed outward or against himself, recalls that of Blake's Urizen:

> Times on times he divided, & measur'd
> Space by space in his ninefold darkness
> Unseen, unknown! changes appeard
> In his desolate mountains rifted furious
> By the black winds of perturbation
>
> For he strove in battles dire
> In unseen conflictions with shapes
> Bred from his forsaken wilderness
> (*The Book of Urizen* 1.2–3)

Frankenstein too is entrapped by his own phantasmagoria. The oppressively close, enveloping tomb world into which he descends is a self-engendered abyss that discloses what our finite bodily ground looks like from the heights to which the spirit has ascended. Transforming an evacuated reality into a grotesque naturalization and the denied natural passions into a perversely eroticized shadow life, the sublime artist's exaggerated distance from things has also transformed him into a graveyard poet. In short, Frankenstein has discovered, or invented, an inchoate version of the Freudian unconscious.

Frankenstein's aggression and perverse perception are inscribed in the Creature's appearance. The artist envisioned something quite different: "How can I ... delineate the wretch whom with such infinite pains and care I had endeavoured to form? His limbs were in proportion, and I had selected his features as beautiful" (p. 57). What *did* Frankenstein intend? Treading "heaven in my thoughts ... exulting in my powers" (p. 211), he conceived the Creature as a

representation of the transfigured creative self, a grandiose embodiment of the creator's mind. But it is also a desperate compromise,
designed to mend an intolerable dualism. The beautiful Creature of
Frankenstein's imaginings is analogous to Sin, the perfect narcissistic
image of Satan, the interior paramour who explodes from his brain
when heaven rolls away from him and with whom he proceeds to
copulate; Frankenstein's dread monster corresponds to Sin's unrecognized "nether shape," but even more closely to Death, that chaotic
"darkness visible," who is the ultimate issue of Satan's deranged spirit,
his love of his own thought. The moving Creature, like Death, is
unrepresentable. However, directly after the infusion of life, while the
Creature is still dazed, Frankenstein ventures the novel's only description of this formless form:

> Beautiful!—Great God! His yellow skin scarcely covered the
> work of muscles and arteries beneath; his hair was of a lustrous
> black, and flowing; his teeth of a pearly whiteness; but these
> luxuriances only formed a more horrid contrast with the watery
> eyes, that seemed almost of the same colour as the dun white
> sockets in which they were set, his shrivelled complexion and
> straight black lips. (p. 57)

An "unearthly" figure (p. 219), the Creature bodies forth the horrid
contrast between heaven and hell that Frankenstein experiences as a
dizzying, instantaneous descent.

How is one to explain this catastrophic turn? The only way to
fathom the Creature's appearance, which is more a rhetorical effect than
a natural fact, is to comprehend how it was made. For Frankenstein,
putting together and dismembering are one. The parts he chooses are
beautiful, but they are monstrous in conjunction—or, rather, since the
Creature lacks a phenomenological center, in their absolute disjunc-
tion. Frankenstein is similarly unbalanced, a confused collectivity. The
daemonized self that initiates the project is a force inimical to form,
and it cannot see or guide properly from the heights. The normative
self, desperately in need of bridging back to reality, patches over the
rift in the fabric of Frankenstein's existence as best it can. But although
its eyeballs start "from their sockets in attending to the details" (p.
55), it cannot recollect the original inspiration. The result of all this
frantic alienated labor is a being geared to self-torment. As such, the

Creature is also a figure that reveals, with more startling accuracy and profundity than discursive reason can command, the existential condition of its progenitor: his relation-disrelation to his world, his thoughts, and himself. The incomplete Creature, unmated and unmatable, an inconceivably lonely freestanding unit whose inside is hopelessly divided from its outside, is indeed a "filthy type" (p. 130) of the modern Prometheus.

Any representation of the creative process, whether the novel's narrative or my analytic account, is bound to distort the experience of the whole self. Suspended between heaven and hell, those absolutely disjoined fictive polarities that are in fact mutually sustaining correlates, the creator is at once ravished and ravaged by sublimity. He is filled and swallowed up, but not entirely full or emptied out; for to be wholly abandoned to the sublime would amount to autism, and there would no longer be a self to experience the uplift or downfall. It is always, to modify Emerson slightly, a case of I *and* the abyss. Since he cannot be the thing itself and cannot be nothing, Frankenstein is a spirit destined to "exult in the agony of the torturing flames" (p. 223). Another name for this giant agony is despair. "Despair," writes Kierkegaard, cannot

> consume the eternal thing, the self, which is the ground of despair, whose worm dieth not, and whose fire is not quenched. Yet despair is precisely *self*consuming, but it is an impotent self-consumption. . . . This is the hot incitement, or the cold fire in despair, the gnawing canker whose movement is constantly inward, deeper and deeper. . . . This precisely is the reason why he despairs . . . because he cannot consume himself, cannot get rid of himself, cannot become nothing. This is the potentiated formula for despair, the rising of the fever in the sickness of the self.[4]

Kierkegaard, dangerously on the verge of becoming the dread itself, is a better guide here than Freud, the great analyst of the concept of dread. As Kierkegaard would have it, Frankenstein is a prisoner of despair because his volatile spirit desires only to augment itself, because the self is not "grounded transparently in the Power which posited it" (p. 19). That Power, which may simply be a potentiated form of the despairing spirit, exists beyond the purview of Mary

Shelley's fiction. But *Frankenstein* is empowered, and at times disabled, by a despair over the human condition, whose limits condemn the creator's sublime quest to the status of an extravagant, desperate wish. The novel's wisdom, not only imperfectly expressed by an advocacy of domestic bliss but in fact undercut by overt moralizing, is that we need "keeping" (p. 19), that we must be concrete in the same measure as we are abstract and that we must abide with the antinomies (life and death, ideality and actuality, will and fate) that constitute our ground. Frankenstein may be said to err in misreading both his own reality and the larger reality that circumscribes his existence. No matter how great the spirit within him, the universal life principle he thinks he has captured, although it is not merely a trick of spirit, can never become his instrument for correcting existence. It "was now within my grasp," he says; he adds, however, that "the information I had obtained was of a nature rather to direct my endeavours so soon as I should point them towards the object of my search. . . . I was like the Arabian who had been buried with the dead, and found a passage to life, aided only by one glimmering, and seemingly ineffectual, light" (pp. 52–53). Dazzled by an obscure revelation, he can only move toward the light, for the power source he taps is a constituent element in an ongoing process, a continuum of animation and deanimation according to whose subtle rhythm of recurrence we live and die every moment. Frankenstein is a thief of fire, and the utmost he can do is to transmit the power to a body capable of sustaining life.

His nervous symptoms become increasingly pathological as the time for the Creature's inspiration nears, and once he is about to perform the deed, finding himself in a recognizably realistic setting, Frankenstein is less anxious than melancholic, as though calamity has already struck. What possible act or object could satisfy the aspirations of the uncreated soul? The dream of the sublime artist's overflowing fullness is grotesquely parodied as Frankenstein sickens into creation: "the rain pattered dismally against the panes, and my candle was nearly burnt out, when, by the glimmer of the half-extinguished light, I saw the dull yellow eye of the creature open" (p. 57). What is bracketed here, at the decisive moment of Frankenstein's reentry into reality, is the infusion of the spark of life. The creative act is a mindless reflex, an indication that the creator has fallen away from his desire into a void that nothing can fill but that somehow must be limited, as in *The Book of Urizen*, by a barrier of "solid obstruction." The Creature, though not quite setting a limit to Frankenstein's nightmare, is hell's bottom. Landing there, Frankenstein sees his Creature for the first time when its eyes open, a negative epiphany revealing to him that he is not alone, that he too is now visible. The nightmare follows, with its horrific climactic emblem of the condition of corporeality, and he wakens to confront the self-impelled Creature, the living image of death this new Orpheus has brought back from the house of the dead. The creator's terror attests to his lack of mastery, the grim fact of his own creatureliness, which is what set the creative process in motion. Beholding the Creature, Frankenstein is back at his original impasse, uncannily subject to the recurrence of his dread of time, space, and the body of death.

It is impossible to know what Frankenstein apprehends at the pivotal instant when his half-extinguished candle is eclipsed by the Creature's dull yellow eye, but the former seeker of the inner light almost immediately fixates on appearances. The overwhelming irony is that Frankenstein has opened up a space in reality for the emergence of something radically new, realizing the power to make literally present that the poets have always dreamed of. A presence so full that it is as unapproachable as light or an absence so great that it confounds the representational faculties, the Creature is the sublime or grotesque thing itself. Frankenstein's all too human failure of response is to petrify his living artifact into an otherness that cannot be restituted by mind. The Creature becomes a blocking agent, standing between Frankenstein and the normative world he longs to rejoin, and an uncanny reminder of the creator's alienated majesty, the sublime experience from which he is henceforth irremediably estranged. This unproductive misreading, though saving him from an encounter with Dread itself, condemns both Creature and creator to anguished incompleteness. Locked into an interminable pursuit of the shadow he has become, Frankenstein emerges as the man who cannot emerge, a prisoner of the passage arrested at the moment of his falling away from his own possible sublimity. The final irony is that his solitude is confirmed. Frankenstein achieves his own separate consciousness of himself as the most wretched of mortals. But even if his egotism is such that he glories in this doom as the token of a special destiny, he has become just another Gothic hero-villain, a tiresome neurotic whose presence impoverishes the larger portion of the novel that bears his name.

III.

There is an intriguing relation between Frankenstein's history and the account of the novel's genesis in the Introduction. Although the vocation of protagonist and novelist is in a sense chosen by their temperaments and circumstances, the origin of the creative enterprise is supremely arbitrary: a spell of bad weather. Confined indoors, Frankenstein is set on the path toward creation after he "chanced to find a volume of the works of Cornelius Agrippa" (p. 39), and Mary Shelley is bestirred after "some volumes of ghost stories"—less threatening models for a literary aspirant than are her companions, Shelley and Byron—"fell into our hands" (p. 7). This archaic matter requires supplementation, and the means of carrying out the project is offered by Waldman's lecture on modern science and by Shelley and Byron's conversation about galvanism. At this juncture, however, two defensive reversals aim to differentiate the careers of active author and passive subject. The sudden light that breaks in upon Frankenstein impels him toward his catastrophic creation scene, but it is only after her waking dream that Mary Shelley experiences her vocational moment: "Swift as light and as cheering was the idea that broke in upon me. 'I have found it!' ... On the morrow I announced that I had *thought of a story*." The vision of the would-be master's victimization is her means of mastery, as though the scene of authorship were already behind her. "And now, once again, I bid my hideous progeny go forth and prosper" (p. 10), she writes, as though the novel were the Creature and she had put on its power to overwhelm others. In the Introduction she passes over the actual writing of *Frankenstein*, and while her creative labor was doubtless less calamitous than Frankenstein's, the novel is necessarily another "imperfect animation" (p. 9). How much, one wonders, was lost in "translation" when the airy book imagination wrote in the mind became the novel we read? But the likelihood is that the ecstatic dream of the book, as represented in the Introduction, is an afterbirth, that now, once again, Mary Shelley is begetting it by replaying both Frankenstein's and *Frankenstein*'s catastrophe of origination. Her mind, too, was the haunt of a terrible idea, which became her means of mastery insofar as it inspired the novel's transcendent or paradigmatic vision of the genesis of any sublime artwork, any uncanny reanimation project.

According to the novel's representation of the creative process, the work emanates from an authorial self whose decisive break with normative experience clears a space for the work to appear. The emergence of this authorizing agency necessitates such a massive withdrawal or sacrifice of the writer's identity that the work is likely to be more estranged from writer than reader. To argue thus is not to deny that Mary Shelley, as mother and mourning mother, was ideally suited to preside over the account of Frankenstein's fearful literal creation. But even if we agree that the novel is informed by her personal experience and that the novel, had it been anonymously published, would be recognizably a woman's book, we cannot necessarily trace its creation back to her empirical self or conclude that its meaning is coextensive with its point of departure in personal experience. The role of the writer's biography and psychobiography in the work is analogous to that of what Freud calls the "day's residue" in the dreamwork. Once the author crosses from the empirical sphere to the transcendent dimension of art, the stuff of ordinary experience is reconstituted as an element in the work's fantastic scenario, and the empirical self, transformed for good or ill by the author's rite of passage, is simply along for the ride. Still, if it is the Real Man or Woman, the Blakean Imagination, that solicits our response in a literary text, we must be careful not to be carried away by Blake's sublime idealizations or capital letters. The authorial self must not be vaporized into an impersonal transcendental consciousness. The writer may be powerfully tempted to become a force refusing all form, but the constitutive subject I am positing has its own complex psychology, determined by its relations to the forms, images, and desires that compose the field of literature. That is to say, the authorial self, like the empirical self, is a living consciousness, not so much disembodied as differently embodied.

What does it mean for the Word to be incarnated, for the work to be written? "When composition begins," writes Shelley, "inspiration is already on the decline, and the most glorious poetry that has ever been communicated to the world is probably a feeble shadow of the original conception of the poet." We recall that when Frankenstein infuses the spark of being into the lifeless thing before him, his candle is "nearly burnt out." Shelley's version is that "the mind in creation is as a fading coal."[5] Composition is at once the shattering of mind and the scattering of dead or dying thoughts, mere leavings, ashes and sparks that are the casual by-products of the 'unextinguished hearth' of original inspiration. Art is a betrayal of its source. Lapsing into discourse, the artist utters a dismembered Word. Alienated by the words intended to mediate it, the Word assumes the opacity of what stands for it and is evacuated by what stands in its place. To be represented by the text is thus to experience a bewildering efface-ment or defacement of the self; the authorial self, in other words, is as much estranged from the work as the empirical self. Of course, it can be argued that the authorial self is merely an effect of textuality, not an originative presence: "Always already"—one hears the insistent murmur of Derrida, echoing Heidegger—textualized. That may be so. But I find it impossible to think about literature without retaining the notion of the creative imagination, if for no other reason than that some such mythic agency is needed to link the completed text to the self that paces about the room and chews pencils. Dr. Johnson, who greatly respected literary power, shows himself to be at least as advanced as the most modern demystifier when he terms imagination a "hunger . . . which preys incessantly upon life" (*Rasselas*, Ch. XXXII). Perhaps, then, it would be more accurate to say that the artist, instead of falling into textuality, falls back on the text to avoid becoming lost in his or her own void. Composing the work, the writer touches ground. Inasmuch as writing is always a reworking of the already written, of literary tradition, it is not the writer's own ground, but it is just as surely the true ground of his or her being, inasmuch as reanimating the dead is the self-alienating labor that constitutes authorship.

However universal Frankenstein's experience may be, his failure as an artist is also particular, a merely personal torment. He counsels Walton not to aspire to be greater than human nature will allow. How great is that? In flight from his catastrophic scene of authorship, Frankenstein seeks consolation in the Alps, declaring that the Power is there, elsewhere, invested in Mont Blanc. Here the human being is a dwarfed latecomer, the sole unquiet thing, and Frankenstein, with dubious ecstasy, yields up his spirit to the "solitary grandeur" (p. 97) presiding over this ancient desolation. But although vowing not "to bend before any being less almighty than that which had created and ruled the elements" (p. 94), he is surprised by his massive and all but omnipotent Creature, the only presence amid this blankness and a fit emblem of his god of Power. Ultimately, the terrific god means "I am terrified"—whether by chaos or the space of absolute freedom remains for the interpreter to decide. Like the speaker of Blake's "Tyger," whose own estranged genius can be read in his distorted visions of a beast and of a beastly creator so fearsome he can be represented only by piecemeal images, Frankenstein is absurdly frightened out of his creative potential by his own creations.

Is it possible to put on power and yet avoid crippling anxiety? Shelley believed so, and his "Mont Blanc" is a serious parody of the "ceaseless ravings" of Coleridge's "Hymn before SunRise," a poem Frankenstein might have written. Shelley himself is nearly overwhelmed by nature's power display and the spectral deity it represents. However, "one legion of wild thoughts," a saving remnant, wanders to "the still cave of the witch Poesy," and from within this zone of calm, carved out of the rock of nature, he recalls the power of his own adverting mind to image and give voice to "the secret Strength of things." In *Prometheus Unbound*, among other things a reply to *Frankenstein*, Shelley exemplifies his hope that an impotently self-consuming despairing man can be therapeutically remembered as an artistic self whose strength derives from the embrace it gives. Bending reality to the shape of his desire, Shelley does not overlook that aspect of the self which cannot participate in a radiant world new-made by mind. Rather, he enjoins a heroic labor of self-creation, an unceasing struggle to redeem "from decay the visitations of the divinity in man" (III, 139) by converting man's spectral component into the medium through which imagination discovers and presents itself. I know that many nowadays regard the Shelleyan creative eros as a phantom. But this supreme fiction, barred from the power that would express it and perhaps coming to be recognized as imagination by virtue of its very inexpressibility, is no lie. The imagination is a real ghost haunting the ceaselessly active mind, and if it can rightly be called a "linguistic fiction," the reason is that this efficacious spirit is the voice that powers the shuttle of representative language.[6] Representation is not only hounded by the curse of mediacy; it can better an original "presence," subliming instead of merely sublimating it, even as Frankenstein engenders a being superior to, or at any rate sublimely other than, his creator.

It is at once peculiar and apt that when we begin reading *Frankenstein* the authoritative voice that addresses us in the Preface is not the author's but her husband's. That the author herself experienced some confusion between mine and thine seems likely. According to James Rieger, Shelley's "assistance at every point in the book's manufacture was so extensive that one hardly knows whether to regard him as editor or minor collaborator" (p. xviii). Is it coincidental that Frankenstein, discovering that Walton "made notes concerning his history ... asked to see them, and then himself corrected and augmented them" (p. 210)? The Shelley–Frankenstein connection has been a frequent source of speculation among the novel's critics, and there is general agreement that Mary Shelley is either deeply divided in her response to Shelley and the entire Romantic enterprise or else downright hostile, using the novel as an instrument of revenge against her (supposedly overidealistic, uncourageous, and insensitive) husband.[7] But in the Introduction, as elsewhere, she deifies Shelley and Shelleyan poetry, writing of his "far more cultivated mind" (p. 6) and ascribing his failure to pursue the ghost-story competition to his annoyance with "the platitude of prose" (p. 8). In part, I suspect, she aggrandizes Shelley here because she wants him out of reach. When she says that "he was for ever inciting me to obtain literary reputation" (p. 6), it sounds like a complaint; and when she maintains that she was indebted to him only for his encouragement, she ignores the challenge that Shelley's literary efforts represented to her and their critical role in the genesis of her novel.

Although the banal note Mary Shelley was to append to *Alastor* belies the extraordinary generative power of that work, Shelley's first major poem, published a year before *Frankenstein*'s conception, exerted a more decisive influence than any of the traditional analogues the novel engages. I think it is safe to say that the focal enigma of *Alastor*, a poem that becomes more difficult to read the better one knows it, is the visionary maid who inspires the Poet's quest. Most obviously, she is an autoerotic projection of the Poet, himself an autoerotic projection of Shelley's authorial self. Both narcissistic double and incestuous twin, she figures forth not only the imaginary other, text or muse, that is the Poet's perfect complement but whatever he lacks. Whether or not there is indeed an answering subject for the Poet to quest after is left unresolved. What is clear, however, is that so long as he remains mortal he can no more capture or merge with her than he can embrace the wind. Hopelessly divided between a historical narrative of disenchantment and a hysterical rage to cast out all that stands between the Poet and his desire, the poem is a kind of moving fixation. Bursting every natural limit that impedes his quest, the Poet keeps encountering new abysses, dangerous centers of power or vacancy that he is daemonically driven toward yet that his daemonic drive to be always ahead of himself keeps impelling him beyond, and in this perpetual self-rending movement the poem profoundly realizes the essence of the quest tradition.

It might seem that, although *Frankenstein* aspires to be a paradigmatic text of texts, *Alastor* is the paradigm defining the novel's vision and scope. Anticipating Frankenstein's career, the Poet renounces home and hearth to pursue "Nature's most secret steps" (I.81); in the midst of the ruins of the past, he is startled by a sudden light, as meaning flashes "on his vacant mind / . . . like strong inspiration" (II.126–27); he is now ready to envision the form of his desire, whereupon his lust to body it forth precipitates him "beyond all human speed" (I.361) while at the same time wasting his "frail . . . human form" (I.350); finally his spirit is wasted too: pursuing the path of a departure to its inevitable terminus (see I.368 and *Frankenstein*, pp. 98, 203), this frightful solitary has become a hollow voice, "Ruin call[ing] / His brother Death" (II.618–19). In one respect Mary Shelley exceeds the literalizing ferocity of her husband's poem. While the visionary maid is a teasingly elusive or illusive literalization of Wordsworth's visionary gleam and Coleridge's Abyssinian maid, the Creature is a figuration that is at once richer and more sublimely literal than its original. This transformation, moreover, suggests that *Frankenstein* may be viewed as a deidealizing critique or misreading of *Alastor*. Retaining the poem's fundamental desire, the novel subverts it by altering the context in which it is lodged. The idealized quest for the epipsyche, or soul out of my soul, engenders the Creature, who is not only a "horrid thing" from which Frankenstein recoils in disgust but a voice of protest against his creator's lack of responsiveness. *Frankenstein*, then, would seem to oppose *Alastor*'s desperate sublime yearnings with a countermyth of continuity and reciprocity.

The main trouble with this reading is that it underestimates the strength, complexity, and sophistication of Shelley's poem, which subverts *Frankenstein* far more powerfully than the novel subverts the poem. What is most remarkable about *Alastor* is that the force of the Shelleyan sublime is great enough to withstand the rugged doubt to which it is always in danger of succumbing. Thomas Weiskel, a superb interpreter of the poem and of the Romantic sublime in general, argues that the energy of Shelley's high style "results almost entirely from what is being denied or suppressed."[8] But I think Shelley neither ignores nor represses what Weiskel terms the "fictionality of desire"; he simply outstrips his own self-consciousness. If the light of sense were to go out in Shelley's moments of glory, he could not gauge how high he had risen or how fast he was going and he would have no limits to mock. Such mockery, which is the utmost the sublime mode can achieve for both writer and reader, applies to the Poet insofar as he affixes his desire to a single image and is in turn mocked, though not canceled, by all that checks the spirit's flight. As the Poet, an "elemental god" (I.351), surges across the ocean in his rifted boat and the tormented element rages below, the self-division that characterizes the scene of writing is rendered more vividly and subtly than in *Frankenstein*. The continually felt presence of the Narrator, at once deeply attracted to and repelled by the Poet's solipsistic quest, is an additional enrichment. Like Mary Shelley's novel, *Alastor* can be reduced to a moral fable advocating human sympathy, but the poem embodies this theme in the Narrator's response and expresses it overtly only in the Preface.

While Shelley gives the overwhelming impression of being the voice of the chasm world of 'Kubla Khan' and at the same time a consummately ironic outsider, Mary Shelley is neither inside nor outside enough. Ultimately, *Frankenstein* is not a masterful representation of Frankenstein's failure, because the author is more bewildered by than secure in her liminal status. She is akin to the Narrator of *Alastor*, who knows the sublime only through the more relentlessly driven Poet, or her Walton, a failed poet who remains susceptible to the allure of the daemonic yet preserves his contacts with home and hopes to regulate his frightening desires. There is, however, no true domestication of desire in Frankenstein, and certainly the novel's praise of domestic affection opens no liberating verbal space. Perhaps Walton will be a wiser man when he returns home, but he will be embittered by all he has failed to achieve. The terrible truth haunting Frankenstein is that, despite its redundant melodramatic excess, 'a voice / is wanting' (*Prometheus Unbound* n.iv.llS-16). According to Walton, Frankenstein is a type of Milton's Raphael: "he possesses . . . an intuitive discernment . . . unequalled for clearness and precision; add to this a facility of expression, and a voice whose varied intonations are soul-subduing music" (p. 29). But we never hear this music, and only the Creature's poignant farewell, a passage that Shelley seems to have been largely responsible for (Rieger, p. xviii), exemplifies the effortless control or grace that is the supreme mark of power. Except for the idea of the

Creature, an instance of the critic's sublime rather than of the reader's, the novel does not achieve sublimity, which remains an alienated episode of Frankenstein's recollected history. Free to fall, the modern Prometheus discovers that on her tongue there is a stone.

NOTES

1. Mary Shelley, *Frankenstein; or, The Modern Prometheus*, ed. M. K. Joseph (London: Oxford Univ. Press, 1969); all page references to the novel, unless otherwise noted, are to this edition and are cited parenthetically in the text.
2. Rubenstein finds here a representation of the uterus (see p. 178). [Marc A. Rubenstein, "'My Accursed Origin': The Search for the Mother in Frankenstein," *Studies in Romanticism*, 15 (1976), 165–94.]
3. See the second section of Freud's *Beyond the Pleasure Principle* for the *fort/da* (gone/here) interplay.
4. Søren Kierkegaard, *The Sickness unto Death*, trans. Walter Lowrie (Princeton: Princeton Univ. Press. 1941), p. 26.
5. Percy Bysshe Shelley, *A Defence of Poetry*, in *Shelley's Prose Works*, ed. Harry Buxton Forman, 4 vols. (London: Reeves and Turner, 1880), III, 137.
6. See Geoffrey Hartman, "The Voice of the Shuttle: Language from the Point of View of Literature," in *Beyond Formalism: Literary Essays 1958–1970* (New Haven: Yale Univ. Press, 1970), pp. 337–55.
7. See Christopher Small, *Ariel like a Harpy: Shelley, Mary and Frankenstein* (London: Gollancz, 1972); Richard Holmes, *Shelley: The Pursuit* (London: Weidenfeld and Nicholson, 1974); and Peter Dale Scott, "Vital Artifice: Mary, Percy, and the Psychopolitical Integrity of *Frankenstein*," in *The Endurance of Frankenstein*, pp. 172–202.
8. Weiskel, *The Romantic Sublime: Studies in the Structure and Psychology of Transcendence* (Baltimore: Johns Hopkins Univ. Press, 1976), p. 156.

"God's Grandeur"
(Gerard Manley Hopkins)

"Elements of the Longinian Sublime in the Poetry of Gerard Manley Hopkins"
by Robert C. Evans, Auburn
University at Montgomery

How did Gerard Manley Hopkins go from being an almost unknown and unappreciated poet when he was alive to being one of the most widely admired and most frequently studied poets of his time a few decades after his death? What accounts for the depth and breadth of the posthumous enthusiasm for his work, and why, in particular, do the writings of such an obviously and openly religious (and even narrowly sectarian) poet appeal so strongly to so many nonreligious readers? Why are so many non-Catholics, and even non-Christians, often so genuinely enthusiastic about the works of a Jesuit priest who made no effort to downplay his strict Catholicism? Clearly the answers to these questions can be neither simple nor straightforward; many factors have helped to contribute not only to Hopkins's popularity with "regular" readers but also to the wide esteem he has won among academic critics. He was perceived, for instance, by many early admirers as a forerunner of literary modernism—a poet who had managed to write in a distinctively cutting-edge style long before the self-proclaimed avant-garde had arrived on the scene. One other factor, though, that may also help to account for Hopkins's high standing is the powerful sublimity of much of his writing—its frequent ability both to describe and to provoke an excited sense of elevation and loftiness. Hopkins's most beloved poems (such as "God's Grandeur" or "The Windhover") are often his most literally sublime works, and it is the sublimity of so much of his poetry that often makes the power of his writings so undeniable and undeniably appealing.

What, however, is meant by "the sublime"? The classic discussion of the term occurs in an ancient Greek treatise titled *On the Sublime*, which is conventionally attributed to a writer named Longinus, although its precise authorship is unknown. Longinus associates sublimity with such effects as elevation, grandeur, power, ecstasy, and the ability to provoke irresistible awe. In an especially memorable passage, he writes that the "effect of elevated language upon an audience is not persuasion but transport. At every time and in every way imposing speech, with the spell it throws over us, prevails over that which aims at persuasion and gratification. Our persuasions we can usually control, but the influences of the sublime bring power and irresistible might to bear, and reign supreme over every hearer" (43). "Sublimity," he says, "flashing forth at the right moment scatters everything before it like a thunderbolt, and at once displays the power of the orator in all its plenitude" (43). Later he notes that, "as if instinctively, our soul is uplifted by the true sublime; it takes a proud flight, and is filled with joy and vaunting, as though it had itself produced what it has heard" (55). In this way, sublime writing convinces us of the power of the writer while also enhancing the reader's own sense of power and loftiness. The effect of the sublime is to "dispose the soul to high thoughts" and to "leave in the mind more food for reflexion than the words seem to convey" (55–57). "For that is really great" (Longinus continues) "which bears a repeated examination, and which it is difficult or rather impossible to withstand, and the memory of which is strong and hard to efface. . . . In general, consider those examples of sublimity, to be fine and genuine which please all and always" (57).

As I hope to suggest, Hopkins's best poems are often sublime in these and various other ways, and it is precisely their sublimity that helps to account for their appeal to so many and such various kinds of readers. Indeed, one of Hopkins's earliest and most enthusiastic academic champions, F.R. Leavis, in 1935 ascribed the power of Hopkins's famous long poem "The Wreck of the Deutschland" precisely to its sublimity. Some readers, Leavis wrote, "may be, indeed have been, disturbed by the fervent irrationalities of its Trinitarianism, Marianism, martyrolatry, and saint-worship; they may, at first, resent the insidious persuasiveness of its appeal; but they will probably be forced to agree with Longinus that 'it is not to persuasion but to ecstasy that passages of extraordinary genius carry the hearer'" (qtd. in Roberts 329). Few subsequent commentators, however, seem to have pursued Leavis's suggestion much further. Todd K. Bender, in his 1966 study *Gerard Manley Hopkins: The Classical Background and Critical Reception of His Work*, does discuss Longinus's justification of the rhetorical device of *hyperbaton* (or transposition)—a device much used in Hopkins's poems—but he tends not to link Longinus to Hopkins in any detailed way (103–106; 115–116). Jerome Bump, in a 1974 article on "'The Wreck of the Deutschland' and the Dynamic Sublime," discusses a particular kind of sublimity at length but mainly in connection to that one long poem. Meanwhile, Lyle H. Smith Jr., in an essay titled "Beyond the Romantic Sublime: Gerard Manley Hopkins," explores some of the lyric poems but not (in general) the most famous ones or the ones that might strike many readers as most obviously "sublime." Finally, in a 1998 essay, Michael Raiger touches briefly on the sublimity of "God's Grandeur" but mostly as a point of entrance to a much lengthier discussion of works by Flannery O'Connor. There seems some value, then, in looking at a few of Hopkins's most memorable lyrics—especially "God's Grandeur"—in light of the extended discussion of sublimity offered by Longinus. After all, as a professor of classical literature who was well schooled in the history of ancient literary theory, Hopkins would surely have known Longinus's treatise, and the traits of many of his poems suggest that he was deliberately aiming for sublime effects, whether or not he was consciously or directly inspired by Longinus.

Few poems by any author seem as undeniably sublime as Hopkins's "God's Grandeur." Its opening line—"The world is charged with the grandeur of God"—seems sublime not only in the lofty connotations of its individual nouns and verb but also in the stately assonance of its sound effects. The line isn't rushed; the pace is leisurely, and each major word is emphasized and rolls on the tongue. Meanwhile, the poem's opening emphasis on the "world" already suggests the grand comprehensiveness of the work's focus; Hopkins begins by dealing not with any small or trivial subject but with the entire "world," a term that refers not only to the entire Earth but may even suggest the entire universe. The verb "charged" already implies enormous energy and force, while the noun "grandeur" is associated, almost by definition, with the awe-inspiring sublimity. Finally, the reference to "God" (which comes in the crucial and heavily-stressed last syllable of the line) is once again sublime almost by fiat, since no subject could be greater, more important, or more literally powerful than an omnipotent deity. The tone of the entire first line is certain, assertive, and assured; the poet pronounces his words with enormous self-confidence, as if no contradiction to his claim is imaginable or possible. Yet his self-confidence is also combined, of course, with an admirable sense of humility, respect, and worshipfulness: Just as the ideal reader will be inspired by and enthusiastic about contemplating Hopkins' poem, so the poet himself seems inspired by and enthusiastic about contemplating "the grandeur of God." The poet thus manages to sound authoritative without sounding egotistical. He manages to sound ecstatic without sounding self-important or self-absorbed. The mere fact that the poet chooses such a topic already suggests that he possesses the "elevation of mind" to which Longinus awarded "the foremost rank" of all the requirements for sublime writing (59). "Sublimity," Longinus wittily quotes (or echoes) himself as having once said, "is the echo of a great soul," and in this poem the "great soul" that inspires Hopkins is the soul of God himself.

God's grandeur, according to the poem's second line, "will flame out, like shining from shook foil"—phrasing that not only amplifies and specifies the imagery implied by the verb "charged" in line 1 but that also recalls Longinus's comparison of the sublime to the effect of a thunderbolt (43). It is "grandeur," Longinus also wrote, "that excites admiration" (137), by which he meant grandeur both in subject matter and in style. In trying to explain the sources of sublime phrasing, he listed five as key: (1) "the power of forming great conceptions"; (2) "vehement and inspired passion"; (3) the "due formation of figures" (i.e., figures of speech, such as metaphors and similes); (4) "noble diction"; and (5) "dignified and elevated composition" (57–59). Even in its first two lines, "God's Grandeur" already seems sublime in all these ways, and that effect of sublimity continues as the poem proceeds. Especially sublime are the poem's "figures," such as the highly vivid and striking reference to "shining from shook foil," as well as the subsequent statement that God's grandeur "gathers to a greatness, like the ooze of oil / Crushed" (ll. 3–4). Here as throughout the poem, Hopkins wonderfully exploits all the various sound effects of the English language, including not only assonance and alliteration but also onomatopoeia (especially in the phrase "ooze of oil / Crushed") as well as the strategic placement of powerful verbs (as in the very beginning of line 4). He also splendidly employs abstract nouns, such as "greatness," that seem to answer Longinus's call for "noble diction" and for "dignified and elevated" phrasing, but he juxtaposes such abstract phrasing with highly memorable concrete comparisons, as in the references to the flaming, shining foil and the oozing oil. The poem manages to be both lofty and precise, both elevated and sensual, both general and particular.

In his treatise, Longinus makes it abundantly clear that the sublime is not merely a matter of rhetoric and phrasing but a matter of character and morals. A bad man cannot be a sublime poet, and a corrupt, materialistic society is unlikely to produce sublime literature. The sublime is a call to personal, social, and spiritual greatness, not simply to elevated but empty rhetoric, and any sublime work of literature is implicitly a critique of the lowly, the trivial, and the unworthy. "Nature," says Longinus in one of the most inspiring passages in a treatise devoted to inspiration, has appointed humans

> to be no base nor ignoble animals; but when she ushers us into life and into the vast universe as into some great assembly, to be as it were spectators of the mighty whole and the keenest aspirants for honour, forthwith she implants in our souls the unconquerable love of whatever is elevated and more divine than we.... Wherefore not even the entire universe suffices for the thought and contemplation within the reach of the human mind, but our imaginations often pass beyond the bounds of space, and if we survey our life on every side and see how much more it everywhere abounds in what is striking, and great, and beautiful, we shall soon discern the purpose of our birth. (133–135)

Sublimity, Longinus continues, raises writers "near the majesty of God" (135), but he also implies that it ideally has the same effect on a writer's audience. The power and beauty and majesty of the sublime thus help explain the puzzlement of Hopkins's speaker in the concluding portion of line 4. Having spent most of the poem's first four lines extolling the majesty and grandeur and omnipotence of God, the speaker now asks, "Why do men then now not reck [i.e., heed] his rod?" How and why can humans apparently ignore, fail to celebrate, and seemingly not even fear a source of power as impressive in every way as God?

"Generations," the speaker continues, "have trod, have trod, have trod" (l. 5)—repetitive phrasing that splendidly evokes the monotonous and literally mundane nature of normal daily existence—existence that has not been vivified by any sublime awareness of God's inspiring grandeur. Even worse, "all" is now "seared with trade; bleared, smeared with toil, / And wears man's smudge, and shares man's smell" (ll. 6–7). Even "the soil / Is bare now, nor can foot feel, being shod" (ll. 7–8). Thus, if the first four lines of the poem evoke, exalt, and exult in the sublimity of God, the second four lines, in contrast, emphasize the *un*sublime nature of everyday life when that life is devoted to mere materialism. Humans have lost contact not only with the creator but also with his creation; they have insulated themselves from contact with the Earth; they have dirtied and polluted everything; and, most significantly, they have lost sight of the source of all true Being. They are behaving, in other words, in ways that strikingly recall phrasing from Longinus, especially the passages from *On the Sublime* in which he defines sublimity by attacking its opposites. Early in the treatise, for instance, he remarks that in "life nothing can be considered great which it is held great to despise. For instance, riches, honours, distinctions, sovereignties, and all other things which possess in abundance the external trappings of the stage, will not seem, to a man of sense, to be supreme blessings, since the very contempt of them is reckoned good in no small degree, and in any case those who could have them, but are high-souled enough to disdain them, are more admired than those who have them" (55). Longinus's condemnation of materialism, however, becomes even more emphatic near the end of his essay, where he writes (among much else in a similar vein) that "the love of money (a disease from which we all now suffer sorely) and the love of pleasure make us their thralls, or rather, as one may say, drown us body and soul in the depths, the love of riches being a malady which makes men petty, and the love of pleasure one which makes them most ignoble" (157–159). "God's Grandeur," then, is sublime not only in what it praises and celebrates but also in what it attacks and disdains, including a life devoted merely to "trade" and "toil."

Hopkins, however, soon switches from such satire back to praise and exaltation, perhaps realizing that the surest way to summon people to higher values is to evoke those values convincingly rather than sourly lamenting or mocking their absence. And so, after four lines of condemning corruption, he shifts in the sestet to further celebration of the beauties of nature and of nature's creator. Genuine "nature," he opines in an effective pun, "is never spent" (i.e., never used up, consumed, or exhausted, but also never paid out, disbursed, or expended in a materialistic sense [l. 9]). Likewise, and with a similar pun on the double-edged connotations of "dearest," he asserts that "There lives the dearest freshness deep down things" (l. 10). God's creation is both precious and inexhaustible because the same is true of God himself. Thus, even though "the last lights off the black West went / Oh, morning, at the brown brink eastward, springs" (ll. 11–12). The world is a globe (a geometrical shape already associated with God's own perfection and his own lack of beginning or end), and the nature of experience is cyclical: Darkness is followed by light; morning literally rises or "springs," and our awareness of the beauties God has built into his creations inspires excited exclamations (such as "Oh" in line 12 and "ah" in line 14). Confronted with the sublime, as Longinus says, our soul is filled with "joy and vaunting" (55), and surely those are the kinds of emotions overwhelmingly aroused by this poem's sestet, which ends by imagining how "the Holy Ghost over the bent / World broods with warm breast and with ah! bright wings" (ll. 13–14). In these final lines, the poem comes full circle: The imagery of light and warmth evoked in the sonnet's first two lines returns here, but now the effect is less one of startling grandeur than of protective intimacy and nurturing love. The most sublime aspect of Hopkins's God in this poem is not so much his overwhelming power as his out-reaching concern and affection for his creation. Sublimity, according to Longinus, may raise us up toward God, but for Hopkins the sublime also involves God's efforts to connect with man—a connection most sublimely achieved, of course, in the incarnation of Christ.

One needn't be a Catholic or even a Christian to feel and appreciate the sublime qualities of Hopkins's best verse; he achieves his sublime effects through the sheer power of his writing, including skillful word choice and word placement and such other elements as the effective use of sound, rhythm, and rhyme. He also achieves sublimity by dealing credibly (rather than bathetically) with inherently lofty topics; one needn't be personally religious to be open to the possibility, at least, of a vast, mysterious, and all-controlling

power. Just as one needn't be a Romantic to appreciate the sublimity
of poems such as Coleridge's "Kubla Khan" or Shelley's "Ode to the
West Wind," one needn't agree with Hopkins's theology to appreciate
the power of his verse. Ultimately, indeed, it is the power of the writer
that makes any potentially sublime work truly sublime; if the writer
lacks the talent and genius to make his work compelling, his choice
of a "sublime" theme will not matter. Only a highly gifted writer can
create the effect of sublimity; otherwise he risks seeming ridiculous.
As Longinus himself observes, "evil are the swellings, both in the body
and in diction, which are inflated and unreal, and threaten us with the
reverse of our aim; for nothing, they say, is drier than a man who has
the dropsy" (i.e., is puffed up with excess fluids [49]). Excess is always
the risk a writer runs in any attempt to achieve sublimity; in striving to
seem lofty, an untalented writer may only produce derisive laughter.

Another famous poem by Hopkins—"The Windhover"—arguably
runs a brief risk of bathos when the speaker, describing the stun-
ning flight of a kestrel falcon, exclaims that he "Stirred for a bird" (l.
8)—phrasing that can perhaps be seen as inapt, inept, and too obvious.
Otherwise, though, the poem seems yet another example of Hopkins's
gift not only for imagining sublime effects but (more importantly)
for getting them down on paper. Certainly the topic itself—a soaring
falcon—is lofty almost by definition, and the poem begins at once
with an assertion of the speaker's own power in the phrase "I caught"
(i.e., literally saw and perhaps also imaginatively grasped). The fact that
the poem is set during the "morning" immediately associates it with
light and with new beginnings, while the description of the falcon as
"morning's minion, king- / dom of daylight's dauphin" links the bird
with royalty, with further light, and with royalty once again, while the
flood of alliteration, the unusual break between the first and second
lines, and the torrent of nouns all help convey (and evoke in the reader)
the speaker's sense of excitement and exultation. The very syntax of the
poem is breathless: The first sentence consumes the first six-and-a-half
lines, as if the speaker can barely pause to catch his breath or collect
his thoughts, and the poem brims with powerful, heavily accented
and active verbs, which are often further emphasized by rhyme (e.g.,
"riding," "striding," "gliding"; ll. 2–3, 6). Hopkins creates vivid, striking,
and extended metaphors (e.g., ll. 2–5) and equally memorable similes
(e.g., l. 6), and the tone of the poem is literally ecstatic (l. 5)—an effect
emphasized by its frequent exclamation marks (e.g., ll. 5, 8, 10, 11) and

by its excited interjections (such as "oh," "O," and "ah"; ll. 9, 11, and 13). There is hardly a word or phrase in this poem (with the possible exception of "stirred for a bird") that does not seem to fit some definition of the sublime as outlined by Longinus.

Lines 2–5, for instance, seem perfectly to exemplify Longinus's assertion that the "proper time for using metaphors is when the passions roll like a torrent and sweep a multitude of them down their resistless flood" (121). Later Longinus explains that "it is the nature of the passions, in their vehement rush, to sweep and thrust everything before them, or rather to demand hazardous turns as altogether indispensable. They do not allow the hearer leisure to criticise the number of the metaphors because he is carried away by the fervour of the speaker ... [so that] there is nothing so impressive as a number of tropes following close one upon the other" (123). The complicated and extended syntax of lines 2–5 can also be justified by Longinus's defense of periphrasis (i.e, circumlocution or roundabout phrasing) as a frequently sublime effect (115), while the whole impact of this entire poem, like the impact of the falcon flight itself, can be partly explained by Longinus's claim that "what is useful or necessary men regard as commonplace, while they reserve their admiration for that which is astounding" (135). Few works of literature by any author better illustrate than does "The Windhover" Longinus's assertion that the purpose of poetical imagery is "enthrallment" (85), and this sonnet, in the sheer rush and apparently unpremeditated sweep of its phrasing, also seems to illustrate Longinus's claim that "an exhibition of passion has a greater effect when it seems not to be studied by the speaker himself but to be inspired by the occasion" (99). The "oh," the "O," and the "ah" of "The Windhover" (among numerous other devices) all suggest that the speaker is so carried away by the excitement of his vision that this perfectly composed poem continually risks slipping out of his control. As Longinus elsewhere puts it, "art is perfect when it seems to be nature, and nature hits the mark when she contains art hidden within her" (103). It would be hard to imagine a better description both of "The Windhover" and of the soaring but graceful falcon that inspired it.

Numerous other poems by Hopkins seem sublime in Longinus's senses of the term (including various senses unexplored here). These poems include such works as "The Starlight Night" (with its ecstatic exclamations), "Spring" (with its description of a thrush's song that "strikes like lightnings"; l. 5), and "Pied Beauty" (with its splendid opening line—"Glory be to God for dappled things"—and its equally splendid and emphatic closing: "Praise him"; ll. 1, 11). Indeed, the sublime seems to be one of the effects Hopkins most frequently sought and (even more significant) most frequently achieved. Surely his reading of Longinus must have helped spur Hopkins's interest in sublime writing, but it was his own peculiar genius that allowed him to achieve so magnificently the undeniable effects of sublimity he sought to convey.

WORKS CITED OR CONSULTED

Bender, Todd K. *Gerard Manley Hopkins: The Classical Background and Critical Reception of His Work*. Baltimore: The Johns Hopkins Press, 1966.

Bump, Jerome. "'The Wreck of the Deutschland' and the Dynamic Sublime." *ELH* 41.1 (1974): 106–129.

Hopkins, Gerard Manley. *The Poetical Works of Gerard Manley Hopkins*. Ed. Norman H. MacKenzie. Oxford: Clarendon Press, 1990.

Longinus. *On the Sublime*. Trans. W. Rhys Roberts. Cambridge: Cambridge University Press, 1899.

Raiger, Michael. "'Large and Startling Figures': The Grotesque and the Sublime in the Short Stories of Flannery O'Connor." *Seeing into the Life of Things: Essays on Literature and Religious Experience*. New York: Fordham University Press, 1998. 242–270.

Roberts, Gerald, ed. *Gerard Manley Hopkins: The Critical Heritage*. London: Routledge & Kegan Paul, 1987.

Smith, Lyle H., Jr. "Beyond the Romantic Sublime: Gerard Manley Hopkins." *Renascence: Essays on Values in Literature* 34.3 (1982): 173–184.

THE POETRY OF HOMER AND SAPPHO

Selection from Longinus's *On the Sublime,*
(*ca.* 1st Century A.D.)

INTRODUCTION

While its author, date of composition, and fragmentary state remain ambiguous, *On the Sublime* (*Peri hypsous*, also translated as *On Great Writing*) has profoundly affected the history of literature, rhetoric, and aesthetic philosophy in manifold ways. After the Greek text (attributed to Longinus) was translated into French and introduced to a wide readership in the seventeenth century, poets and critics alike began to form sentiments, works of art, and aesthetic theories that lauded and attempted to capture the sublime. Longinus's notions of what makes poetry and speech truly and powerfully great have informed generations of authors, giving poets and critics the promise of criteria by which to judge, consume, and produce art. For Longinus, successful writing and speaking do not merely persuade but transport their readers and listeners into a recognition of their creator's greatness, an ecstatic state where the boundary between self and other is overcome by powerful emotion. In this selection, Longinus cites passages

---

Longinus. Chapters 8–10. *On the Sublime; the Greek text edited after the Paris manuscript.* Ed. and trans. W. Rhys Roberts. Cambridge: Cambridge UP, 1899. 57–75.

from Homer's and Sappho's poetry that evoke sublimity and enumerates their characteristics.

ॐ

VIII.

There are, it may be said, five principal sources of elevated language. Beneath these five varieties there lies, as though it were a common foundation, the gift of discourse, which is indispensable. First and most important is the power of forming great conceptions, as we have elsewhere explained in our remarks on Xenophon. Secondly, there is vehement and inspired passion. These two components of the sublime are for the most part innate. Those which remain are partly the product of art. The due formation of figures deals with two sorts of figures, first those of thought and secondly those of expression. Next there is noble diction, which in turn comprises choice of words, and use of metaphors, and elaboration of language. The fifth cause of elevation—one which is the fitting conclusion of all that have preceded it—is dignified and elevated composition. Come now, let us consider what is involved in each of these varieties, with this one remark by way of preface, that Caecilius has omitted some of the five divisions, for example, that of passion. 2. Surely he is quite mistaken if he does so on the ground that these two, sublimity and passion, are a unity, and if it seems to him that they are by nature one and inseparable. For some passions are found which are far removed from sublimity and are of a low order, such as pity, grief and fear; and on the other hand there are many examples of the sublime which are independent of passion, such as the daring words of Homer with regard to the Aloadae, to take one out of numberless instances,

> Yea, Ossa ill fury they strove to upheave on Olympus on high,
> With forest-clad Pelion above, that thence they might step to
> the sky.[1]

And so of the words which follow with still greater force:—

> Ay, and the deed had they done.[2]

3. Among the orators, too, eulogies and ceremonial and occasional addresses contain on every side examples of dignity and

elevation, but are for the most part void of passion. This is the reason why passionate speakers are the worst eulogists, and why, on the other hand, those who are apt in encomium are the least passionate. 4. If, on the other hand, Caecilius thought that passion never contributes at all to sublimity, and if it was for this reason that he did not deem it worthy of mention, he is altogether deluded. I would affirm with confidence that there is no tone so lofty as that of genuine passion, in its right place, when it bursts out in a wild gust of mad enthusiasm and as it were fills the speaker's words with frenzy.

IX.

Now the first of the conditions mentioned, namely elevation of mind, holds the foremost rank among them all. We must, therefore, in this case also, although we have to do rather with an endowment than with an acquirement, nurture our souls (as far as that is possible) to thoughts sublime, and make them always pregnant, so to say, with noble inspiration. 2. In what way, you may ask, is this to be done? Elsewhere I have written as follows: 'Sublimity is the echo of a great soul.' Hence also a bare idea, by itself and without a spoken word, sometimes excites admiration just because of the greatness of soul implied. Thus the silence of Ajax in the Underworld is great and more sublime than words.[3] 3. First, then, it is absolutely necessary to indicate the source of this elevation, namely, that the truly eloquent must be free from low and ignoble thoughts. For it is not possible that men with mean and servile ideas and aims prevailing throughout their lives should produce anything that is admirable and worthy of immortality. Great accents we expect to fall from the lips of those whose thoughts are deep and grave. 4. Thus it is that stately speech comes naturally to the proudest spirits. [You will remember the answer of] Alexander to Parmenio when he said 'For my part I had been well content'. . . the distance from earth to heaven; and this might well be considered the measure of Homer no less than of Strife. 5. How unlike to this the expression which is used of Sorrow by Hesiod, if indeed the *Shield* is to be attributed to Hesiod:

Rheum from her nostrils was trickling.[4]

The image he has suggested is not terrible but rather loathsome. Contrast the way in which Homer magnifies the higher powers:

> And far as a man with his eyes through the sea-line haze may
>   discern,
> On a cliff as he sitteth and gazeth away o'er the wine-dark deep,
> So far at a bound do the loud-neighing steeds of the Deathless
>   leap.[5]

He makes the vastness of the world the measure of their leap. The sublimity is so overpowering as naturally to prompt the exclamation that if the divine steeds were to leap thus twice in succession they would pass beyond the confines of the world. 6. How transcendent also are the images in the Battle of the Gods:—

> Far round wide heaven and Olympus echoed his clarion of
>   thunder;
> And Hades, king of the realm of shadows, quaked thereunder.
> And he sprang from his throne, and he cried aloud in the
>   dread of his heart.
> Lest o'er him earth-shaker Poseidon should cleave the ground
>   apart,
> And revealed to Immortals and mortals should stand those
>   awful abodes,
> Those mansions ghastly and grim, abhorred of the very Gods.[6]

You see, my friend, how the earth is torn from its foundations, Tartarus itself is laid bare, the whole world is upturned and parted asunder, and all things together—heaven and hell, things mortal and things immortal—share in the conflict and the perils of that battle!

7. But although these things are awe-inspiring, yet from another point of view, if they be not taken allegorically, they are altogether impious, and violate our sense of what is fitting. Homer seems to me, in his legends of wounds suffered by the gods, and of their feuds, reprisals, tears, bonds, and all their manifold passions, to have made, as far as lay within his power, gods of the men concerned in the Siege of Troy, and men of the gods. But whereas we mortals have death as the destined haven of our ills if our lot is miserable, he portrays the

gods as immortal not only in nature but also in misfortune. 8. Much superior to the passages respecting the Battle of the Gods are those which represent the divine nature as it really is—pure and great and undefiled; for example, what is said of Poseidon in a passage fully treated by many before ourselves:—

> Her far-stretching ridges, her forest-trees, quaked in dismay,
> And her peaks, and the Trojans' town, and the ships of Achaia's
>   array,
> Beneath his immortal feet, as onward Poseidon strode.
> Then over the surges he drave: leapt sporting before the God
> Sea-beasts that uprose all round from the depths, for their king
>   they knew,
> And for rapture the sea was disparted, and onward the car-steeds
>   flew.[7]

9. Similarly, the legislator of the Jews, no ordinary man, having formed and expressed a worthy conception of the might of the Godhead, writes at the very beginning of his Laws, 'God said'—what? 'Let there be light, and there was light; let there be land, and there was land.' 10. Perhaps I shall not seem tedious, friend, if I bring forward one passage more from Homer—this time with regard to the concerns of *men*—in order to show that he is wont himself to enter into the sublime actions of his heroes. In his poem the battle of the Greeks is suddenly veiled by mist and baffling night. Then Ajax, at his wits' end, cries:

> Zeus. Father, yet save thou Achaia's sons from beneath the
>   gloom,
> And make clear day, and vouchsafe unto us with our eyes to see!
> So it be but in light, destroy us![8]

That is the true attitude of an Ajax. He does not pray for life, for such a petition would have ill beseemed a hero. But since in the hopeless darkness he can turn his valour to no noble end, he chafes at his slackness in the fray and craves the boon of immediate light, resolved to find a death worthy of his bravery, even though Zeus should fight in the ranks against him. 11. In truth, Homer in these cases shares the full inspiration of the combat, and it is neither more nor less than true of the poet himself that

> Mad rageth he as Ares the shaker of spears, or as mad flames
>   leap
> Wild-wasting from hill unto hill in the folds of a forest deep,
> And the foam-froth fringeth his lips.[9]

He shows, however, in the Odyssey (and this further observation deserves attention on many grounds) that, when a great genius is declining, the special token of old age is the love of marvellous tales. 12. It is clear from many indications that the Odyssey was his second subject. A special proof is the fact that he introduces in that poem remnants of the adventures before Ilium as episodes, so to say, of the Trojan War. And indeed, he there renders a tribute of mourning and lamentation to his heroes as though he were carrying out a long-cherished purpose. In fact, the Odyssey is simply an epilogue to the Iliad:—

> There lieth Ajax the warrior wight, Achilles is there,
> There is Patroclus, whose words had weight as a God he were;
> There lieth mine own dear son.[10]

13. It is for the same reason, I suppose, that he has made the whole structure of the Iliad, which was written at the height of his inspiration, full of action and conflict, while the Odyssey for the most part consists of narrative, as is characteristic of old age. Accordingly, in the Odyssey Homer may be likened to a sinking sun, whose grandeur remains without its intensity. He does not in the Odyssey maintain so high a pitch as in those poems of Ilium. His sublimities are not evenly sustained and free from the liability to sink; there is not the same profusion of accumulated passions, nor the supple and oratorical style, packed with images drawn from real life. You seem to see henceforth the ebb and flow of greatness, and a fancy roving in the fabulous and incredible, as though the ocean were withdrawing into itself and was being laid bare within its own confines. 14. In saying this I have not forgotten the tempests in the Odyssey and the story of the Cyclops and the like. If I speak of old age, it is nevertheless the old age of Homer. The fabulous element, however, prevails throughout this poem over the real. The object of this digression has been, as I said, to show

how easily great natures in their decline are sometimes diverted into absurdity, as in the incident of the wine-skin and of the men who were fed like swine by Circe *(whining porkers*, as Zoilus called them), and of Zeus like a nestling nurtured by the doves, and of the hero who was without food for ten days upon the wreck, and of the incredible tale of the slaying of the suitors.[11] For what else can we term these things than veritable dreams of Zeus? 15. These observations with regard to the Odyssey should be made for another reason—in order that you may know that the genius of great poets and prose-writers, as their passion declines, finds its final expression in the delineation of character. For such are the details which Homer gives, with an eye to characterisation, of life in the home of Odysseus; they form as it were a comedy of manners.

X.

Let us next consider whether we can point to anything further that contributes to sublimity of style. Now, there inhere in all things by nature certain constituents which are part and parcel of their substance. It must needs be, therefore, that we shall find one source of the sublime in the systematic selection of the most important elements, and the power of forming, by their mutual combination, what may be called one body. The former process attracts the hearer by the choice of the ideas, the latter by the aggregation of those chosen. For instance, Sappho everywhere chooses the emotions that attend delirious passion from its accompaniments in actual life. Wherein does she demonstrate her supreme excellence? In the skill with which she selects and binds together the most striking and vehement circumstances of passion:—

2. Peer of Gods he seemeth to me, the blissful
   Man who sits and gazes at thee before him,
   Close beside thee sits, and in silence hears thee
       Silverly speaking,

   Laughing love's low laughter. Oh this his only
   Stirs the troubled heart in my breast to tremble!
   For should I but see thee a little moment,
       Straight is my voice hushed;

Yea, my tongue is broken, and through and through me
'Neath the flesh impalpable fire runs tingling;
Nothing see mine eyes, and a noise of roaring
    Waves in my ear sounds;

Sweat runs down in rivers, a tremor seizes
All my limbs, and paler than grass in autumn,
Caught by pains of menacing death, I falter,
    Lost in the love-trance.

3. Are you not amazed how at one instant she summons, as though they were all alien from herself and dispersed, soul, body, ears, tongue, eyes, colour? Uniting contradictions, she is, at one and the same time, hot and cold, in her senses and out of her mind, for she is either terrified or at the point of death. The effect desired is that not one passion only should be seen in her, but a concourse of passions. All such things occur in the case of lovers, but it is, as I said, the selection of the most striking of them and their combination into a single whole that has produced the singular excellence of the passage. In the same way Homer, when describing tempests, picks out the most appalling circumstances. 4. The author of the *Arimaspeia* thinks to inspire awe in the following way:—

A marvel exceeding great is this withal to my soul—
Men dwell on the water afar from the land, where deep seas
    roll.
Wretches are they, for they reap but a harvest of travail and
    pain,
Their eyes on the stars ever dwell, while their hearts abide in
    the main.
Often, I ween, to the Gods are their hands upraised on high,
And with hearts in misery heavenward-lifted in prayer do they cry.

It is clear, I imagine, to everybody that there is more elegance than terror in these words. 5. But what says Homer? Let one instance be quoted from among many:—

And he burst on them like as a wave swift-rushing beneath black
    clouds,

Heaven huge by the winds, bursts down a ship, and the wild
　foam shrouds
From the stem to the stern of her hull, and the storm-blast's
　terrible
　breath
Roars in the sail, and the heart of the shipmen shuddereth
In fear, for that scantly upborne are they now from the clutches
　of death.[12]

6. Aratus has attempted to convert this same expression to his own use:—

And a slender plank averteth their death.

Only, he has made it trivial and neat instead of terrible. Furthermore, he has put bounds to the danger by saying *A plank keeps off death*. After all, it *does* keep it off. Homer, however, does not for one moment set a limit to the terror of the scene, but draws a vivid picture of men continually in peril of their lives, and often within an ace of perishing with each successive wave. Moreover, he has forced into union, by a kind of unnatural compulsion, prepositions not usually compounded. He has thus tortured his line into the similitude of the impending calamity, and by the constriction of the verse has excellently figured the disaster, and almost stamped the expression the very form and pressure of the danger, ["they are borne forth from death"].
7. This is true also of Archilochus in his account of the shipwreck, and of Demosthenes in the passage which begins 'It was evening,' where he describes the bringing of the news.[13] The salient points they winnowed, one might say, according to merit and massed them together, inserting in the midst of nothing frivolous, mean, or trivial. For these faults mar the effect of the whole, just as though they introduced chinks or fissures into stately and co-ordered edifices, whose walls are compacted by their reciprocal adjustment.

Notes

1. *Odyss.* XI. 315, 316.
2. *Odyss.* XI. 317.
3. *Odyss.* XI. 543.

4. Hesiod, *Scut.* 267.
5. ll. v. 770.
6. *ll.* XXI. 388, XX. 61–65.
7. *ll.* XIII. 18. XX. 60. XIII. 19. XIII. 27–29.
8. *ll.* XVII. 645–647.
9. *ll.* XV. 605–607.
10. *Odyss.* III. 109–111.
11. *Odyss.* IX. 182, X. 17, X. 237, XII. 62, XII. 447. XXII. 79.
12. *ll.* XV. 624–628.
13. Demosth. *De Cor.*, 169.

THE POETRY OF JOHN KEATS

"The Tragic Sublime of Hazlitt and Keats"
by W.P. Albrecht, in
Studies in Romanticism (1981)

INTRODUCTION

In this essay from *Studies in Romanticism*, W.P. Albrecht delineates John Keats's conception and use of the Romantic sublime by first pointing out how Keats diverges from his contemporaries. Albrecht argues that Keats's sublime is similar to that of William Hazlitt (a contemporary critic who Keats greatly admired), particularly Hazlitt's views regarding Shakespearean tragedy. Albrecht also distinguishes Keats and Hazlitt's ideas of sublimity from those of Coleridge, Wordsworth, Shelley, and noted classical scholar Richard Payne Knight. In his discussion of Keats's contemporaries, Albrecht provides a valuable and clear analysis of Romantic sublimity by tracing its similarities with the influential aesthetic theory of German philosopher Immanuel Kant (a major influence on Coleridge's critical writings) and addressing important psychoanalytical studies of the subject by Thomas Weiskel and Stuart Ende. According to Albrecht, Keats rejected many notions commonly held about the sublime: that it is essentially distinct from experiencing beauty, that it is exclusively occasioned by feelings of

Albrecht, W.P. "The Tragic Sublime of Hazlitt and Keats." *Studies in Romanticism* 20.2 (Summer 1981): 185–201.

terror and awe, and that it can only be found in the solitary and
meditative contemplation of natural grandeur.

ᘯᗘ

Beauty sustains mülteity in unity, said Coleridge, whereas the sublime
"unshapes" both whole and parts in its vision of "endless allness."[1]
Provided we know what "unshapes" means, this is a good definition
of the Romantic sublime—or, more specifically, a good definition of
its structure. Its content, however, differs among Romantic critics and
poets. Thus we can distinguish the religious sublime of Coleridge and
Wordsworth, the amoral sublime of Richard Payne Knight, the comic
sublime of Blake and—sometimes—of Shelley, and the tragic sublime.
The tragic sublime may be found in *Manfred*, *The Cenci*, and *Death's
Jest-Book*, but it is most clearly defined by Hazlitt and Keats.

The religious sublime, firmly articulated by John Dennis in 1704,[2]
remained immaculate in Wordsworth and Coleridge, although in
other hands it had often lapsed into secularity. Addison and Burke
added pleasures that had nothing to do with religion apart from their
sponsorship by a complaisant God. Eventually the sublime not only
dispensed altogether with divine power but, to offer redemption or
consolation in a painful world, substituted the mind's affirmation of
its own power. This sort of affirmation marks both the comic and what
I have chosen to call the tragic sublime. Blake's comic vision makes
evil a delusion of fallen man, from which he can escape if imagination
restores his mind to innocent wholeness. The tragic sublime, on the
other hand, must face up to the persistence of evil.

Recent scholarship has described tragic emotions as compromising
the sublime or as countering its excesses. These judgments come of
looking at the sublime as illusion—a view which was not, of course,
current in English Romanticism. By examining what Romantic writers
themselves meant by *sublimity*, we may construct a definition ample
enough to include the tragic. But more is at stake than taxonomy: the
tragic sublime is not the least of Hazlitt's contributions to Romantic
criticism or to a comprehension of Keats's poetry.

I

For Thomas Weiskel in *The Romantic Sublime: Studies in the Structure
and Psychology of Transcendence* (1976) the sublime stands apart from

empirical reality.[3] Weiskel's model is Kant. Aesthetic form, according to Kant, must impress the judgment as purposefully disinterested. Thus, judgment links understanding with the transcendental faculty of reason. *Beauty* engages reason when the mind bases its judgment on the interplay of visible forms. Therefore the imagination must *succeed* in representing these forms to the understanding. *Sublimity*, on the other hand, requires the imagination to fail. Before the mind can call on reason for an intuition of absolute magnitude or power, it must reject, as futile, the imagination's effort to represent these qualities. Therefore only by "subreption"—that is, only by an acknowledged *mis*representation—can a sensible object be allowed to symbolize infinite oneness. In order to sustain the sublime moment, the interplay of mind and object must continue to put down the sensory imagination. The "displeasure" (*Unlust*) in the imagination's failure and the "pleasure" (*Lust*) in reason's triumph alternately repel and attract the mind.[4] Keeping an eye on this altercation, Weiskel builds a similar embarrassment into the structure of the Romantic sublime. In Wordsworth, however, it is not the imagination's failure to grasp the external object, but the object's failure to represent the mind's ideas, that Weiskel sees as provoking a cognitive crisis. Consequently, sensory particulars must lose their reality in a fog of self-projection (pp. 24, 26, 59, 68). In other words, the Romantic sublime can't win. It either sacrifices empirical reality to the noumenal reason, as in Kant, or smothers it with "overdetermination," as in Wordsworth. But, having crippled the Romantic sublime with Kantian subreption or "Wordsworthian fade-out," Weiskel rescues Romantic poetry with "*de*sublimation" (pp. 31–32, 47–49, 56–58, 129–32). Desublimation refunds the moral cost of the sublime. It occurs when Collins, Coleridge, Shelley, Keats, and even Wordsworth become skeptical of their mind's projections—when, for instance, Keats strips the nightingale of the immortality his "dream" has given it (p. 57). Desublimation reverses a poem from illusion to disillusion: a day-return to the healthful climate of reality.

To furnish a model for the Romantic sublime, Coleridge will serve better than Kant (although Kant supplied Coleridge with some useful parts). Since an object cannot simultaneously keep and lose its "shape," says Coleridge, it cannot be both "sublime and beautiful at the same moment to the same mind"; but a beautiful object, such as a circle, becomes sublime when Coleridge "contemplates eternity under that figure" ("Marginalia" p. 341; Raysor, p. 532–33). What this process does to empirical reality Coleridge describes in "Hymn before Sun-rise in the Vale of Chamouni." Here all the images of Mont Blanc merge into infinite oneness as the mountain becomes a "kingly Spirit," a "dread Ambassador from Earth to Heaven." Yet, while their *separateness* (a less ambiguous word than Coleridge's "shapeliness") "vanishes from . . . thought," all these forms remain "visible to the bodily sense," as indeed they must in order to sustain the dialectic of metaphor.[5] When Coleridge analyzes imagination at work, he makes it clear just what objects lose and what they keep. For Coleridge, we must recall, the imagination is not the faculty that Kant finds wanting; that is, it is not merely the faculty that combines sensory impressions and reproduces them to the understanding.[6] Coleridge gives the imagination direct access to reason and the power to render sensory images "consubstantial" with the truths of reason.[7] When the imagination seeks to reconcile opposites—such as "Shadow" and "Substance" in Milton's description of death[8]—the imagination "repels" and again "calls forth what it again negatives . . . to substitute a grand feeling of the unimaginable for a mere image." What the mind repels and again calls forth are the images of fancy, wherein the mind's contribution of thought and feeling is minimal. What the mind rejects, however, is not the empirical reality of fancy but the abstract unreality of ideas "fixed" in the "understanding."[9] This is the dialectic of both beauty and sublimity. Both draw on reason to inform sensory objects with some principle beyond time and space. But whereas a beautiful object does this by displaying separate parts unified within a determinate whole,[10] the sublime dismisses *all thought* confined by space or time. That is to say, although the sublime, like the beautiful, *repels* images as yet inchoate, it altogether *rejects* the kind of separateness that the understanding imposes on ideas. Neither beauty nor sublimity has any use for "a mountain," which is an abstraction frozen outside of reality. Beauty, nevertheless, must keep "this particular mountain" distinct from "that particular cloud"; while sublimity repels all "mountains" and all "clouds" into anonymous sensation. Sensory objects, unnamed but still unfaded, remain present to the senses, their reality extended but visually unimpaired. Blake's microcosmic grain of sand would still feel gritty between even the most innocent fingers.

At this point a definition of the Romantic sublime, as generalized from Coleridge, seems to be in order: *Sublimity is a quality, bestowed by the mind, which extends the reality of external objects by repudiating the*

boundaries of time and space in an intuition of endless power or magni-
tude; this intuition acquires content from the interaction of mind and object
as the mind, through the synthesizing power of the imagination, tries to
comprehend the infinite through an awareness of the finite. This definition,
which applies to the psychological structure of the sublime, allows
room for a considerable variety of content. My purpose is to define
the tragic sublime of Hazlitt and Keats by showing that, although it
shares this structure, its content is its own.

II

Coleridge's sublime envisions the "one Life" of God's infinite presence.[11] It always reaches toward those "obscure" and ultimately
religious ideas "necessary . . . to the moral perfection of the human
being."[12] Wordsworth also, as he contemplates the "Power at once
awful & immeasurable" that lies at the heart of his sublime, feels the
humility, reverence, awe, dread, or exaltation appropriate to God's
nearness. The sublime moment presupposes the intactness of "our
moral Nature."[13] Although the religious sublime assumed God's
omnipresence, it had always found certain kinds of terrain more
helpful to vision than others. These favorable locations were likely to
be remote, craggy, and partly covered by clouds.[14] The Lake District
fitted into this tradition very nicely. Wordsworth was aware that he
selected his materials narrowly and that this narrowness discouraged
readers. But he found support in the religious sublime of John Dennis.
In the 1815 Preface, following a distinction made by Dennis in 1701
and 1704, Wordsworth "contra-distinguishes" the "enthusiastic and
meditative Imagination . . . from human and dramatic Imagination"
(*PW*, III, 33–34).[15] It is the former that leads to the sublime. Both
poet and reader find this a difficult path to follow because the meditative imagination requires a specially endowed mind with the special
experience of contemplative solitude. The "practice and the course of
life" is "remote . . . from the sources of sublimity, in the soul of Man
. . ." (*PW*, III, 83).

Because of the narrowness of his materials, Wordsworth's
sublime came under fire from Blake, Hazlitt, and Keats. Weiskel
lines up Blake and Keats against the "Wordsworthian fade-out,"
but Wordsworth is no more guilty than Coleridge of repelling
his images into obscurity. The only "indefiniteness" toward which

he believed imagination must "recoil" describes ideas, not images (*PW*, III, 36–37. Cf. *Friend*, I, 106). If, as Wordsworth remembers his Simplon Pass crossing, the "light of sense goes out" (*Prelude*, VI, 600–601), it is only because sensory differences have vanished from his "thought" and not from his visual memory. What Blake and Keats—and Hazlitt as well—object to is not a fadeout but a blackout. To Blake, clouded details signal a divisive respect for the faculty of understanding.[16] Wordsworth is man divided, but for a different reason. In the "Recluse" passage which closes Wordsworth's Preface to *The Excursion*, Blake finds Wordsworth too willing to accept "the external World" as beautiful. The world and the mind are so "exquisitely" fitted to each other, Wordsworth says, that even "madding passions" and brooding sorrow "have their authentic comment."[17] Wordsworth, Blake replies, has fitted the world "not to Mind, but to the Vile Body only & to its Laws of Good & Evil & its Enmities against the Mind" (pp. 655–56). This is overkill, but the target was vulnerable. The "Recluse" fragment seems only to excuse the tragic, instead of transforming it into vision.

When Hazlitt wrote of Wordsworth's "intense intellectual egotism" and when Keats defined the "wordsworthian or egotistical sublime," they were looking farther into the Wordsworthian blackout.[18] If Wordsworth's sublime is illusion, this is not because self-projection blurs his details into unreality or because he turns nature into a vision of moral order, but because his vision excludes too much of human experience. Wordsworth's feelings, says Hazlitt, are "deep" but "narrow." Solitary contemplation has sequestered him from "the passions and events of the real world"—from all its sensuality and all its drama (5.131; 11.89, 94; 19.9–12, 18–19). Keats's "poetical Character . . . has no self . . . it lives in gusto, be it foul or fair, rich or poor, mean or elevated—It has as much delight in conceiving an Iago as an Imogen" (1, 386–87). Hazlitt's and Keats's remarks show the direction of the tragic sublime, and it is at this point that Hazlitt and Keats diverge from Blake. Blake's vision wipes out entirely the distinction between good and evil that tragedy must sustain. Evil is a delusion from which man can escape as his imagination restores his wholeness.[19] On the other hand, although the tragic sublime may take a moral position, it assumes in human nature a moral ambiguity that remains unresolved even in the sublime moment. In this respect it differs from both the comic and the religious sublime.

III

Hazlitt and Keats, therefore, have no trouble in reversing Dennis's and Wordsworth's priorities. Now it is "human and dramatic imagination," with all its variety and intensity, that accounts for sublimity. Hazlitt's distinction between the *ideal* and the *dramatic* describes qualities that set his sublime apart from Kant's, Coleridge's, and Wordsworth's. The "ideal" aspires "after pure enjoyment and lofty contemplation alone. . . ." In its "continued approximation to the *great* and the *good*," the mind "rejects as much as possible not only the petty, the mean, and disagreeable, but also the agony and violence of passion, the force of contrast, and the extravagance of imagination." The "dramatic," on the other hand, may include all of these and must include the last three (20.304–5). It is this intensity in diversity that, according to Hazlitt, unites the tragic and the sublime. Structurally, however, the tragic sublime is still within the definition generalized from Coleridge: in an intuition of endless power or magnitude the temporal and spatial separateness of sensory forms disappears from thought. But in the interaction of mind and object Hazlitt has replaced "reason" with "reasoning imagination"—that is, with imagination so conditioned by sympathetic experience that it immediately combines selected particulars into "truth" and "reality" (1.19n, 21; 8.32–42; 9.58; 18.158–59). Since accumulated experience recognizes the persistent reality of evil as well as good, the "endless allness" intuited by the tragic sublime no longer has beneficent auspices or entirely reassuring effects.

Hazlitt's use of *sublime* and *beautiful* is not, to be sure, always the same. In his clearest definition of these words, he calls sublimity or "grandeur . . . the principle of connexion between different parts," whereas "beauty is the principle of affinity between different forms, or their gradual conversion into each other. The one harmonises, the other aggrandises, our impressions of things" (18.164). "Affinity" depends on relationships in space or time such as "continuity," "symmetry," and variety in unity (18.165; 4.74; 12.357). "Connexions," on the other hand, join "extremes" so deficient in visual links that their union requires an "excess of power" or "strength." Hazlitt gives two illustrations, one from the Elgin Marbles and the other a painting by Titian. "The Ilissus, or Rivergod, is floating in his proper element and is, in appearance, as firm as a rock, as pliable as a wave of the sea." The firmness of the god's flesh has been "unshaped" into the infinitude of his realm. In the second example, although Titian has painted in precise outline the "sharp" and "angular" features of Ippolito de' Medici, intensity of feeling discloses the "unity of intention in nature, and in the artist" (18.163; see also 10.225). Even irregular particulars are rendered absolute by the imagination (18.158–59).

In the power that makes connexions, tragic passions excel all others (4.268; 5.51–54; 18.164–65).[20] Coleridge and De Quincey, though not altogether barring tragedy from the sublime, recognize a higher claim in the Bible and in *Paradise Lost*.[21] To the select company of the Scriptures and Milton, Wordsworth adds only Spenser (*PW*, III, 82). But it is in tragedy that Hazlitt finds the greatest sublimity. "Tragic poetry, which is the most impassioned species . . . , strives to carry on the feeling to the utmost point of sublimity or pathos" (5.5). In the context of the tragic sublime, "pathos" means the intensity of shared emotion. "The concluding events [of *Lear*] are sad, painfully sad; *but* their pathos is extreme" (4.270; my italics. See also 4.268). Most of the works that Hazlitt calls "sublime" or "grand" are tragic dramas, and among these the one he most frequently mentions as sublime is King Lear.[22] It is "the best of all Shakespear's plays" (4.257), distinguished by "the greatest depth of passion" (4.233; 5.185). On at least six occasions Hazlitt uses the word "sublime" to describe Lear, and at least five of these illustrate what he calls "the *sublime* of familiarity," which staggers the mind with materials foreign to the religious sublime (18.334).

Lear discovers a good deal about evil before it finally destroys him. But the audience sees evil more plainly, as imagination brings extremes of folly and wisdom, malice and compassion, anger and forbearance, into an intuition of indeterminate but ordered magnitude. The tragic sublime—unlike Wordsworth's sublime—holds no promise that "[evil] power may be overcome or rendered evanescent" (*PW*, II, 356). In the portrait of Ippolito de' Medici, says Hazlitt, Titian has painted "a face which you would beware of rousing into anger or hostility, as you would beware of setting in motion some complicated and dangerous machinery" (12.286–87). The sublimity of the portrait lies in capturing the "unity of intention" in a "nature" as irregular morally as Ippolito's features are diverse visually. Likewise, the "absolute truth and identity" of Macbeth's character emerges from "an unruly chaos of strange and forbidden things" as Shakespeare's imagination explores "the farthest bounds of nature and passion" (4.191–92; see also 5.206). The imaginative stretch that combines images outside their usual associations extends itself to unify divergence within and among characters (5.54; 12.342). The characters of Othello, Desdemona, Iago, Cassio, and Roderigo, as well as "the images they stamp upon the mind are the farthest asunder possible ... : yet the compass of knowledge and invention which the poet has shown in embodying these extreme creations ... is only greater than the truth and felicity with which he has identified each character with itself, or blended their different qualities together in the same story" (4.200–201). This "truth and felicity" in character and action defines the tragic sublime's comprehension of the infinite through an awareness of the finite.

This comprehension, although it excludes any Providential intent to favor good over evil, offers consolation. The ending of *Lear*, Hazlitt explains in the *Characters of Shakespear's Plays*, relieves its painful sadness not only "by the very interest we take in the misfortunes of others," but also by "the reflections to which they give birth" (4.270). The first of these two phrases echoes Edmund Burke, as does Hazlitt's final—and rather loosely appended—statement in this essay, where he argues that tragedy releases a comforting flood of benevolence and simultaneously elevates the audience to a strengthened "desire of good" (4.271–72; see also 5.6–7).[23] But in the second phrase, "reflections" suggest a tragic "pleasure" that is both intellectually fuller and more original. As it "rouses the whole man within us," Hazlitt points out in "On Poetry in General," tragedy tests the reality of evil in all its dimensions.

> We do not wish the thing to be so; but we wish it to appear such as it is. For knowledge is conscious power; and the mind is no longer, in this case, the dupe, though it may be the victim of vice or folly. (5.6–8; cf. 6.355)

Tragedy brings the discriminating and organizing force of thought and feeling to bear on evil, and in the mind's power to know evil—both its strength and its limits—the audience finds reassurance.

In short, tragic passion overcomes "separateness"—in images, association, character, or action—to produce an intuition of absolute oneness. Thus Hazlitt's tragic sublime conforms to the structure of the Romantic sublime. Its content, although excluding any supernatural interest in the matter, affirms the truth of intense experience as transcending evil and thereby offering reassurance in a tragic world. A tragic character—like Manfred, Cain, or Beatrice—may contribute to this reassurance through some sort of moral triumph over death, but moral triumph on the part of a character is not necessary to the tragic sublime. All that is necessary is that the mind—of reader or spectator—simultaneously create, test, and accept a version of truth so firm that, in Keats's words, it is also beautiful. *Thus* tragedy defamiliarizes familiar pain.

IV

Before going on to Keats, it is hardly practical or necessary to examine many more Romantic poets or critics. But it may help clarify the tragic sublime to mention Richard Payne Knight and Shelley. Tragedy is sublime, said Knight, but neither tragedy nor any other work of art has much to do with morality. Knight did not recognize a faculty like Hazlitt's reasoning imagination which can comprehend large designs of thought and feeling. What an audience enjoys is only the vigor and energy of tragic emotions.[24] Knight's amoral sublime leaves the tragic disagreeables outside the theater; the tragic sublime always puts them on stage.

Shelley's sublime is neither amoral nor always tragic. *Sublimity*, in Shelley's most general sense, seems to mean loftiness in beauty and virtue. Shelley applies the word so sparingly to specific pieces of literature that his discovery of the sublime in *Antigone, Oedipus the King, Oedipus at Colonus, King Lear*, and "the dramatic poem entitled *Job*" is worth noting.[25] Unfortunately his comments on these tragedies include little analysis. We do know that Shelley ranked tragedy above other kinds of poetry in breadth of moral power and that he regarded virtue and beauty as equally reflective of eternal oneness.[26] Furthermore, the prefaces to *Prometheus Unbound* and *The Cenci* recall two distinctions already encountered in this article: first, Dennis's and Wordsworth's between "enthusiastic" and "dramatic" imagination and, second, Hazlitt's between the "ideal" and the "dramatic." In *Prometheus Unbound* Shelley proposes "to familiarize the highly refined imagination of the more select classes of poetical readers with the beautiful idealisms of moral excellence."[27] Prometheus is not a tragic character. After Act III, scene iii, the poem celebrates his immortality and immutability. Whether or not the closing scenes sustain this vision of man's triumph has been questioned, but Shelley's intention takes his poem outside the tragic sublime.[28] In *The Cenci*, on the other hand, Shelley will deal with "a sad reality" idealized to "mitigate" the actual horror of events but not so much as to keep their moral force from "the multitude."[29] The world of *The Cenci* is that of the tragic sublime. Beatrice's avowed faith in gentleness and tears and patience as the way back to innocence takes its moral force from the tragic ambiguity which she shares with all humankind (V.V.143–45).[30] Here evil has not been idealized out of Shelley's vision.

Dennis considered the drama, with its "Vulgar" passions, more generally instructive than the poetry of "Enthusiastick Passion" but inferior to it in religious insight.[31] Since Shelley, however, had no reason to believe that the drama acquires its breadth of moral effect only at the cost of spiritual insight, he did not follow Dennis and Wordsworth in elevating non-dramatic above dramatic poetry. But if he rejected Dennis's and Wordsworth's priorities, he did not—like Hazlitt—invert them. Roomy enough for both "sad reality" and "beautiful idealisms," Shelley's sublime does not offer tragedy superior accommodations.

On the other hand, in Keats's later poetry the sublime has rejected the ideal in favor of the tragic. Late in 1817 Keats wrote: "I have the same Idea of all our Passions as of Love they are all in their sublime, creative of essential Beauty." In this context the word "all," emphasized by repetition, is unique to the tragic sublime. Sorrow, fear, anger, and love are all equally sublime in creating "the truth" that "imagination seizes as Beauty" (I, 184). "Essential" does not describe a special kind of beauty—all beauty, for Keats, captures essence.[32] This essence does not exist before, but emerges from, the creative act. Keats's "mighty abstract Idea . . . of Beauty" is neither abstract in the Lockean sense nor ideal in the Kantian sense. It is abstract only in its remoteness from less passionate experience. Its permanence is relative to its temporal context. The poet, his imagination excited by passion in its "sublime," selects and combines sensory details to catch the "verisimilitude" which an object or experience has for him at that moment (I, 193–94). If there is aggrandizement, empirical reality shares in it. The imagination has brought all the mind's resources of thought and feeling into a cognitive surge that raises sensory perception to "essential Beauty."

Keats does not separate the sublime from the beautiful except as "sublime" may mean the intensity of emotion necessary to beauty.[33]

However, within the "verisimilitude" that Keats calls beautiful we may distinguish the structures of both "sublimity" and "beauty" as defined by both Coleridge and Hazlitt. Keats has Endymion tell us that happiness lies in "a sort of oneness" with nature through poetry or, more intensely and fully, in the melting "radiance" of love (I, 777–816). In such intensity visual and aural configuration is unshaped.

> ... who, of men, can tell
> That flowers would bloom, or that green fruit would swell
> To melting pulp, that fish would have bright mail,
> The earth its dower of river, wood, and vale,
> The meadows runnels, runnels pebble-stones,
> The seed its harvest, or the lute its tones,
> Tones ravishment, or ravishment its sweet,
> If human souls did never kiss and greet?
>   (I, 835–42)

The temporal and spatial contiguity of these images as well as the rhythm and syntax provide (to use Hazlitt's terms) "affinities" which make the passage "beautiful." But, jumping from "affinities" to "connexions," Endymion wonders whether these natural objects could exist without the power of love. To a lover the radiance of his love gives all things a new and less fragile life in essential beauty. Now reflecting their oneness with the lover, these things claim the immortality that Endymion assigns to love (I, 843–49). Endymion's "love" may lack the powerful auspices of Coleridge's love through faith in the "one Life," but it unshapes particulars in the same way. In the closing lines, Endymion's description rises from "beauty" to "sublimity." Here I am using these two words not as Keats did but as Hazlitt—and as far as structure is concerned—Coleridge distinguished between them.

Obviously the content of Keats's "essence," even when sensory forms are unshaped, is not always "dramatic," as Hazlitt defines that quality. But in Keats's greatest poetry the unshaping emotion is not only dramatic but tragic. In the passage just quoted, of course, the content of essence is "happiness." Endymion acknowledges the destructiveness of process (the "green fruit" swelling to "melting pulp") but doesn't worry about it. For the moment, the fruit is safe in the aura of love. A few lines earlier Endymion had been testy on this score, defending the "ardent listlessness" that tolerates the "slime" of "human serpentry"

(816–25). But neither Endymion nor Keats could sustain the rapture of love's radiance, and in later poems Keats would become more and more occupied with the grimmer depths of "poetry" that in 1816 he had contrasted with the pleasures of "sleep." In 1817 he had already been examining, in scientific terms related to sublimation, the power of beauty over tragic disagreeable.[34] "The excellence of every Art," he wrote, "is its intensity, capable of making all disagreeables evaporate, from their being in close relationship with Beauty & Truth—Examine King Lear & you will find this examplified throughout ..." (I, 192). Keats was commenting on Benjamin West's *Death on the Pale Horse*, in which, he says, "there is nothing to be intense upon." Very likely Keats had read Hazlitt's criticism (18.138–40) that West's painting lacks "gusto"—that is, "power or passion defining [the internal character or truth of] an object" (4.77). West's painting fails to please, not because it deals with death, but because its images fail to excite the imagination into grasping the essential truth of death. In "West's picture we have unpleasantness without any momentous depth of speculation excited, in which to bury its repulsiveness" (I, 192). "Widening speculation," in other words, "helps ... ease the Burden of the Mystery" which we feel when "we see not the ballance of good and evil" (I, 277, 281; see also II, 102–3). Keats does not specify the speculation excited in *Lear*, but presumably it includes the comprehension, of good and evil, that Lear's pain and sorrow "in their sublime" are "creative of." Keats, of course, is not asking the speculative mind to strike a balance in favor of good but, in Hazlitt's words, to make evil "appear such as it is." Essential truth, or beauty, can be nothing but "agreeable" to the mind creating it. Not only in his letters but also in his major poems, as Ronald A. Sharp has demonstrated, Keats was aware of replacing traditional belief with "his own ... untraditional humanized religion" of beauty.[35]

As early as "Sleep and Poetry" (1816), Keats describes a poet's choice between the "happy" sounds and "cheerful" images of nature, on the one hand, and "the agonies," "strife," and "dark mysteries" of human souls on the other. This is a hard choice, not because the poet must compromise his search for "essential beauty," but because he must distill essential beauty from more recalcitrant materials. "Poetry" threatens a kind of discontinuity, although not quite the same kind, I think, as Stuart A. Ende describes in *Keats and the Sublime* (1976).[36] Ende's insights are original and admirable (and I am indebted to them), but his definition of "poetic sublimity" should not be taken for Keats's. Ende sees the sublime as an illusion—not "morally sinister," as Weiskel calls it, but aesthetically perverse.[37] "In Keats and in Yeats," says Ende, the "sometimes indistinguishable ideals" of "'Eternal Being,' beauty, [and] one's idea of the great men who have gone before … constitute … poetic sublimity, the state of being to which poetic ecstasy may transport [the poet]" (p. xiv). Keats's professed "humility" toward these three ideals need not, however, confirm his acceptance either of this definition or of the kind of "otherness" it implies (I, 266). This "otherness," Ende believes, is beyond the human exigencies of both pleasure and pain (pp. 5–12, 32, et passim). Therefore, to avoid the insubstantiality and isolation of merely contemplative poetry, a poet must settle for something less than sublimity (pp. 46–59, 166–67). According to Ende, Keats reached his ultimate solution in the "sublime pathetic," which, without completely sacrificing the search for otherness, retains a "commitment to sorrow" (pp. 90–91, 96, 100, 107).

Ende calls the "sublime pathetic" an oxymoron, but we cannot be sure that Keats thought so when he wrote that phrase in the margin of *Paradise Lost* (Ende, frontispiece). Ende describes pathos as "blind feeling," a "condition of loss that brings no compensatory inflooding of vision" (p. 104). Hazlitt, of course, must have had some feeling of loss in mind when he cited the fallen angels in *Paradise Lost* as the poem's most "perfect example of mingled pathos and sublimity" (5.66); and apparently it was Hazlitt's phrasing that suggested a similar juxtaposition of terms to Keats. Yet we need not infer that, for Hazlitt, the pathos of the fallen angels was a "condition of loss" at odds with vision and that, therefore, Hazlitt and Keats understood pathos and sublimity as opposing or diminishing each other. Hazlitt's sublime does not permit any passive acceptance of sorrow; tragedy must heighten "pathos" to the intensity demanded by the sublime (4.270; 5.5).[38] If we accept this correlation of pathos and sublimity—and there is little reason to think that Keats did not—the direction from "sleep" to "poetry" is not from the pathetic to the sublime. It is simply toward wider-ranging, often uncomfortable materials and the emotional intensity needed to evaporate their disagreeables. Fortunately for evaporation, the passions arising from "agony" and "strife" are extraordinarily intense. Therefore, as Keats uses the word "sublime"—that is, to mean both intensity of emotion and the resulting beauty—sleep as well as poetry may lay claim to sublimity. We cannot say that poetry is more sublime or more essential than sleep unless we mean that it is more intensely capacious in grasping difficult truths. We do not, I think, need to be any more doleful than Keats himself was in turning to tragic materials and emotions. The choice is well argued in his letters, without any evident feeling of compromise. The poetical character's delight in "an Iago" does not taint Keats's search for essential beauty any more than it damages his human sympathies.

"Pathos" and "mortality" alone, Ende concludes from his analysis of *The Fall of Hyperion*, cannot sustain the imagination. Watching Saturn "degraded, cold, upon the sodden ground," the dreamer thinks only of death. "The poet as poet," continues Ende, "needs these large-limbed visions, these cloudy symbols of romance," but, unfortunately for the dreamer, Saturn and Thea have lost the "illusory dignity" the poet demands of them (p. 157). Moneta must come up with some still romantic and inspiring symbol—conveniently at hand in Hyperion. The dreamer's problem with Saturn and Thea might, however, be defined a bit differently. It lies not so much in feeling their defeat as in sharing their dejection—an emotion which, as Coleridge knew, cripples the imagination. The dreamer's "mortality" is weak as he staggers under his load of gloom. His passions, like Saturn's and Thea's, are not "in their sublime." A tragic protagonist—and Keats and Moneta are talking about tragedy—must be diligent as he goes to school in "a World of Pains and troubles." He must not let himself be bullied by reality or lured away from it. He can be neither a tame nor a truant scholar if he is to affirm that "Identity" which distinguishes a "soul" from an unschooled "Intelligence" (n, 102–3). The sublime "otherness" of tragedy lies in this distinction and in the emotional and intellectual force necessary to it. Identity is secure only as *"Mind and Heart"* continue to *act* "on each other" in a world where "the heart must feel and suffer in a thousand diverse ways" (II, 102). In the "Ode to a Nightingale" the bird has to fly away before the speaker can take his imagination back to the classroom. If the speaker is finally perplexed by his experience, Keats does not share his doubt: in the first four stanzas the nightingale has offered a "dream"; in the next four, a "vision." Likewise, the Grecian urn is "a friend to man" because it has known an eternity of both ecstasy and surfeit, of both love and death. As it makes its final claim to permanence, it is no longer just the happy urn of the first three stanzas.

In *The Fall* the dreamer takes a long time to get beyond the early nightingale and the preliminary urn. As, depressed by the image of Saturn, he pities his "own weak mortality," his imagination has not yet given Moneta's oxymorons their full range of death-bound deathlessness. He has still failed, in fact, to establish his credentials as a poet. Moneta had promised him a vision "free from all pain, if wonder pain thee not," but Saturn's immortal endurance and Thea's enduring love only fill the dreamer with despair. He is not yet seeing "as a god sees." Still trying to believe that godhead ought to be above pain, he decides, like the speaker in the "Nightingale," that death has a lot to offer. But "a benignant light" in Moneta's eyes promised more. Moneta knows all about Ruth's tears, the generations of folk circling the urn, and, of course, soul making. So she points to "Blazing Hyperion" as he defies the "aching" horrors that close in on him. The otherness of Hyperion comes more from his passion than from his large-limbed divinity. He is angry; and, unlike dejection, anger is creative. Now the dreamer has something "to be intense upon." Hyperion is no Lear. Though stout of heart, he cannot match Lear in mind. But his "earthly fire" coalesces extremes of loss and fulfillment with the same sureness of touch and something of the same complexity of thought as Lear's fusion of "a madman" with "a king, a king." The reader's imagination searches out and combines multiple allusions throughout the whole work, submerging unpleasantness in speculation. Now, standing in the "clear light" of the imagination, the dreamer actually does "see as god sees."

> Anon rush'd by the bright Hyperion;
> His flaming robes stream'd out beyond his heels,
> And gave a roar, as if of earthly fire,
> That scar'd away the meek ethereal hours
> And made their dove-wings tremble: on he flared.
> (II, 57–61)

The poem ends with the sublime—the tragic sublime of course. At least the dreamer has filled in Moneta's oxymorons. Deathlessness has become more than passive endurance or hopeless love. Now it includes identity passionately asserted in the face of inexorable loss. As Hyperion's roar frightens away the hours, pain and aspiration embrace eternity.

"Keats," says Weiskel, "moved quickly away from the blandishments of sublimation, and there is a profound critique of it in *The Fall of Hyperion*" (p. 57). Keats, in other words, rejected the self-aggrandizing fiction that Weiskel puts at the heart of the Romantic sublime. But in Keats's own terms *The Fall* does not desublimate. For Keats, the sublime cannot exist apart from empirical reality. It simply heightens this reality into essential beauty, regardless of any unpleasant materials reality may include. The tragic sublime welcomes the disagreeables so that it may evaporate them. To look for vision beyond pain, Keats discovered, is to end up loving death; but to embrace even pain in vision, is to find sublimity in life.

Although the tragic sublime may make moral judgments, it comprises, in its particular kind of infinite oneness, the moral extremes that make up the world's uneasy balance of good and evil. So defined, the tragic sublime has much the same content as Ende's "sublime pathetic." The difference, other than in language, is that the tragic sublime draws its exciting emotions from a wide range of experience, while the "sublime pathetic" takes its initial impulse from an ideal beyond general experience—an ideal which it must eventually compromise. Such an ideal threatens the kind of alienation from nature that Yeats objects to:

> All art is sensuous, but when a man puts only his contemplative nature and his more vague desires into his art, the sensuous images through which it speaks become broken, fleeting, uncertain, or are chosen for their distance from general experience, and all grows unsubstantial and fantastic.[39]

Yeats had Shelley in mind, but he sounds like Hazlitt and Keats on the egotistical sublime or, indeed, like Wordsworth himself on the remoteness of his sublime materials. The tragic sublime does not run the risk of such insubstantiality. Its delight in life is as copious as the poetical character's. Regardless of what sort of beauty his protagonists may, on occasion, be looking for, at least by 1817 Keats had stopped believing that "essential Beauty" had to be remote from pain and sorrow or from any other sort of tragic emotion. All that makes Keats's sublime—the tragic sublime—remote from suffering is the intensity that firms images of pain into truth and beauty.

NOTES

1. *Table Talk and Omniana* (London: Oxford U. Press, 1917), pp. 442–43. See also J. Shawcross, "Coleridge's Marginalia," *Notes and Queries*, 10th series, 4 (1905), 341–42; and T.M. Raysor, "Unpublished Fragments on Aesthetics by S. T. Coleridge," *Studies in Philology*, 22 (1925), 532–35.

2. *Critical Works*, ed. E.N. Hooker, 1 (Baltimore: Johns Hopkins U. Press, 1939), 338–40, 361–73.

3. (Baltimore: Johns Hopkins U. Press, 1976), esp. pp. 41, 53–54. My debt to this valuable study will be obvious; but I must agree with those reviewers who believe that Weiskel defines the Romantic sublime too narrowly: Frances Ferguson, *The Wordsworth Circle*, 8 (1977), 240–41; Hugh Haugton, *TLS*, 24 Dec. 1976, p. 1619; Raimonda Modiano, "Coleridge on the Sublime," *The Wordsworth Circle*, 9 (1978), 112–13.

4. *Critique of Judgement*, ed. J.C. Meredith (Oxford: Clarendon Press, 1973), esp. pp. 91–106, 110–14, 120.

5. *Complete Poetical Works* (*CPW*), ed. E. H. Coleridge (Oxford: Clarendon Press, 1912), I, 376–80.

6. For Kant the imagination is the faculty that synthesizes sense perceptions according to the a priori concepts of the understanding (the "categories"). In its "productive function" it is the a priori power of synthesis exerted on these concepts. In its "reproductive function" it "apprehends" sense impressions, combining them according to the laws of association (*Critique of Pure Reason*, trans. N. K. Smith [London: Macmillan, 1929], pp. 111–13, 122–25, 131–32, 143–46).

7. *Lay Sermons*, ed. R. J. White, in *Collected Works* (*CC*), VI, (Princeton U. Press, 1972), 29.

8. *Paradise Lost*, II, 669.

9. *Coleridge on Shakespeare: The Text of the Lectures of 1811–12*, ed. R.A. Foakes (Charlottesville: U. Press of Virginia, 1971), p. 82.

10. "On Poesy and Art" (1818), in *Literary Remains*, ed. H. N. Coleridge, I (London: W. Pickering, 1836), 222.

11. *Collected Letters* (*CL*), ed. E. L. Griggs (Oxford: Clarendon Press, 1956–62), II, 866. See also I, 349–50, 354, 461–62, 625; and *CPW*, I, 110–11, 113–14.

12. *The Friend*, ed. Barbara E. Rooke (1969), in *CC*, IV, vol. I, 106.

13. *Prose Works* (*PW*), ed. W. J. B. Owen and J. W. Smyser (Oxford: Clarendon Press, 1974), II, 349–60.

14. See Coleridge, *CL*, I, 349; "Marginalia," p. 342.

15. See Dennis, *Critical Works*, I, 216, 338–40.

16. *Poetry and Prose of William Blake*, ed. David V. Erdman (Garden City, N.Y.: Doubleday and Doubleday, 1970), pp. 635–38, 647–50. All references will be to this edition.

17. *Poetical Works*, ed. E. de Selincourt and H. Darbishire, 2nd ed., V (Oxford: Oxford U. Press, 1959), 3–6. See Weiskel, pp. 46–47.

18. *Complete Works of William Hazlitt*, ed. P.P. Howe (London: J.M. Dent and Sons, 1930–34), 19.11 (all references will be to this edition); *Letters of John Keats*, 1814–1821, ed. H.E. Rollins (Cambridge: Harvard U. Press 1938), I, 387. Unless otherwise shown, references to Keats will be to the *Letters*.

19. See Northrop Frye, *Fearful Symmetry* (Princeton: Princeton U. Press, 1969), p. 304. Blake does not call tragedy either "sublime" or "beautiful" (words which in general he uses interchangeably). In fact, although he admired Shakespeare, he mentions tragedy only three times, once to disparage its Burkean pleasures (p. 181).

20. See also 5.63–66; 6.3 17; 17.64; 20.304. For fuller discussion, see my articles "Hazlitt, Passion, and *King Lear*," *SEL*, 18 (1978), 611–24; and "Hazlitt and the Romantic Sublime," *The Wordsworth Circle*, 10 (1979), 59–68.

21. *CL*, I, 281; *Table Talk and Omniana*, pp. 33–34, 91, 210; *Coleridge's Miscellaneous Criticism*, ed. T. M. Raysor (Cambridge: Harvard U. Press, 1936), pp. 163–64 (but c.f. *CL*, I, 122); *Collected Writings of Thomas De Quincey*, ed. David Masson (Edinburgh: A. & C. Black, 1889–90), II, 72; V, 400–402; X, 300; XI, 24.

22. Hazlitt uses either "sublime" or "grandeur" in describing the following tragic poets, plays, and actors: *King Lear* (12.341, 342; 16.61, 63; 18.334, 335); *Macbeth* (5.206, 207); *Coriolanus* (18.290); *Antony and Cleopatra* (4.230, 231; 5.191); Kean (5.210), in *Richard III* (5.182), in *Othello* (5.271, 272), in *Lear* (18.336); Raymond in *Hamlet* (5.189); Kemble (5.379); Mrs. Siddons (5.312); Marlowe, *Tragedy of Dr. Faustus* (6.202–3); Webster, *Duchess of Malfi* (6.246); Greek tragedy (16.63–64),

Aeschylus, *Prometheus Bound* (16.73); Seneca (6.230); Chapman, *Bussy d'Ambois* (6.230); Goethe, *Iphigenia* (6.363). Hazlitt also calls Hector's death in *Troilus and Cressida* "sublime" (4.224).

23. See Edmund Burke, *A Philosophical Enquiry into the Origin of Our Ideas of the Sublime and Beautiful*, ed. J.T. Boulton (London: Routledge and Kegan Paul, 1958), pp. 44–48.

24. An Analytical Inquiry into the Principles of Taste, 2nd. ed. (London: T. Payne and J. White, 1805), esp. pp. 259, 270–75, 354–55.

25. *Letters of Percy Bysshe Shelley*, ed. F.L. Jones (Oxford: Clarendon Press, 1964), II, 364; Preface to *The Cenci, Complete Works of Percy Bysshe Shelley*, ed. R. Ingpen and W.E. Peck (Julian ed., London: Ernest Benn, 1927–30), II, 70–71; *Defence of Poetry, Complete Works*, VII, 119–20; "Essay on Christianity," *Complete Works*, VI, 229.

26. *Defence of Poetry*, pp. 112–13, 119–22.

27. *Complete Works*, II,174–75. See also *Letters*, II, 388.

28. See Frye, p. 305.

29. *Complete Works*, II, 67, 70; *Letters*, II, 174. See also Earl Wasserman, *Shelley: A Critical Reading* (Baltimore: Johns Hopkins U. Press, 1971), p. 101.

30. See also Preface to *The Cenci*, pp. 70–71; *Defence of Poetry*, p. 121; Wasserman, pp. 105–6, 122–23.

31. *Critical Works*, I, 338–39; II, 401.

32. Keats's letters usually support this definition of beauty (I, 192, 194, 266, 388, 403, 405). It is not contradicted by other letters that mention beauty (II, II, 126, 263).

33. For *sublime*, the *Concordance to the Poetry of John Keats*. ed. D. L. Baldwin. J. W. Hebel. et al. (Washington: Carnegie Institution. 1917) lists eight appearances. I have counted thirteen more in the *Letters*: 1, *173*, *184*, 200, *261*, 304, 322, *325*, 387, *398* (2), 403; II, *94*. The italicized page numbers show the more specific uses of the word. These, as well as Endymion, III. 329–32, and "Dear Reynolds . . . ," II. 67–72, suggest a state of mind remote from ordinary perception dulled, as it is, by self-centeredness, materialism, and the confusion of daily cares. Apparently sublime may apply either to intense emotion or to the version of reality this emotion helps create. For the text of Keats's

poems I have used *The Poems of John Keats*, ed. Jack Stillinger (Cambridge: Harvard U. Pres. 1978).

34. See Stuart M. Sperry, *Keats the Poet* (Princeton U. Press. 1973), pp. 37–49.

35. "'A Recourse Somewhat Human': Keats's Religion of Beauty," *Kenyon Review*, New series, 1 (1979), 22–24, 32. Sharp treats the subject more fully in *Keats, Skepticism, and the Religion of Beauty* (Athens: U. of Georgia Press, 1979).

36. (New Haven: Yale U. Press, 1976).

37. See Weiskel, p. 54.

38. See Ende, pp. 28, 190n. In his edition of *Select English Poets* (cited by Ende) Hazlitt says that Milton did not attain sublimity and pathos to an equal degree. Nevertheless we need not infer any tension between these two qualities as Hazlitt defines them (9.237. See also 9.241). Above all other things in *Paradise Lost*, says Hazlitt, it is Satan's "daring ambition and fierce passions," his power of "action" as well as "suffering," that give rise to "unmixed sublimity and beauty" (5.63–66).

39. "Discoveries," *Essays and Introductions* (New York: Macmillan, 1961), p. 293. Quoted in Ende, p. 166.

KING LEAR
(WILLIAM SHAKESPEARE)

"Othello; MacBeth; Lear"
by Edward Dowden, in *Shakspere:*
A Critical Study of His Mind and Art (1881)

INTRODUCTION

In his lengthy study of Shakespeare's plays and Shakespeare's development as an artist and thinker, Edward Dowden characterizes *King Lear* as a tragedy in which "everything . . . [is] in motion, and the motion is that of a tempest." The moral ambiguity of the play's cosmos constitutes, for Dowden, a kind of verisimilitude where "the mysteries of human life" are rendered both sublime and grotesque. Remarking on Cordelia's undeserved fate and Lear's harsh punishment, Dowden asserts that Shakespeare "does not attempt to answer these questions. . . . [because] the heart is purified not by dogma, but by pity and terror." Thus, Dowden concludes that Shakespeare presents readers and audiences of *King Lear* with a Stoic universe, one where "human existence is a vast piece of unreason and grotesqueness" that can only be mitigated by an indifferent "devotion to the moral idea, the law of the soul, which is forever one with itself and with the highest reason." By authoring a universe filled with "inexplicable

Dowden, Edward. "*Othello; MacBeth; Lear.*" *Shakspere: A Critical Study of His Mind and Art.* New York: Harper Brothers, 1881.

riddles" and capturing our capacity for evil-doing and loving devotion in his characterizations, Shakespeare, according to Dowden, has created a sublime drama whose "effect cannot be received at second-hand; it cannot be described; it can hardly be suggested."

III.

The tragedy of *King Lear* was estimated by Shelley, in his "Defence of Poetry," as an equivalent in modern literature for the trilogy in the literature of Greece with which the *Oedipus Tyrannus*, or that with which the *Agamemnon* stands connected. *King Lear* is, indeed, the greatest single achievement in poetry of the Teutonic, or Northern, genius. By its largeness of conception and the variety of its details, by its revelation of a harmony existing between the forces of nature and the passions of man, by its grotesqueness and its sublimity, it owns kinship with the great cathedrals of Gothic architecture. To conceive, to compass, to comprehend, at once in its stupendous unity and in its almost endless variety, a building like the cathedral of Rheims, or that of Cologne, is a feat which might seem to defy the most athletic imagination. But the impression which Shakspere's tragedy produces, while equally large—almost monstrous—and equally intricate, lacks the material fixity and determinateness of that produced by these great works in stone. Everything in the tragedy is in motion, and the motion is that of a tempest. A grotesque head, which was peering out upon us from a point near at hand, suddenly changes its place and its expression, and now is seen driven or fading away into the distance with lips and eyes that, instead of grotesque, appear sad and pathetic. All that we see around us is tempestuously whirling and heaving, yet we are aware that a law presides over this vicissitude and apparent incoherence. We are confident that there is a logic of the tempest. While each thing appears to be torn from its proper place, and to have lost its natural supports and stays, instincts, passions, reason, all wrenched and contorted, yet each thing in this seeming chaos takes up its place with infallible assurance and precision.

In *King Lear*, more than in any other of his plays, Shakspere stands in presence of the mysteries of human life. A more impatient intellect would have proposed explanations of these. A less robust spirit would have permitted the dominant tone of the play to become an eager or pathetic wistfulness respecting the significance of these hard riddles in the destiny of man. Shakspere checks such wistful curiosity, though it exists discernibly; he will present life as it is. If life proposes inexplicable riddles, Shakspere's art must propose them also. But, while Shakspere will present life as it is, and suggest no inadequate explanations of its difficult problems, he will gaze at life not only from *within*, but, if possible, also from an extra-mundane, extra-human point of view, and, gazing thence at life, will try to discern what aspect this fleeting and wonderful phenomenon presents to the eyes of gods. Hence a grand irony in the tragedy of *Lear*; hence all in it that is great is also small; all that is tragically sublime is also grotesque. Hence it sees man walking in a vain shadow; groping in the mist; committing extravagant mistakes; wandering from light into darkness; stumbling back again from darkness into light; spending his strength in barren and impotent rages; man in his weakness, his unreason, his affliction, his anguish, his poverty and meanness, his everlasting greatness and majesty. Hence, too, the characters, while they remain individual men and women, are ideal, representative, typical; Goneril and Regan, the destructive force, the ravening egoism in humanity which is at war with all goodness; Kent, a clear, unmingled fidelity; Cordelia, unmingled tenderness and strength, a pure redeeming ardor. As we read the play we are haunted by a presence of something beyond the story of a suffering old man; we become dimly aware that the play has some vast impersonal significance, like the *Prometheus Bound* of Aeschylus, and like Goethe's *Faust*. We seem to gaze upon "huge, cloudy symbols of some high romance."

What was irony when human life was viewed from the outside, extra-mundane point of view becomes, when life is viewed from within, Stoicism. For to Stoicism the mere phenomenon of human existence is a vast piece of unreason and grotesqueness, and from this unreason and grotesqueness Stoicism makes its escape by becoming indifferent to the phenomenon, and by devotion to the moral idea, the law of the soul, which is forever one with itself and with the highest reason. The ethics of the play of *King Lear* are Stoical ethics. Shakspere's fidelity to the fact will allow him to deny no pain or calamity that befalls man. "There was never yet philosopher that could endure the toothache patiently."[1] He knows that it is impossible to

> "Fetter strong madness in a silken thread,
> Charm ache with air, and agony with words."

He admits the suffering, the weakness, of humanity; but he declares that in the inner law there is a constraining power stronger than a silken thread; in the fidelity of pure hearts, in the rapture of love and sacrifice, there is a charm which is neither air nor words, but, indeed, potent enough to subdue pain and make calamity acceptable. Cordelia, who utters no word in excess of her actual feeling, can declare, as she is led to prison, her calm and decided acceptance of her lot:

> "We are not the first
> Who, with best meaning, have incurred the worst;
> For thee, oppressed king, I am cast down;
> Myself could else out-frown false fortune's frown."[2]

But though ethical principles radiate through the play of *Lear*, its chief function is not, even indirectly, to teach or inculcate moral truth, but rather, by the direct presentation of a vision of human life and of the enveloping forces of nature, to "free, arouse, dilate." We may be unable to set down in words any set of truths which we have been taught by the drama. But can we set down in words the precise moral significance of a fugue of Handel or a symphony of Beethoven? We are kindled and aroused by them; our whole nature is quickened; it passes from the habitual, hard, encrusted, and cold condition into "the fluid and attaching state"—the state in which we do not seek truth and beauty, but attract and are sought by them; the state in which "good thoughts stand before us like free children of God, and cry 'We are come.'"[3] The play or the piece of music is not a code of precepts or a body of doctrine[4]; it is "a focus where a number of vital forces unite in their purest energy."

In the play of *King Lear* we come into contact with the imagination, the heart, the soul of Shakspere, at a moment when they attained their most powerful and intense vitality. "He was here," Hazlitt wrote, "fairly caught in the web of his own imagination." And being thus aroused about deeper things, Shakspere did not in this play feel that mere historical verisimilitude was of chief importance. He found the

incidents recorded in history and ballad and drama; he accepted them
as he found them. Our imagination must grant Shakspere certain
postulates, those which the story that had taken root in the hearts
of the people already specified. The old "Chronicle History of King
Leir" had assigned ingenious motives for the apparently improb-
able conduct ascribed to the King. He resolves that upon Cordelia's
protesting that she loves him he will say, "Then, daughter, grant me
one request—accept the husband I have chosen for you," and thus
he will take her at a vantage. It would have been easy for Shakspere
to have secured this kind of verisimilitude; it would have been easy
for him to have referred the conduct of Lear to ingeniously invented
motives; he could, if he had chosen, by psychological fence have
turned aside the weapons of those assailants who lay to his charge
improbability and unnaturalness. But then the key-note of the play
would have been struck in another mode. Shakspere did not at all
care to justify himself by special pleading and psychological fence. The
sculptor of the Laocoon has not engraved below his group the lines of
Virgil which describe the progress of the serpent towards his victims;
he was interested in the supreme moment of the father's agony, and
in the piteous effort and unavailing appeal of the children. Shakspere,
in accordance with his dramatic method, drove forward across the
intervening accidents towards the passion of Lear in all its stages, his
wild revolt against humanity, his conflict with the powers of night and
tempest, his restoration through the sacred balm of a daughter's love.

Nevertheless, though its chief purpose be to get the forces of the
drama into position before their play upon one another begins, the first
scene cannot be incoherent. In the opening sentence Shakspere gives us
clearly to understand that the partition of the kingdom between Albany
and Cornwall is already accomplished. In the concluding sentences we
are reminded of Lear's "inconstant starts," of "the unruly waywardness
that infirm and choleric years bring with them." It is evidently intended
that we should understand the demand made upon his daughters for
a profession of their love to have been a sudden freak of self-indulged
waywardness, in which there was something of jest, something of
unreason, something of the infirmity which requires demonstrations of
the heart.[5] Having made the demand, however, it must not be refused.
Lear's will must be opposeless. It is the centre and prime force of his little
universe. To be thrown out of this passionate wilfulness, to be made a
passive thing, to be stripped first of affection, then of power, then of home

or shelter, last, of reason itself, and, finally, to learn the preciousness of true love only at the moment when it must be forever renounced—such is the awful and purifying ordeal through which Lear is compelled to pass.

Shakspere "takes ingratitude," Victor Hugo has said, "and he gives this monster two heads, Goneril ... and Regan." The two terrible creatures are, however, distinguishable. Goneril is the calm wielder of a pitiless force, the resolute initiator of cruelty. Regan is a smaller, shriller, fiercer, more eager piece of malice. The tyranny of the elder sister is a cold, persistent pressure, as little affected by tenderness or scruple as the action of some crushing hammer; Regan's ferocity is more unmeasured, and less abnormal or monstrous. Regan would avoid her father, and, while she confronts him alone, quails a little as she hears the old man's curse pronounced against her sister:

> "O the blest gods! so will you wish on me
> When the rash mood is on."

But Goneril knows that a helpless old man is only a helpless old man, that words are merely words. When, after Lear's terrible malediction, he rides away with his train, Goneril, who would bring things to an issue, pursues her father, determined to see matters out to the end.[6] To complete the horror they produce in us, these monsters are amorous. Their love is even more hideous than their hate. The wars of

> "Dragons of the prime
> That tare each other in their slime"

formed a spectacle less prodigious than their mutual blandishments and caresses.

> "*Regan.* I know your lady does not love her husband;
> I am sure of that: and at her late being here
> She gave strange oeillades and most speaking looks
> To noble Edmund."

To the last Goneril is true to her character. Regan is despatched out of life by her sister; Goneril thrusts her own life aside, and boldly enters the great darkness of the grave.

Of the secondary plot of this tragedy—the story of Gloucester and his sons—Schlegel has explained one chief significance: "Were Lear alone to suffer from his daughters, the impression would be limited to the powerful compassion felt by us for his private misfortune. But two such unheard-of examples taking place at the same time have the appearance of a great commotion in the moral world; the picture becomes gigantic, and fills us with such alarm as we should entertain at the idea that the heavenly bodies might one day fall from their appointed orbits."[7] The treachery of Edmund, and the torture to which Gloucester is subjected, are out of the course of familiar experience; but they are commonplace and prosaic in comparison with the inhumanity of the sisters and the agony of Lear. When we have climbed the steep ascent of Gloucester's mount of passion, we see still above us another *via dolorosa* leading to that

> "Wall of eagle-baffling mountain,
> Black, wintry, dead, unmeasured,"

to which Lear is chained. Thus the one story of horror serves as a means of approach to the other, and helps us to conceive its magnitude. The two, as Schlegel observes, produce the impression of a great commotion in the moral world. The thunder which breaks over our head does not suddenly cease to resound, but is reduplicated, multiplied, and magnified, and rolls away with long reverberation.

Shakspere also desires to augment the moral mystery, the grand inexplicableness of the play. We can assign causes to explain the evil in Edmund's heart. His birth is shameful, and the brand burns into his heart and brain. He has been thrown abroad in the world, and is constrained by none of the bonds of nature or memory, of habit or association.[8] A hard, sceptical intellect, uninspired and unfed by the instincts of the heart, can easily enough reason away the consciousness of obligations the most sacred. Edmund's thought is "active as a virulent acid, eating its rapid way through all the tissues of human sentiment."[9] His mind is destitute of dread of the Divine Nemesis. Like Iago, like Richard III, he finds the regulating force of the universe in the *ego*—in the individual will. But that terror of the unseen which Edmund scorned as so much superstition is "the initial recognition of a moral law restraining desire, and checks the hard bold scrutiny of imperfect thought into obligations which can never be proved to have any sanctity in the absence of feeling." We can, therefore, in some degree account for Edmund's bold egoism and inhumanity. What obligations should a child feel to the man who, for a moment's selfish pleasure, had degraded and stained his entire life? In like manner, Gloucester's sufferings do not appear to us inexplicably mysterious.

> "The gods are just, and of our pleasant vices
> Make instruments to plague us;
> The dark and vicious place where thee he got
> Cost him his eyes."

But, having gone to the end of our tether, and explained all that is explicable, we are met by enigmas which will not be explained. We were, perhaps, somewhat too ready to

> "Take upon us the mystery of things
> As if we were God's spies."[10]

Now we are baffled, and bow the head in silence. Is it, indeed, the stars that govern our condition? Upon what theory shall we account for the sisterhood of a Goneril and a Cordelia? And why is it that Gloucester, whose suffering is the retribution for past misdeeds, should be restored to spiritual calm and light, and should pass away in a rapture of mingled gladness and grief,

> "His law'd heart,
> Alack! too weak the conflict to support,
> 'Twixt two extremes of passion, joy and grief,
> Burst smilingly;

while Lear, a man more sinned against than sinning, should be robbed of the comfort of Cordelia's love, should be stretched to the last moment upon "the rack of this tough world," and should expire in the climax of a paroxysm of unproductive anguish?

Shakspere does not attempt to answer these questions. The impression which the facts themselves produce, their influence to "free, arouse, dilate," seems to Shakspere more precious than any proposed explanation of the facts which cannot be verified. The heart is purified not by dogma, but by pity and terror. But there are other questions which the play suggests. If it be the stars that govern our conditions; if that be, indeed, a possibility which Gloucester, in his first shock and confusion of mind, declares,

> "As flies to wanton boys are we to the gods;
> They kill us for their sport;"

if, measured by material standards, the innocent and the guilty perish by a like fate—what then? Shall we yield ourselves to the lust for pleasure? Shall we organize our lives upon the principles of a studious and pitiless egoism?

To these questions the answer of Shakspere is clear and emphatic. Shall we stand upon Goneril's side or upon that of Cordelia? Shall we join Edgar or join the traitor? Shakspere opposes the presence and the influence of evil not by any transcendental denial of evil, but by the presence of human virtue, fidelity, and self-sacrificial love. In no play is there a clearer, an intenser manifestation of loyal manhood, of strong and tender womanhood. The devotion of Kent to his master is a passionate, unsubduable devotion, which might choose for its watchword the saying of Goethe, "I love you; what is that to you?" Edgar's nobility of nature is not disguised by the beggar's rags; he is the skilful resister of evil, the champion of right to the utterance. And if Goneril and Regan alone would leave the world unintelligible and desperate, there is

> "One daughter,
> Who redeems nature from the general curse
> Which twain have brought her to."

We feel throughout the play that evil is abnormal; a curse which brings down destruction upon itself; that it is without any long career; that evil-doer is at variance with evil-doer. But good is normal; for it the career is long; and "all honest and good men are disposed to befriend honest and good men, as such."[11]

> "*Cordelia.* O thou good Kent, how shall I live, and work,
> To match thy goodness! My life will be too short,
> And every measure fail me.
> *Kent.* To be acknowledged, madam, is o'erpaid,
> All my reports go with the modest truth;
> Nor more, nor clipped, but so."

Nevertheless, when everything has been said that can be said to make the world intelligible, when we have striven our utmost to realize all the possible good that exists in the world, a need of fortitude remains.

It is worthy of note that each of the principal personages of the play is brought into presence of those mysterious powers which dominate life and preside over human destiny; and each, according to his character, is made to offer an interpretation of the great riddle. Of these interpretations, none is adequate to account for all the facts. Shakspere (differing in this from the old play) placed the story in heathen times, partly, we may surmise, that he might be able to put the question boldly, "What are the gods?" Edmund, as we have seen, discovers no power or authority higher than the will of the individual and a hard trenchant intellect. In the opening of the play he utters his ironical appeal:

> "I grow; I prosper—
> Now gods stand up for bastards."[12]

It is not until he is mortally wounded, with his brother standing over him, that the recognition of a moral law forces itself painfully upon his consciousness, and he makes his bitter confession of faith:

> "The wheel is come full circle, I am here."

His self-indulgent father is, after the manner of the self-indulgent, prone to superstition; and Gloucester's superstition affords some countenance to Edmund's scepticism. "This is the excellent foppery of the world, that when we are sick in fortune—often the surfeit of our own behavior—we make guilty of our disasters the sun, the moon, and the stars, as if we were villains by necessity; fools by heavenly compulsion; knaves, thieves, and treachers by spherical predominance; drunkards, liars, and adulterers by an enforced obedience of planetary influence; and all that we are evil in by a divine thrusting-on."

Edgar, on the contrary, the champion of right, ever active in opposing evil and advancing the good cause, discovers that the gods are upon the side of right, are unceasingly at work in the vindication of truth and the execution of justice. His faith lives through trial and disaster, a flame which will not be quenched. And he buoys up, by virtue of his own energy of soul, the spirit of his father, which, unprepared for calamity, is staggering blindly, stunned from its power to think, and ready to sink into darkness and a welter of chaotic disbelief. Gloucester, in his first confusion of spirit, exclaims bitterly against the divine government:

> "As flies to wanton boys are we to the gods;
> They kill us for their sport."

But before the end has come he "shakes patiently his great affliction off," he will not quarrel with the "great opposeless wills" of the gods; nay, more than this, he can identify his own will with theirs, he can accept life contentedly at their hands, or death. The words of Edgar find a response in his own inmost heart:

> "Thou happy father,
> Think that the clearest gods, who make them honors
> Of men's impossibilities, have preserved thee."

And as Edgar, the justiciary, finds in the gods his fellow-workers in the execution of justice, so Cordelia, in whose heart love is a clear and perpetual illumination, can turn for assistance and co-operancy in her deeds of love to the strong and gentle rulers of the world:

> "O you kind gods,
> Cure this great breach in his abused nature."

Kent possesses no vision, like that which gladdens Edgar, of a divine providence. His loyalty to right has something in it of a desperate instinct, which persists, in spite of the appearances presented by the world. Shakspere would have us know that there is not any devotion to truth, to justice, to charity, more intense and real than that of the man who is faithful to them out of the sheer spirit of loyalty, unstimulated and unsupported by any faith which can be called theological. Kent, who has seen the vicissitude of things, knows of no higher power presiding over the events of the world than fortune. Therefore, all the more, Kent clings to the passionate instinct of right-doing, and to the hardy temper, the fortitude which makes evil, when it happens to come, endurable. It is Kent who utters his thought in the words—

> "Nothing almost sees miracles
> But misery."

And the miracle he sees, in his distress, is the approaching succor from France, and the loyalty of Cordelia's spirit. It is Kent, again, who, characteristically making the best of an unlucky chance, exclaims, as he settles himself to sleep in the stocks,

> "Fortune, good night; smile once more, turn thy wheel."

And again:

> "It is the stars,
> The stars above us, govern our conditions."

And again (of Lear):

> "If Fortune brag of two she loved and hated,
> One of them we behold."

Accordingly, there is at once an exquisite tenderness in Kent's nature, and also a certain roughness and hardness, needful to protect, from the shocks of life, the tenderness of one who finds no refuge in communion with the higher powers, or in a creed of religious optimism.

But Lear himself—the central figure of the tragedy—what of him? What of suffering humanity that wanders from the darkness into light, and from the light into the darkness? Lear is grandly passive—played upon by all the manifold sources of nature and of society. And though he is in part delivered from imperious self-will, and learns, at last, what true love is, and that it exists in the world, Lear passes away from our sight, not in any mood of resignation or faith or illuminated peace, but in a piteous agony of yearning for that love which he had found only to lose forever. Does Shakspere mean to contrast the pleasure in a demonstration of spurious affection in the first scene with the agonized cry for real love in the last scene, and does he wish us to understand that the true gain from the bitter discipline of Lear's old age was precisely this—his acquiring a supreme need of what is best, though a need which finds, as far as we can learn, no satisfaction?

We guess at the spiritual significance of the great tragic facts of the world, but, after our guessing, their mysteriousness remains.

Our estimate of this drama as a whole, Mr. Hudson has said, depends very much on the view we take of the Fool; and Mr. Hudson has himself understood Lear's "poor boy" with such delicate sympathy that to arrive at precisely the right point of view we need not go beyond his words: "I know not how I can better describe the Fool than as the soul of pathos in a sort of comic masquerade; one in whom fun and frolic are sublimed and idealized into tragic beauty.... His 'laboring to outjest Lear's heart-struck injuries' tells us that his wits are set a-dancing by grief; that his jests bubble up from the depths of a heart struggling with pity and sorrow, as foam enwreathes the face of deeply troubled waters.... There is all along a shrinking, velvet-footed delicacy of step in the Fool's antics, as if awed by the holiness of the ground; and he seems bringing diversion to the thoughts, that he may the better steal a sense of woe into the heart. And I am not clear whether the inspired antics that sparkle from the surface of his mind are in more impressive contrast with the dark, tragic scenes into which they are thrown, like rockets into a midnight tempest, or with the undercurrent of deep tragic thoughtfulness out of which they falteringly issue and play."[13]

Of the tragedy of *King Lear* a critic wishes to say as little as may be; for, in the case of this play, words are more than ordinarily inadequate to express or describe its true impression. A tempest or a dawn will not be analyzed in words; we must feel the shattering fury of the gale, we must watch the calm light broadening.[14] And the sensation experienced by the reader of *King Lear* resembles that produced by some grand natural phenomenon. The effect cannot be received at second-hand; it cannot be described; it can hardly be suggested.[15]

NOTES

1. *Much Ado About Nothing*, Act V., Sc. 1.
2. Compare also, as expressing the mood in which calamity must be confronted, the words of Edgar:
   > "Men must endure
   > Their going hence, even as their coming hither;
   > Ripeness is all."

3. Goethe's "Conversations with Eckermann," Feb. 24, 1824.

4. Flathe, who ordinarily finds all preceding critics wrong and himself profoundly right, discovers in *King Lear* Shakspere's "warning letter against naturalism and pseudo-rationalism;" the play is translated into a didactic discourse on infidelity.

5. Coleridge writes, "The first four or five lines of the play let us know that the trial is but a trick; and that the grossness of the old King's rage is in part the natural result of a silly trick suddenly and most unexpectedly baffled and disappointed." Dr. Bucknill maintains that the partition of the kingdom is "the first act of Lear's developing insanity." *Shakespeare-Jahrbuch*, vol. II, contains a short and interesting article by Ulrici on "Ludwig Devrient as King Lear." That great actor, if Ulrici might trust his own impression, would seem to have understood the first scene of the play in the sense in which Ulrici himself explains it—viz., that Lear's demand for a declaration of his daughter's love was sudden and sportive, made partly to pass the time until the arrival of Burgundy and France. Having assigned their portions to Goneril and Regan, there could not be a serious meaning in Lear's words to Cordelia:

> "What can you say to draw
> A third more opulent than your sisters?"

The words were said with a smile, yet, at the same time, with a secret and clinging desire for the demonstration of love demanded. All the more is Lear surprised and offended by Cordelia's earnest and almost judicial reply. But Cordelia is at once suppressing and in this way manifesting her indignation against her sisters' heartless flattery.

6. It is Goneril who first suggests the plucking-out of Gloucester's eyes. The points of contrast between the sisters are well brought out by Gervinus.

7. "Lectures on Dramatic Art," translated by J. Black, p. 412.

8. Gloucester (Act I, Sc. 1) says of Edmund, "He hath been out nine years, and away he shall again."

9. This and the quotation next following will be remembered by readers of "Romola;" they occur in that memorable chapter entitled "Tito's Dilemma."

10. Words of Lear (Act V, Sc. 3).

11. Butler, " Analogy," Part I, Ch. III.

12. Compare Edmund's words (uttered with inward scorn) spoken of Edgar:

> "I told him the revenging gods
> 'Gainst parricides did all their thunders bend."

13. "Shakespeare's Life, Art, and Characters," Vol. II, pp. 351, 352. What follows, too long to quote, is also excellent.

14. In Victor Hugo's volume of dithyrambic prophesying entitled "William Shakespeare," a passage upon *King Lear* (ed.1869, pp. 205–209) is particularly noteworthy. His point of view—that the tragedy is "Cordelia," not " King Lear," that the old King is only an occasion for his daughter—is absolutely wrong; but the criticism, notwithstanding, catches largeness and passion from the play. [...].

15. In addition to the medical studies of Lear's case by Doctors Bucknill and Kellogg, we may mention the "König Lear" of Dr. Carl Stark (Stuttgart, 1871), favorably noticed in *Shakespeare-Jahrbuch*; Vol. VI; and again by Meissner, in his study of the play, *Shakespeare-Jahrbuch*, Vol.VII., pp. 110–115.

"Kubla Kahn"
(Samuel Taylor Coleridge)

"The Sublime in Coleridge's 'Kubla Khan'"
by Robert C. Evans,
Auburn University at Montgomery

Among all the poems in the English language that might be considered sublime, surely "Kubla Khan" by Samuel Taylor Coleridge must rank very high on any list. Few poems are more impassioned, more exciting to read, or more memorable once they are read; few poems are more lofty, more mysterious, or more compelling. "Kubla Khan" exhibits many of the qualities often associated with the sublime, including a sense of irresistible elevation, of transcendence, and of enraptured, ravished, and ravishing power; yet rarely has the poem been discussed as "sublime" at any length in any of the obviously expected or easily accessible sources. Thus a search of "'Kubla Khan' and 'sublime'" in the Modern Language Association online bibliography, for instance, turns up only one brief article, published in Poland in 1992 (Rachwal), while the index of Raimonda Modiano's book *Coleridge and the Concept of Nature* (which contains more than 30 pages discussing Coleridge and the sublime) reveals no reference to "Kubla Khan." Likewise, Thomas Weiskel's seminal work *The Romantic Sublime* devotes a number of pages to Coleridge but doesn't mention "Kubla Khan," while Allan Grant, in his *Preface to Coleridge*, devotes several pages to the sublime (29–33) without discussing "Kubla Khan" in that connection (although he does later make two brief references to the sublime when he treats the poem at some length) (132–33). Philip Shaw's valuable conceptual overview, *The Sublime*, mentions neither Coleridge nor "Kubla Khan" (even though it includes a chapter on "The Romantic Sublime"), while David Vallins's invaluable compilation of writings by Coleridge—including poems and prose both in and about the sublime mode—contains no reference to or excerpt from "Kubla Khan."

There seems some value, then, in providing a brief discussion of "Kubla Khan" as a sublime lyric, but the first problem that immediately presents itself is how to define "the sublime," and the second problem is how to determine the ways in which Coleridge himself defined (or thought about) the term. Definitions of "the sublime" usually begin with the classic (and classical) treatise attributed to the first-century author Longinus. Titled *Peri hypsous* in Greek and usually translated as *On the Sublime*, this text is deservedly one of the great classics of literary criticism; but whether, when, and with what results Coleridge may have read this work are all matters that are difficult to determine. Surprisingly, Vallins's superb compilation of writings by Coleridge about the sublime contains no reference to Longinus. Evidence survives that Coleridge did indeed read Longinus (e.g., *Literary Remains*, 1:166), but whether he embraced any or much of Longinus's thinking about sublimity is far less clear. In fact, during Coleridge's era there were numerous and sometimes competing definitions of the sublime (see Ashfield and de Bolla), and it is hard to know how Coleridge in general, or "Kubla Khan" in particular, may have been affected by any of them.

Perhaps the best way to begin a discussion of "Kubla Khan" as a sublime poem is to survey briefly some of Coleridge's own ideas about the sublime as they are compiled in Vallins's superb book. Some of Coleridge's comments seem especially relevant to "Kubla Khan," even though those comments were sometimes written long after the poem was initially composed. Thus, in a letter addressed to Robert Southey and dated 13 July 1794 (several years *before* the composition of "Kubla Khan" in 1797 or 1798), Coleridge recounts a walk over mountains, which he describes as "most sublimely terrible!"—a comment suggesting that he, like many of his contemporaries, sometimes associated the sublime with a sense of awe-inspiring fear (Vallins 37). Likewise, later in the same letter (in language that almost seems to foreshadow "Kubla Khan" itself), Coleridge mentions "cataracts [i.e., waterfalls] most astonishing," and he reports that "the sun was reflected in the river, that winded through the valley with insuffer-able brightness" (Vallins 38). Clearly, then, Coleridge often associated the sublime with astonishingly awe-inspiring natural features—the same sorts of features that appear later in his famous poem. In a letter dated 22 August 1796, for instance, he describes a place called "Dove-Dale" as, "without question, tremendously sublime" (Vallins 38), while in a manuscript dated November 1800 he describes a view of "bits and edges" of "Mountains . . . in the most sublime style" (Vallins 44). Repeatedly, however, in his comments on landscapes, it is moving water (often in the form of waterfalls) that Coleridge seems to consider sublime, and in some cases his reports uncannily resemble the descriptions of bursting water in "Kubla Khan." Thus, in one letter dated 6 August 1802, he mentions "a most splendid waterfall" (Vallins 50), and then, a little later in the same letter, the following passage occurs, which strikingly resembles phrasing in his great poem:

> . . . at length two streams burst out & took their way down, one on [one] side a high Ground upon this Ridge, the other on the other—I took that to my right . . . & soon the channel sank all at once, at least 40 yards, & formed a magnificent Waterfall— and close under this a succession of Waterfalls 7 in number, the third of which is nearly as high as the first. (Vallins 51)

Similar passages occur in later letters as well (e.g., Vallins 54, 67), and in general the selections reprinted in Vallins's chapter titled "Coleridge and the Sublimity of Landscape" are frequently reminiscent of the kind of sublime landscapes and natural features depicted in "Kubla Khan."

It was not only nature, however, that Coleridge sometimes praised as sublime. Thus, in his chapter on "Transcendence in Literature and the Visual Arts," Vallins quotes a passage in which Coleridge describes the poet as "one who carries the simplicity of childhood into the powers of manhood; who, with a soul unsubdued by habit, unshackled by custom, contemplates all things with the freshness and wonder of a child," particularly with "the childlike feeling of devout wonder" (85; see also 86)—the same sort of devout wonder that seems amply on display in "Kubla Khan." Even more strikingly relevant to the poem is another passage in which Coleridge proclaims that "Gothic art is sublime. On entering a cathedral, I am filled with devotion and with awe; I am lost to the actualities that surround me, and my whole being expands into the infinite; earth and air, nature and art, all swell up into eternity, and the only sensible impression left is, 'that I am nothing!'" (Vallins 87). Perhaps nowhere better than here does Coleridge more succinctly sum up the qualities and feelings he associates with sublimity, and certainly the words he uses to describe the impact of a Gothic cathedral might just as easily describe some of the impact of his own "Kubla Khan." Likewise, when he later mentions "that sublime faculty, by which a great mind becomes that which it meditates on" (Vallins 98–99), his words almost recall some of the impression conveyed by the closing lines of his own great lyric.

Interestingly enough, one of the passages in Vallins's book that seems most strikingly relevant to "Kubla Khan" was composed at around the very same time when Coleridge claims that he was at work on the poem. In a letter to John Thelwell dated 14 October 1797, Coleridge reports that his mind "feels as if it ached to behold and know something *great*, something *one* and *indivisible*. And it is only in the faith of that that rocks and waterfalls, mountains or caverns, give me the sense of sublimity or majesty! But in this faith *all things* counterfeit infinity" (Vallins 125). "[R]ocks and waterfalls, mountains and caverns": Such phrases cannot help but recall "Kubla Khan" itself, and here those phrases and images are explicitly linked with the sublime, and the sublime itself is explicitly identified with a sense of "majesty." It would, of course, have been helpful for our present purposes if Coleridge had written a lengthy essay on the sublime, or if he had left detailed responses to his reading of Longinus, or if he had discussed explicitly the connections between the sublime as a concept and "Kubla Khan" as a poem. In the absence of such commentaries, however, we are left with his scattered remarks on sublimity (helpfully compiled by Vallins) and with the splendidly sublime poem itself.

Before turning, finally, to that poem, it may be useful to report a few of the summary comments of David Vallins concerning Coleridge's notions of the sublime. Perhaps no one today is in a better position than Vallins to describe what the sublime meant to Coleridge. Thus Vallins begins his book by asserting that "[n]o other British Romantic focuses so consistently as Coleridge on the importance of transcending the material, the everyday, or the mundanely comprehensible in favor of a confrontation with the infinite forces which, like many of his contemporaries, he sees as underlying both human consciousness and the natural world" (1). A few sentences later, Vallins associates Coleridge's views of the sublime with feelings of "elevation and excitement" and also with "a liberating sense of calmness and freedom from merely temporal concerns" (1). "For Coleridge as much as for any Romantic" (Vallins later continues), "the feeling of the sublime is the feeling of life itself, intuited through the medium of our own mental activity and striving" (4). In responding to sublime landscapes, Coleridge often emphasizes the "grandeur, remoteness, wildness, and savagery of mountain regions" (Vallins 6), while in his early writings in and about the sublime, Coleridge seeks "to promote forms of insight" designed to bring human beings "closer to the deity Himself" (Vallins 14). Indeed, in responding to sublime landscapes, Coleridge tends to emphasize "the intuition of something that lies beyond or behind them and which the mind can never know or comprehend so clearly or directly as any part of the physical world" (Vallins 36), while in responding to the sublime in literature and art he tends to emphasize a liberating sense of elevation, excitement, and transcendence of the everyday" (Vallins 81). As will soon be clear, nearly all these ideas seem relevant to the sublimity Coleridge both describes and achieves in "Kubla Khan," a poem that may be "sublime nonsense" (as Charles Rosen has called it [77]) but which seems undeniably, beautifully, and powerfully sublime nonetheless.

"Kubla Khan" has been read in so many various and often contradictory ways (see, for a sample, Milton 17–35) that there seems no point here in trying to offer yet another particular interpretation of its meaning. Instead it seems to make more sense to discuss, in general terms, the aspects of the poem that almost any interpreter might consider sublime, especially the qualities of its diction, imagery, rhythms, and sounds. These sublime qualities begin already with the opening line ("In Xanadu did Kubla Khan"), in which the names both of the place and of the person immediately convey a sense of mystery, remoteness, and power—a kind of literal and figurative remoteness from familiar, mundane life. This sense is then enhanced in the second line ("A stately pleasure-dome decree"), where the adjectives, noun, and verb all imply a sense of loftiness and potency. Whatever pleasures are associated with Xanadu are not trivial or mundane but "stately," impressive, or august; they are dignified rather than superficial. Meanwhile, the fact that Kubla Khan has merely to "decree" something to make it happen already suggests his almost godlike authority. Similarly, the reference to "Alph, the sacred river" (l. 3) again contributes to a sense of elevation. The name "Alph" seems neither mundane nor predictable; rather, it seems almost literally primal, while the fact that the river is "sacred" not only reinforces the connotations of "stately" (used in the previous line) but also introduces a sense of literal holiness, as if a river—the most natural of things—is somehow also supernaturally sacred.

The fact that the river runs through "caverns" that are "measureless to man" makes those caverns (almost like the Grand Canyon) seem all the more awe-inspiring and impressive; one is reminded of the response Coleridge said he felt upon entering a Gothic cathedral: "'I am nothing!'" (Vallins 87). Likewise, the fact that the river runs "Down to a sunless sea" (l. 5) has a similar impact: obviously the word "sea" is an exaggeration or bit of hyperbole, but its purpose is to suggest a lake too vast and too intensely dark to be measured by any mere human. The effect, here as elsewhere when Coleridge is describing sublime landscapes (or seascapes), is to imply the immensity of nature and the relative puniness of man—unless, of course, that man happens to be as powerful as Kubla Khan. Indeed, no sooner does Coleridge stress the awesomeness of nature than he quickly implies the Khan's efforts to tame it or impose his own order upon it: "So twice five miles of fertile ground / With walls and towers were girdled round" (ll. 6–7). This is an enclosure project that would surely be impressive even in the present day, and it would have seemed all the more impressive to Coleridge and his contemporaries. The reference to "twice five miles" manages to be both precise and impressively vague at the same time. (A more exact measurement, such as "52,800 feet," would seem exact but trivial.) Meanwhile, the fact that the enclosed ground is "fertile" suggests its potential, its latent power, its ability both to produce and to nourish life. The landscape, like the demideity who presides over it, seems sublimely powerful.

The "walls and towers" with which the Khan encircles his property are quite literally elevated; they serve the function of demarcating his dominion, of setting it off as special and distinct, as an area of supremely personal authority. Within that dominion are "gardens bright with sinuous rills" (l. 8), a line in which the word "gardens" is especially important. That word immediately suggests beauty, fertility, and vitality, but it also implies man not only cooperating with nature to nurture life but also imposing his control on nature. Man and nature combine in mutual creativity, but man exercises the crucial creative power. The fact that these are gardens "Where blossomed many an incense-bearing tree" suggests a heightening of the senses of sight and smell, while the fact that the Khan's dominion also consists of "forests ancient as the hills" which nevertheless enfold "sunny spots of greenery" (ll. 9–11) suggests that he presides over a land that is both supremely old as well as one that is constantly renewing itself.

Perhaps one of the most obviously sublime moments in a generally sublime poem is the sudden shift of tone that occurs in the switch to lines 12–13: "But oh! that deep romantic chasm which slanted / Down the green hill athwart the cedarn cover!" Here the poem becomes abruptly and explicitly exclamatory; the tone is now one of even more clearly heightened emotion. Words are no longer sufficient, by themselves, to convey the speaker's excitement, and normal syntax breaks down: Lines 12–13 are literally a fragment. Normal punctuation and sentence structure can no longer accurately communicate the speaker's heightened feelings, while the words "deep" and "chasm" already imply perceptions that are unusual and out of the ordinary. Even more vitality than has already been implied is suggested by the reference to the "green hill athwart a cedarn cover," while the sudden description of the landscape as "A savage place!" that is also somehow also "holy and enchanted" not only adds to the fragmentary syntax but also suggests that all the normal, expected, logical, and mundane categories of description are inadequate for the speaker's attempts to describe this almost magical place. Here, as often in Romantic concepts of the sublime, an element of fear is suggested through the adjective "savage," but here, too, the words "holy" and "enchanted" convey the more obviously sublime connotations of something supernatural and sacred.

No sooner does Coleridge emphasize a place that is "holy and enchanted," however, than he instantly shifts to a different and darker sense of the supernatural: this is a place that seems as holy and enchanted "As e're beneath a waning moon was haunted / By woman wailing for her demon lover!" (ll. 15–16). Intense emotion is once more suggested here, but for the first time that emotion seems potentially base, immoral, perverse, and merely sensual. For all these reasons the phrasing now seems briefly disturbing and less than obviously ennobling. The verb "wailing" makes the woman sound almost animalistic, while the adjective "demon" suggests that her lover may be a supernatural power of a distinctly "lower" sort. The language of the ensuing lines likewise sounds powerful but also dangerous, and many readers have heard sexual overtones in the comment that it was "As if this earth in fast thick pants were breathing" (l. 18). In any case, there is a sense of heightened emotional excitement that is typical of most of the poem, and when the "mighty fountain momently [is] forced" (l. 19), the language sounds both orgasmic and volcanic. We are suddenly in the presence of enormous, awe-inspiring, but also potentially dangerous power, although the excitement eventually subsides when the speaker describes how the outburst flings up "momently the sacred river," whose leisurely movement is then depicted: "Five miles meandering with a mazy motion / Through wood and dale the sacred river ran, / Then reached the caverns measureless to man, / And sank in tumult to a lifeless ocean" (ll. 25–28). This whole description of the outburst of water and the impressiveness of the subsequent waterfall clearly seems connected to the similar descriptions of sublime landscapes recorded in Coleridge's prose.

In its emphasis on alliteration, assonance, and constantly repeated images, "Kubla Khan" has an almost hypnotic effect, while its fragments and exclamations and its literal and figurative outbursts make it seem sublime (i.e., transcendent, irresistible) in other ways as well. The poem alternates between passages suggesting intense (but usually also very lofty) sensual pleasures and dangerous threats, especially in the sudden reference to mysterious "ancestral voices prophesying war!" (l. 30). These voices suggest power of their own, but they also suggest limits to the power of the Khan; at the same time, the fact that Kubla can hear them suggests his own power once more. Soon, however, the emphasis shifts from the power of the Khan to the power of the poet, who recounts how "A damsel with a dulcimer / In a vision once I saw" (ll. 37–38). Almost by definition his "vision" was an ecstatic and transcendent experience—precisely the kind of experience traditionally defined as "sublime." The "damsel" and her beautiful singing seem a potent contrast with the almost animalistic "woman wailing for her demon-lover" who was mentioned earlier (l. 16), and indeed the later "damsel" is explicitly described as "an Abyssinian maid" (or virgin) "Singing of Mount Abora" (ll. 39, 41), so that she seems morally chaste and her song seems literally elevated in its subject matter. The maid intones a "symphony and song" that the poet longs to "revive" within himself—a desire that signals his own aspiration to achieve something grand, inspiring, and transcendent (concepts especially suggested by the word "symphony").

The poet explicitly desires to feel "deep delight," which he hopes to express through "music loud and long" (ll. 44–45)—language that once more implies a desire to transcend anything that is merely ordinary, mundane, or trivial. He seeks a music that is heightened in volume and lengthy in duration, and, in contemplating the possibility of such power, he reminds us that he has already, in composing the present poem, actually achieved it: "I would build that dome in air, / That sunny dome! Those caves of ice!" (ll. 46–47). But, of course, those imposing structures have already been built in this very lyric; indeed, they exist in actuality nowhere else but in "Kubla Khan" itself. The poem has already achieved precisely the sublime effects it presently and explicitly longs for, and in the very intensity with which those longings are now expressed, the poem becomes even more sublime (even more heightened, even more lofty and transcendent in tone) than it has been already. As the poem closes, the speaker imagines that his hoped-for sublime powers will make him seem somewhat frightening and intimidating (ll. 48–54) so that he will seem, in some ways, far more imposing and impressive a figure than even the Khan himself. Most readers, however, will also feel an enormous sense of gratitude to a poet capable of writing in such an intensely sublime fashion and capable of communicating, so convincingly, that sense of the sublime to others. Ultimately, the creator of "Kubla Khan" seems a far more imposing figure than the imagined Khan himself, precisely because the Khan and his splendid dominions are indeed the obvious product of the poet's very own sublime imagination.

WORKS CITED OR CONSULTED

Ashfield, Andrew and Peter de Bolla, eds. *The Sublime: A Reader in British Eighteenth-Century Aesthetic Theory*. Cambridge: Cambridge University Press, 1996.

Coleridge, Samuel Taylor. *The Complete Poems*. Ed. William Keach. New York: Penguin, 1997.

———. *The Literary Remains of Samuel Taylor Coleridge*. Ed. Henry Nelson Coleridge. 4 vols. London: W. Pickering, 1836–1839.

Grant, Allan. *A Preface to Coleridge*. London: Longman, 1972.

Milton, Mary Lee Taylor. *The Poetry of Samuel Taylor Coleridge: An Annotated Bibliography of Criticism, 1935–1970*. New York: Garland, 1981.

Modiano, Raimonda. *Coleridge and the Concept of Nature*. Tallahassee: Florida State University Press, 1985.

Rachwal, Tadeusz. "Textuality Unltd." *Boundary of Borders*. Ed. Tadeusz Slawek. Cieszwy: Proat, 1992. 63–70.

Rosen, Charles. *The Romantic Generation*. Cambridge, MA: Harvard University Press, 1995.

Shaw, Philip. *The Sublime*. New York: Routledge, 2006.

Valins, David, ed. *On the Sublime*, by Samuel Taylor Coleridge. New York: Palgrave Macmillan, 2003.

Weiskel, Thomas. *The Romantic Sublime: Studies in the Structure and Psychology of Transcendence*. Baltimore: The Johns Hopkins University Press, 1976.

"LINES WRITTEN A FEW MILES ABOVE TINTERN ABBEY" (WILLIAM WORDSWORTH)

"A Poem About Interiors"
by Albert O. Wlecke, in
Wordsworth and the Sublime (1973)

INTRODUCTION

For Albert Wlecke, the Wordsworthian sublime deals with the interior world: "We might say, therefore, that whatever else 'sublime' awareness, or 'sublime' intentionality, is in 'Tintern Abbey', it seems to involve an act in which consciousness senses itself penetrating an interior." Wlecke calls the Wordsworthian sublime a sort of *sacred horror* in which individual autonomy and notions of self dissolve in a visionary moment: "To be haunted by a passion is to be haunted by his love, his desire to encounter the visionary underworld of creative power. And he is simultaneously afraid of this love, of staring too directly into the awe-engendering underworld of consciousness—an underworld from which, however, he cannot quite turn his face away in the patent 'deep and gloomy wood' of Tintern Abbey." Thus, for Wlecke, Wordsworth, in depicting the grandeur of nature, explores the sublime depths of consciousness imagining itself.

Wlecke, Albert O. "A Poem About Interiors." *Wordsworth and the Sublime.* Berkeley: University of California Press, 1973. 20–46.

I

"Tintern Abbey" resembles the classical religious meditation in that it begins with a careful description of a scene, with what Saint Ignatius would have called "the composition of place." It also shows Wordsworth employing those three powers of the mind designated by the ultimately Augustinian psychology from which the religious meditation was derived: memory, understanding, and will. In the poem we find Wordsworth struggling to understand what his memory so poignantly reveals: his perception of nature has irrevocably changed with the passing of years. We also find him making certain promises: he shall continue to turn to nature as the "guide, the guardian of my heart, and soul / Of all my moral being" (ll. 110–111). But despite these similarities with the religious meditation, the atmosphere of Wordsworth's poem is vastly different. The scene that is "composed" is significant only because of the private resonances Wordsworth discovers in it. It carries in its texture none of the traditional dimensions of meaning that scenes from scripture had for the disciple of Saint Ignatius. Moreover, as Louis Martz has pointed out, the kind of understanding "applied" is associative rather than, as in a meditation by Donne, dialectic.[1] And the moment of illumination toward which this ruminating understanding gropes lacks the benefit of an orthodox theology by which to guide itself. Finally, the resolution Wordsworth makes, his pledge of continuing fealty to nature, is based exclusively upon his past experience. His wish derives none of its force or point from any traditionally sanctioned moral directive.

Perhaps it is this complete absence of any perspective other than the private which makes the total impression of Wordsworth's poem so different from the impression left by a classical religious meditation. We may, for example, find Donne struggling in his meditations with grave doubts about his own possibilities for salvation, but the fundamental coordinates of his universe are secure. And his precisely defined orthodoxy more often than not provides the alembic in which his doubts are resolved. In "Tintern Abbey," however, Wordsworth's universe and his resolution are far more tentative. The essential elements of his vision of nature are questioned a number of times in the poem. And his wish to find continuing sustenance in nature, a wish that grows out of his tentative vision, has none of that certainty of fulfillment that Donne can feel in the Christian promises. In the concluding lines of the poem, Wordsworth even finds it necessary to project his sister Dorothy into the uncertain future: *she* will, he hopes, sustain the necessary relationship with saving nature even if he no longer can do so. Both the poet's faith in nature and the version of "salvation" that faith implies are so shot through with ambiguities that it is easy to agree with what one critic has suggested, namely, that the "dominating mood of the greater part" of Wordsworth's meditation along the banks of the Wye is "one of perplexity."[2] This perplexity quietly intrudes into what appears to be the most affirmative passage of the poem: Wordsworth can find no better name for the principle of cosmic oneness which he intuits than "something."

We can examine the sources of Wordsworth's perplexity by posing the following question: to what extent can we see, in the whole activity of mind which the meditation describes, reflections of that act of vision during which Wordsworth encounters an interfusing cosmic presence; an encounter that dissolves distinctions between the activity of consciousness and the activity of its intended object; an encounter that finally, I have argued, is a manifestation of imaginative consciousness becoming reflexively aware of its own ubiquitous energies? This thesis, it must now be admitted, suggests that Wordsworth, even at that moment when his rhetoric indicates a mind at the highest pitch of intuitive certitude, is still struggling unawares with a perplexity: a consciousness of transcendence without the proper name for what is indeed the transcendent agent—his own mind. The tentative quality of Wordsworth's vision and hope in "Tintern Abbey" is thus not simply the result of the privacy of that vision and hope, their lack of sanction in terms of a traditional orthodoxy. Within the poet's very privacy there is a failure of recognition. He displaces his "sense sublime" of the power of his own imaginative consciousness into a "something" dwelling throughout the universe. And this displacement is but the most extreme of a series of displacements of the recognition of imaginative activity which pervades the entire meditation.

To clarify and support these generalities, I consider the poem from two points of view: (1) as a poem about interiors; (2) as a meditation that proceeds as a continuing exploration of the sense of interiors. The first point of view will bring us up against Wordsworth's persistent characterization of imaginative activity as a creation of a sense of immanence, of a "within," in phenomenal nature, and also up against the question of how indeed this activity proceeds from a "depth" of the mind far below the surface of ordinary consciousness. The second point of view will enable us to see the associative progressions of the poem as controlled, in part at least, by an explorative movement of the poet's mind from one "interior" of consciousness to the next: a journey through a variety of mental depths. These two approaches will not permit us to unravel every strand of meaning in the poem, nor answer every question, and what follows is not to be regarded as an effort toward total explication (I exclude, for example, any consideration of the last verse paragraph). But they will at least serve to describe, in a way corroborative of my thesis, the grounds of Wordsworth's haunting perplexity.

II

"Tintern Abbey" is a poem preoccupied with the insides of things, with a sense of immanent power lurking beneath the surface of phenomena.[3] The "something," of course, is "deeply interfused" and dwells within all things. But even in Wordsworth's opening "composition of place" (ll. 1–22), the poet's eye and ear encounter a landscape permeated with immanence. The mountain springs of the Wye are heard as rolling with a "soft inland murmur," the word "inland" not only supplying a reason for the softness of the murmur but also obliquely evoking a much more extensive region than that seen in the poem, a region *within which* the immediate landscape around Tintern Abbey is located. The "wild secluded scene" of this landscape is seen by the poet as somehow impressed by "steep and lofty cliffs" with "Thoughts of a more deep seclusion," as if the elements of the scene were in themselves enacting the poet's sense of intensifying solitude. Wordsworth finds himself located in a kind of interior: "I again repose / Here, under this dark sycamore." He observes "orchard-tufts" which because of their "one green hue" seem almost to be submerging as they "lose themselves / 'Mid groves and copses." The "pastoral farms" of the scene barely emerge from the lush, enclosing landscape: they are "Green to the very door." The poet, noticing suggestive "wreaths of smoke" drifting up from among the trees with "some uncertain notice," begins to shape hypotheses about the immanence of the woods. Perhaps the uncertain notice is of "vagrant dwellers in the houseless woods." The quiet oxymoron "vagrant dwellers" prefigures the curious way in which Wordsworth will later attempt to fix the location of the "something":

its "dwelling" turns out to be everywhere. Here, at the opening of the meditation, the "dwellers" of the woods, perhaps gypsies, are in fact wandering (L. *vagari*, to wander); and it seems only fitting that they be located where there are no fixed human locations. Their potential ubiquity within the "houseless" woods resembles the ubiquity of the "something" within its universal dwelling-places.

Finally Wordsworth surmises a "Hermit" sitting alone at the quiet heart of the landscape. This surmise completes the centripetal movement of the poem's first verse paragraph. The Hermit's presence is envisaged as not only within the landscape (itself surrounded by a larger, unseen region) but also within an enclosure itself by the woods—a "Hermit's cave." This last interpretation by Wordsworth of the "uncertain notice" is also the last refinement of his "Thoughts of more deep seclusion." The "wild secluded scene," at the moment when Wordsworth is about to turn away from a direct contemplation of it, is thus sensed as possessing an immanence—and is perhaps not so wild after all. For the solitude enclosed within the landscape is surmised as a human solitude.

We might also characterize the progression of Wordsworth's mind in his initial meditative act as a movement downward and inward: from the sight of "steep and lofty cliffs" to a sense, beyond the reach of sight, of an immanent human presence deep in the woods. And if we try to characterize this progression in terms of a larger context of metaphorical implication, we find useful Northrop Frye's observation that the "metaphorical structure of Romantic poetry tends to move inside and downward instead of outside and upward, hence the creative world is deep within, and so is heaven or the place of the presence of God."[4] Thus, we are tempted to ask of Wordsworth's composition of place whether it in fact is symbolic of a movement of his mind toward the sources of his creativity, whether the poet's preoccupation with the immanence of phenomena is not really a preoccupation with the creative power immanent within his own mind, and whether, finally, the movement downward and inward does not prefigure the poet's later encounter with his transcendent "something." To investigate these questions, we must step momentarily away from "Tintern Abbey" and consider at large Wordsworth's metaphorical geography of introspection.

I say "geography" because Wordsworth consistently tends to speak of his mind in metaphors implying spatial extent; thus the acts of introspection, of memory, of consciousness in general, all of which take place *within* this spatialized mind, can be likened to a movement within a special kind of spatial dimension or even to a journey through a certain region. What, then, are the main (physical and psychological) features of Wordsworth's interior landscape? We might say, first of all, that since Frye's observation suggests a metaphorical equation between the place where imaginative power is to be found and the place where— to borrow a term from Rudolf Otto—the "Holy" is to be encountered,[5] the journey into what has been referred to in Wordsworth as the "abysses of the subjective consciousness" is simultaneously a journey toward the numinous, the transcendent, even the awful.[6] And in terms of this geography of introspection, Wordsworth at times approaches his power of imagination with something of the same mixture of dread and desire that a soul of an earlier tradition might have experienced in feeling himself translated to the otherworld.

In the fragment of *The Recluse* which Wordsworth includes in the preface to the 1814 edition of *The Excursion*, the poet deliberately recalls the Christian tradition of vision, only to express, with a certain bravado, his emotional indifference to it:

> Jehovah—with his thunder, and the choir
> Of shouting Angels, and the empyreal thrones—
> I pass them unalarmed.

Instead, Wordsworth discovers his terror of the "Holy" in the journey "inside and downward"—in the visionary act of introspection. In lines immediately following his almost contemptuous dismissal of Jehovah's "shouting Angels," he writes:

> Not Chaos, not
> The darkest pit of lowest Erebus,
> Nor aught of blinder vacancy, scooped out
> By help of dreams—can breed such fear and awe
> As fall upon us often when we look
> Into our Minds, into the Mind of Man—
> My haunt, and the main region of my song.[7]

Wordsworth's otherworld is thus an underworld, not that created by Miltonic vision but that discovered by consciousness turning inward upon itself. The negative comparisons of these lines curiously suggest that this underworld, while totally devoid of form or shape, is still a space, a "haunt," an almost sacred spot filled with the presence of awesome power. Since, in terms of Wordsworth's metaphors, there is nothing to be *seen* in this haunt—no palpable shape upon which the mind can establish a purchase—reflexive consciousness discovers no limiting contours to its introspective plunge and thus finds itself upon a fearful journey into an open-ended abyss.

This kind of interior space is quite different from the confining space of Locke's *camera obscura*. This earlier metaphor for the mind reflects both Locke's rejection of the theory of innate ideas, which were often described by the Cambridge Platonists as kinds of inner light, and his restriction of the sources of knowledge to the not always certain reports of the senses.[8] Wordsworth's metaphor of the mental abyss, however, intimates a theory of the mind which goes far beyond Locke's careful empiricism. For immanent throughout the poet's interior space is the numinous power of the imagination—sometimes referred to by him as a mist or vapor, sometimes as a stream, sometimes as nothing more than the sound made by an unseen stream. In Book XIV of *The Prelude*, for example, Wordsworth characterizes his history of the growth and development of his imagination as the tracing of a "stream / From the blind cavern whence is faintly heard / Its natal murmur."[9] Earlier in the same book, where Wordsworth discovers in the mountain vision (also a vision of depths) from the top of Snowdon a "perfect image of a mighty Mind," he sees in a "blue chasm" in the outspread mist below a "breach / Through which the homeless voice of waters rose." And in this "dark deep thoroughfare," he goes on, "had Nature lodg'd / The Soul, the Imagination of the whole."[10] We note in these lines, incidentally, a suggestion of the same oxymoron of home / homeless—the "vagrant dwellers" of the "houseless" woods, the something's "dwelling" ubiquitously—which we saw in "Tintern Abbey": here the "homeless voice of waters" is "lodg'd" as an auditory emblem of the "Imagination" in the "blue chasm" in the mist.

In Book VI of *The Prelude*, after Wordsworth describes his discovery of having crossed the Alps without realizing it, the poet is suddenly confronted directly by his imagination:

> here the Power so called
> Through sad incompetence of human speech,

> That awful Power rose from the mind's abyss
> Like an unfathered vapour that enwraps,
> At once, some lonely traveller.[11]

The imagery here is especially involved. Not only does the imagination rise from the by now familiar subjective abyss; but the mind itself, confronted suddenly by its immanent power, is enclosed (imagination "enwraps" the traveler) by the intensity of its reflexive awareness. Consciousness is both the container that in its depths contains imagination and, now that imagination has leapt forth from these depths, the contained. Imagination is described as this confining, enclosing mist because so potent is its abrupt intrusion into awareness that the phenomenal world is lost. As Wordsworth tells us a few lines later: "the light of sense / Goes out."[12] The phrase "light of sense" recalls of course the Lockean epistemology and his notion of the mental *camera obscura* into which sensation, as it were, beamed its message. But when this light is extinguished for Wordsworth, there is discovered by the poet an innate power of the mind undreamt of in Locke's philosophy.

This direct, unmediated confrontation with imaginative power is rare in Wordsworth. The poet's primary aim, he tells us in the preface to *The Excursion*, is to sing a "spousal verse" celebrating the marriage of his mind to nature.[13] Such a marriage would inevitably have to avoid a prolongation of that state of mind brought about when the light of sense has gone out, for this kind of awareness necessarily involves a break with nature, a divorce of consciousness from the phenomenal world. Nature, the chosen partner of Wordsworth's mind, demands that the light of sense be maintained. The obvious difficulty in meeting this demand—from the point of view of the metaphors we have been examining—is that his creative power, the power whereby he seeks to blend his mind with nature, includes a tendency to force Wordsworth's awareness back toward the abysses of subjective consciousness, to halt and enwrap the mental traveler. The mind's awareness of its own imaginative power tends to be the antithesis of its awareness of nature. And even when the power discovered in the abysses of the mind has been somehow synthesized with consciousness of nature, it threatens always to destroy nature by its own exuberance. Wordsworth complains in *The Prelude*:

> Oh! why hath not the Mind
> Some element to stamp her image on
> In nature somewhat nearer to her own?
> Why, gifted with such powers to send abroad
> Her spirit, must it lodge in shrines so frail?[14]

In these lines we again see Wordsworth's concern with a dwelling: his "spirit" of imagination is to "lodge" in nature, however "frail" its "shrines" may prove to be. (The lodges of nature are appropriately "shrines" because the imagination is a numinous power.) In these lines we also see a metaphorical paradigm of how Wordsworth attempts to solve the problem posed by his scheme of marriage. Reflexive imaginative consciousness is to be mediated by an awareness of nature, to be experienced *sub specie naturae*. The poet will transfer ("stamp") onto nature the image of his mind as a place wherein lurks an immanent power. Nature now must become a dwelling, a lodge, a home, and also, therefore, a place of immanence. We might say that the sense of the abyss of the mind is converted into a sense of the depths of nature, but of course nature exhibits these depths only insofar as imagination has been sent abroad, as it were, to deepen nature. As Hartman has put it, in commenting upon Wordsworth's "obsession with specific place," "consciousness of self" is to be "buried in nature."[15] Consciousness allows itself to become aware of imagination's power by displacing that power into a shrine (or lodge, or home, or house, and so on) in the phenomena supplied by the light of sense. This relationship between consciousness and nature is inevitably oxymoronic: the "homes" provided by nature, although limited in terms of their phenomenal surface, must simultaneously possess an immanent open-ended space adequate to the nature of the numinous power of imagination whose original dwelling-place was the infinite underworld of Wordsworth's mind. The poet's "natural mysticism," therefore, might be characterized as a consciousness of this underworld opening out beneath the surface of the natural world.

By now it should be apparent toward what conclusions about the opening landscape of "Tintern Abbey" this brief account of Wordsworth's metaphors of immanence is leading. The sense of interiors that so fascinates the poet in his composition of place is in fact a sense of his own creative power enclosed within nature. This sense of interiors, of something far more deeply interfused, is what Wordsworth's eye attempts to resolve as it scans a landscape shot through with unseen presence and as the landscape itself seems to dissolve into the pervasive green of the season. The gradual focus of his eye upon the "uncertain notice" of the wreaths of smoke, and then the passing of his mind beyond the reach of sight into the depths of the green woods where he postulates "vagrant dwellers" in the "houseless" forest and a Hermit sitting alone in a cave,[16] are actions that recall in a remarkably distilled and naturalistic fashion the metaphors of consciousness we have been tracing: the imagination as a mysterious vapor rising from the depths, the oxymoronic dwelling in an unconfined space, the mind as a cave wherein lurks a secret power. And just as in the Alps the imagination enclosed Wordsworth's awareness like a mist and extinguished the light of sense, so here the rising smoke from the depths of the landscape beckons Wordsworth beyond the phenomenal world into the immanence of the forest, into the underworld of his own mind.[17]

III

We now can analyze what Professor Martz has characterized as the "associative" understanding of Wordsworth's meditation. After the composition of place of the first verse paragraph, the poet turns away from a direct contemplation of his scene and begins to explore the significance for himself of the "beauteous forms" (l. 22) of the landscape, an exploration that brings him to thoughts of both his past and his future, and also to an encounter with "something far more deeply interfused."

The language of this exploration suggests a continuing sense of the mind as a kind of interior space, a space into which the poet seeks to sink, escaping from the "heavy and weary weight / Of all this unintelligible world" (ll. 39–40). For the most part this escape, this inward sinking, is mediated through a vision of phenomenal nature, a vision that requires sensation or at least the memory of sensation before the poet can turn inward upon himself. At the end of the fourth verse paragraph, phenomenal nature, the nature revealed through the "language of the sense," is described by Wordsworth as the "guide, the guardian" of his heart, and finally as the "soul" of all his moral being (ll. 108–111). This characterization suggests the poet's recognition of nature's role in restoring him to a sense of his own heart, his own soul—to a sense of what is most essentially inward in himself. That nature is granted the epithet "soul," as if Wordsworth were saying that nature at least in one respect was his very essence, is but another manifestation of his habit of displacing his own inwardness into nature. But this displacement turns out to be reciprocal: having transferred his sense of self into nature, Wordsworth finds that nature made immanent leads him back toward himself.

At the beginning of the second verse paragraph, we find an example of such a backward turning. After having surmised an unseen Hermit at the heart of the landscape, Wordsworth continues to move beyond the immediacies of the scene by directing his consciousness toward his past: he transforms his sense of a human presence enclosed in the woods into an explicit memory of himself "in lonely rooms, and 'mid the din / Of towns and cities" (ll. 25–26). The cave of nature becomes a room in London, the identity of whose inhabitant is now no longer disguised. The poet's envisaging of hidden solitude is converted, through a process of association, into an overt memory of his own past solitude. This transformation makes more understandable the grounds of the sense of pervading immanence of the opening landscape. Consciousness of self is lodged throughout the scene because, as Wordsworth's eye passes over it, he is simultaneously aware, however subliminally, of the previous encounters of his mind with the scene. There was a direct encounter in the year 1793, the time of his first visit to Tintern Abbey, and then a series of indirect encounters made possible by his recalling, through the agency of affective memory, the "beauteous forms" during the period between 1793 and July 13, 1798, the day of his return and his meditation. The landscape, therefore, so strangely immanent, is not simply being seen, but is being seen "again"—the word is repeated four times in the first twenty-two lines. And so it is filled with an implicit history of the poet's past conscious experiences with its forms. We might say that it is the richness of the sense of "being seen again" which is, as it were, spatialized into the immanencies of the scene. We might also say, from this point of view, that Wordsworth's image of himself in a lonely city room is an image that was, up to a point in the poem, buried in the unseen spaces of the landscape: one of his earlier undefined thoughts of "more deep seclusion." The image now becomes emergent and explicit.

The seclusion of the city, as Wordsworth remembers it, also was characterized by movements of consciousness describable in terms suggesting a movement into an interior. Since Wordsworth apparently found in the phenomena of the city nothing more than "many shapes / Of joyless daylight" (ll. 51–52)—an oppressive experience of the "burthen of the mystery" of things (l. 38)—he would turn for "tranquil restoration" (l. 30) to his memories of the phenomena of the landscape around Tintern Abbey. He tells us that he owed to these remembered forms:

> sensations sweet,
> Felt in the blood, and felt along the heart;
> And passing even into my purer mind,
> With tranquil restoration.
>
> [ll. 27–30]

The language of these lines suggests a movement of awareness from a purely sensory state ("sensations sweet / Felt in the blood"), to a state of more diffused emotion ("felt along the heart"), and finally to a state that seems to transcend the physicality of sensation and emotion. The "sensations sweet" are said to pass somehow "even" into Wordsworth's "purer mind," as if these sensations were penetrating a region of interior consciousness where sensation is not normally found. These lines become more intelligible if we take them as descriptive of a movement of consciousness, by means of a contemplation of the remembered "beauteous forms," from a state that is almost exclusively sensory to a state that, though dependent upon remembered sensation, is more enclosed, more self-contained, more inward than the state of sensory awareness in which consciousness is principally directed toward the remembered objects of sensation. In other words, this description of sensations passing into Wordsworth's "purer mind" suggests a movement of consciousness implicitly analogous to the movement of the poet's mind described in the first verse paragraph: from the surface of phenomena (though in "lonely rooms," a remembered surface) to a sense of enclosed immanence. And this meditative recall by the Wordsworth of 1798 of his earlier acts of remembering continues the process of inwardly deepening consciousness implicit in the poem from its very inception.

An even more intense form of this kind of consciousness is delineated in the final lines of the second verse paragraph. Wordsworth claims that he owes to his memories of the "beauteous forms" "another gift, / Of aspect more sublime" (ll. 36–37). This "aspect" is a certain kind or power of vision (L. *aspectus*, a seeing, a looking, a power of vision), and is described in language intimating an encounter with an immanent presence. This encounter occurs in

> that serene and blessed mood,
> In which the affections gently lead us on,—
> Until, the breath of this corporeal frame
> And even the motion of our human blood
> Almost suspended, we are laid asleep
> In body, and become a living soul:
> While with an eye made quiet by the power
> Of harmony, and the deep power of joy,
> We see into the life of things.
>
> [ll. 41–49]

Wordsworth shifts in these lines into the first person plural, a rhetorical heightening that seems to universalize the availability of the kind of vision he is describing: "we," all of us, are capable of such an "aspect," such a power of vision. But this shift in point of view also suggests that it is of the nature of this kind of encounter with "the life of things" to convert the sense of "I" into a sense of "we," to attenuate the awareness of the self as a single, isolated ego. Such an awareness is thus analogous to the poet's awareness later in the poem of a ubiquitous, all-pervading "something" that lies in the innermost space of all things, including the mind of man: all identities tend to be lost in the universally immanent "something." Here the "aspect more sublime," this vision of "the life of things," is, we note, a seeing "into." And the language describing the movement of consciousness toward the moment of such seeing "into" indicates an awareness that passes beyond bodily sensation ("we are laid asleep / In body") toward an intensity of inward vision ("and become a living soul"). The eye that then sees "into" is of course not the corporeal eye—that along with the body has been "laid asleep"—but the inward eye of meditative introspection, an eye that has been made tranquil by a "power / Of harmony" and a "power of joy" which, we also note, is "deep." This word that Wordsworth uses to describe the sense of joy accompanying his vision suggests not simply the intensity of the joy but, more importantly from the point of view of the poem's language of immanence, the interior of consciousness in which harmony, joy, and a vision "into the life of things" are to be experienced. Finally, we might observe that this "aspect" is "more sublime" than that state of awareness in which he felt "sensations sweet" passing into his "purer mind." The comparative form of the adjective tells us that *both* structures of inward consciousness described in the second verse paragraph are "sublime"—a characterizing term that appears elsewhere in the poem only in Wordsworth's account of a "sense sublime" of "something far more deeply interfused." We might say, therefore, that whatever else "sublime" awareness, or "sublime" intentionality, is in "Tintern Abbey," it seems to involve an act in which consciousness senses itself penetrating an interior. And implicitly, we might also conclude, Wordsworth's surmise at the end of his composition of place of a hermit enclosed within the landscape is a movement of his mind toward sublimity.

What exactly is this "life of things" into which Wordsworth claims he has seen? The question cannot be easily answered, for Wordsworth's retrospective emphasis is almost entirely upon the *state* of consciousness which sees "into" rather than upon the intended *object* of that state of consciousness. It is this structure of awareness which he claims is one of the principal gifts of his memories of the "beauteous forms." Moreover, as the third verse paragraph tells us, while the poet is certain both of having undergone this visionary experience and of the "method" of moving toward such a vision, the precise content of that vision, the presumed encounter with the "life of things," is not so certain after all:

> If this
> Be but a vain belief, yet, oh! how oft—
> In darkness and amid the many shapes
> Of joyless daylight; when the fretful stir
> Unprofitable, and the fever of the world,
> Have hung upon the beatings of my heart—
> How oft, in spirit, have I turned to thee,
> O sylvan Wye / thou wanderer thro' the woods,
> How often has my spirit turned to thee!
>   [ll. 49–57]

These lines come as a dramatic turn in the poet's meditative action. (In a note to the second edition of the *Lyrical Ballads*, Wordsworth claims that the poem roughly resembles an ode in its "impassioned music" and in "the transitions"; it might be said that here is an impassioned example of the "antistrophe," or the "turning against," of that form.)[18] Until this point Wordsworth's awareness—first as he scanned the scene, then as he recalled the quality of his retrospective encounters with the scene—had been growing progressively more inward. But now it appears as if the very language of his meditation—the very articulation of his deepest intuition—has triggered a seizure of doubt. Certitude is abruptly converted into the uncertainty of a hypothesis. It is not the experience itself which might be "a vain belief." Instead, the question is whether he can characterize this vision as indeed a seeing "into the life of things." That phrase, though ringing with an almost metaphysical assurance, is at the same time so vague and extensive in its reference as to be potentially meaningless. What exactly, Wordsworth suddenly seems to inquire, am I to make out of this "aspect more sublime"? Can I base such a sweeping claim on such a private experience? Wordsworth's perplexity here prefigures the later perplexity hidden in his use of the groping term "something" to designate the indwelling spirit of all the cosmos. The poet's deepest intuitions can make no clarifying appeal to traditional myth or to a discursively worked out set of dogmatic formulations. And as he leaves behind the concrete sources of these intuitions, his memories of the "beauteous forms" of the landscape of Tintern Abbey, and as he works his way through his memory of these memories toward a statement of his vision, his language grows progressively more abstract, more generalized, and finally, even to himself, dubious.[19]

Yet this experience of doubt is momentary. The "antistrophe" of the third verse paragraph almost as quickly becomes an "anti-antistrophe." Lacking the support of a traditional myth or dogma, Wordsworth again turns to the undeniable facts of his experience and finds support against his doubts by recalling the genuine solace of his memories when he was oppressed by the "fever of the world" in the midst of "joyless daylight." But this appeal to the past is simultaneously an appeal to the present and to the immediate locale of his meditation. For out of this new memory of his acts of remembering, he apostrophizes the "sylvan Wye" flowing directly before him in the landscape. His appeal, in other words, combines the experiential testimony of both the past and the present. His second-person address to the Wye as "thou wanderer thro' the woods" evokes yet another image of immanence—but an image that draws the poet's eye back into the specific scene and recalls him from the wavering expressed in his suddenly intruding hypothesis. This return to the concrete as an anodyne for doubt is an action that the poet later formulates as a fundamental requirement of his consciousness: Wordsworth writes in lines 107 through 109 that he is "well pleased to recognize / In nature and the language of the sense / The anchor" of his "purest thoughts." An anchor, of course, achieves a purchase upon stability by sinking into the depths of the sea; and here Wordsworth stabilizes himself, escapes from the wavering hypothesizing of one of his "purest thoughts," by addressing his awareness to an immediately given image of an action proceeding through an interior.[20] Vision is to be preserved by an adhesion to sensation, and his eye returns to an image of the immanence of the woods.

At the end of the third verse paragraph, Wordsworth has thus completed an almost circular movement of his consciousness: from present to past back to present; from landscape to a history of the relationships of his mind to that landscape back to landscape; from outward awareness to inward awareness back to outward awareness. This circular movement might almost be compared to an exploration of Chinese boxes: Wordsworth "opens" the strangely immanent landscape and discovers himself in the "box" of a room in the city. He recalls, almost seems to reexperience, the exploration by his past mind (trapped within that city box) into the remembered "beauteous forms." Immanence leads to deeper immanence. At the moment of deepest penetration, there occurs a vision "into" something he terms "the life of things." And immediately, at this moment of climax, the lid of this ultimate interior slams shut, and Wordsworth is left wondering whether he is guilty of a "vain belief." His anxiety is dispelled, or at least he attempts to dispel it, by a return through his memories to the surface of the landscape. This action of consciousness is similar in part to that poignant moment of introspection in Book XII of *The Prelude* where Wordsworth also uses the language of immanence to delineate an intense moment of perplexing introspection:

Oh! mystery of man, from what a depth
Proceed thy honours. I am lost . . .

. . . .
            The days gone by
Return upon me almost from the dawn
Of life: the hiding-places of man's power
Open; I would approach them, but they close.[21]

In "Tintern Abbey" Wordsworth's search into the depths of subjectivity, a downward and inward journey that seems to carry him to a sight of what Frye, as we have noticed, has called "the creative world" or the "place of the presence of God," is terminated by a scrupulous hypothesis. I have already suggested that one reason for the poet's sudden worry about a "vain belief"—as if a question of doctrine were at issue—was the fact that Wordsworth's poetic articulation of his vision, his rendering of his "aspect more sublime" into statement, exposed the vision to the kinds of questions that can be asked of any statement, but are especially likely to be asked of any affirmations about the "life of things." But perhaps a still more fundamental reason can be offered to explain Wordsworth's abrupt upsurge of anxious uncertainty. Perhaps his anxiety is a displaced, brief, and somewhat muted expression of the "fear and awe" that, according to his preface to *The Excursion*, he claims to experience when he approaches the "haunt" and "main region" of his song, namely, his own mind. Perhaps the "life of things" is the numinous presence in the creative underworld of his mind—a presence I have already called the power of "imagination"[22]—and his fearful turning for comfort to the "sylvan Wye" wandering through the woods is but another attempt to find a lodge for his imagination in the phenomena of nature. Going too far beyond, or rather within, these phenomena can lead to a "serene and blessed mood." But the "Holy"—the "life of things"—is also "awful," and can breed anxiety and confusion.

IV

In the fourth verse paragraph Wordsworth plunges again into the past, but to a time even prior to the period of his solacing introspection "in lonely rooms." The poet attempts a picture of what he "was when first" he "came among these hills," that is, on his walking tour of 1793 (ll. 66–67). But what he was in that year, at least as "Tintern Abbey" describes it, was essentially a certain structure of consciousness immersed in the depths of the phenomenal world, a mind almost totally one with nature. He claims that "like a roe" he

> bounded o'er the mountains, by the sides
> Of the deep rivers, and the lonely streams,
> Wherever nature led: more like a man
> Flying from something that he dreads than one
> Who sought the thing he loved.
>
> [Ll. 67–72]

We have here another image of depths ("deep rivers") and of seclusion ("lonely streams"). We also have a curious implication in the simile that concludes the passage: Wordsworth suggests through the comparative form of the figure that though his relationship to nature at that time might be compared to the pursuit by a lover (himself) of his beloved (nature), a better characterization of this relationship is the simile of himself as the pursued fearing and flying from an unknown pursuer ("something"). But of course if the pursuer is only a vague "something," how can this simile be taken—as it indeed seems to offer itself—as delineating the relationship between his mind and nature? That this dreadful "something" was not nature, although at first reading it might be taken as such, is indicated by line 70 which tells us that it was nature who "led" the young poet, and therefore was in a certain sense at least not "behind," the proper place for all pursuers. Perhaps even the "thing he loved" cannot be taken to refer to nature. These lines really do not provide enough to solve the puzzle, and all we can safely infer is that at this time Wordsworth's consciousness was a curiously ambivalent and contradictory mixture of the sense of being led (by nature), of the sense of his own loving pursuit (of nature?) and, most strikingly and memorably, of the fearful sense of being pursued—by "something." Perhaps it is his awareness of these riddles of his past state of mind which prompts Wordsworth to say: "I cannot paint / What then I was" (ll. 75–76).

What he paints instead is a picture of nature in which the phenomena of the landscape are almost identical with certain structures of consciousness:

> The sounding cataract
> Haunted me like a passion: the tall rock,
> The mountain, and the deep and gloomy wood,
> Their colours and their forms, were then to me
> An appetite; a feeling and a love,
> That had no need of a remoter charm,
> By thought supplied, nor any interest
> Unborrowed from the eye.
>
> [Ll. 76–83]

Wordsworth's language presents a world in which there is no distinction to be made between his intentionality and his intended objects. The "directions" of consciousness at this time were totally equivalent to the elements of the landscape. These "forms" quite simply—and the equation is startling—"were" for Wordsworth an "appetite; a feeling and a love." Thus there would be no need for "any interest / Unborrowed from the eye." The simple act of sensation, the mere act of looking, would be sufficient to involve Wordsworth's awareness in a range of conscious experiences far richer than the experience of ordinary seeing. To see is not to produce an occasion for possible emotion; to see is in itself to feel emotion. Phenomena *are* feelings, and feelings *are* phenomena. And to hear a "sounding cataract" is directly to be "Haunted" by a "passion," as if the "sounding cataract" in itself were a certain structure of consciousness (the experience of a "passion") impinging upon awareness. This image of the "sounding cataract"—an image of a dislocated sound—I take to be another image of immanence: it is analogous to the "soft inland murmur" of line 4 in that because its source is unseen, it suggests something hidden away from sight, an interior behind the surface of phenomena. It is precisely this sense of an interior which enables Wordsworth to describe the "sounding cataract" as if it were in itself a structure of consciousness. For, as we have already seen, the sense of immanence is for Wordsworth the sense of his own mind hidden in the landscape. And insofar as phenomena convey this sense of immanence, he is made dimly aware, in this case "Haunted," by the underworld of his mind which he has displaced into nature.

The previously noticed riddles of Wordsworth's curious comparative simile can now be unraveled. Both the term "something" and the term "thing" belong to the poem's language of perplexity (the most obvious example of this language is of course the poem's only other "something," that which is "far more deeply interfused"). This perplexity, I have been arguing, relates to Wordsworth's reflexive consciousness of the activity of his own mind; a consciousness that in Book XIII of the 1805 *Prelude* is the "highest bliss" of those poetic minds whose

> consciousness
> Of whom they are [is] habitually infused
> Through every image, and through every thought,
> And all impressions.[23]

The precise source of Wordsworth's perplexity in "Tintern Abbey" is the fact that, though the meditation explores how his mind is immanent in nature, infused through "every image" and "all impressions," he never can quite bring himself to recognize this infusion. To be sure, the landscape makes him think a great deal *about* his mind, its transactions with itself and with nature in the past, the present, and the future. But during this "thinking about," which constitutes the action of the meditation, Wordsworth does not seem *explicitly* to recognize that the special resonance of his perceptions, both in the present and in the chambers of memory, derives from the fact that frequently these acts of perception are simultaneously acts of apperception; that frequently the intended objects of his consciousness tend to become indistinguishable from the intentionality, the direction of consciousness, which grasps them. Apperception, the reflexive sense of the mind's activity, is lodged in perception, and thus nature becomes immanent.

Now, as we also have seen, Wordsworth is afraid of staring too directly at his mind—afraid of too unmediated an act of apperception. His mind is a "haunt," a sacred region filled with a numinous presence, and thus it fills him with awe and dread. But this mind that is experienced as a "haunt," as the place of the "Holy," is not the mind he thinks *about*, the mind he constitutes as the direct object of his meditation; it is rather the immediately "living" mind he encounters more or less obliquely in the act of apperception. While the Wordsworth of 1805 may have decided this structure of consciousness was "highest bliss," the Wordsworth of 1793 was flying from "something" that he dreaded—in much the same way a soul of an earlier tradition might flee from the awful majesty of God.[24] And just as this soul might also pursue his God with love, so the Wordsworth of 1793 was pursuing the numinous presence of the underworld of his mind in a landscape where phenomena and structures of awareness were identical. But, of course, as the comparative form of Wordsworth's simile indicates, the sense of fear predominated. Perhaps the image of the "sounding cataract" haunting him like a passion most adequately summarizes the paradoxical doubleness of Wordsworth's relationship to his act of reflexive self-awareness infusing itself throughout the phenomena of nature. To be haunted by a passion is to be haunted by his love, his desire to encounter the visionary underworld of creative power. And he is simultaneously afraid of this love, of staring too directly into the awe-engendering underworld of consciousness—an underworld from which, however, he cannot quite turn his face away in the patent "deep and gloomy wood" of Tintern Abbey.

The Wordsworth of 1798, looking back at this time of "aching joys" and "dizzy raptures" (ll. 84–85), does not quite know what to make of it ("I cannot paint"), except finally to say it is "now no more" (l. 84). Certainly the immediate intensity of the 1793 experience is past. But has the experience been completely lost or has it simply been attenuated? The very power of the poet's description of the experience suggests that, in the words of the "Immortality Ode," in the "embers" of his memory "Is something that doth live."[25] Perhaps the difference between his consciousness of 1793 and his consciousness of 1798 can be metaphorically depicted as the difference between the sound of the "sounding cataract" of the past and the sound of the "soft inland murmur" of the present. In other words, attenuation, not total loss. For Wordsworth still senses the landscape as immanent, though it is no longer seen and at the same time felt as a structure of consciousness. At this point in his life, it appears, he has so deeply lodged his self-awareness inside nature, that when he encounters it, as he does again shortly in the so-called "pantheistic" lines of the fourth verse paragraph, he does not know what to call it—especially since this "something" is "far more deeply interfused" than any of the other immanencies of the poem.

We must look upon the metaphor of "dwelling" in these lines as not only Wordsworth's most succinct description of the relationship of his mind and nature—a metaphor of extraordinary tension, yoking into a single precarious focus unbounded objects of perception (sky, air, ocean) with an apperception ubiquitously interfused. The metaphor can also be taken as Wordsworth's most explicit attempt in the poem to define his strangely immanent "something." Kenneth Burke has observed, in *A Grammar of Motives*, that to "tell what a thing is, you place it in terms of something else. This idea of locating, or placing, is implicit in our very word for definition itself: to *define*, or *determine* a thing, is to mark its boundaries, hence to use terms that possess, implicitly at least, contextual reference."[26] That Wordsworth feels he has resolved his perplexity—using the entire universe as a vehicle for contextually defining the unrecognized immanence of his consciousness—is indicated by his surprising "Therefore" which begins the sentence immediately following his vision of the "spirit" that "rolls through all things" (ll. 100, 102). Why, we might ask, a "Therefore"? Is a hidden syllogism being brought to a finish? Why, suddenly, this rhetoric of resolution?

The answer seems to be that Wordsworth has convinced himself that he has uncovered a way out of his difficulties. His experience of transcendence, of the hidden "life of things," is not a "vain belief" so long as he can contextually define, mark the boundaries of, this experience by reference to the phenomena of nature—a strategy of definition which uses the "language of the sense." Nature will provide what traditional myth or religious dogma no longer provides: a way both of making intelligible the visionary world and of mediating its terrors. Wordsworth is "still / A lover of the meadows and the woods, / And mountains"—the polysyndeton of these lines (102–104) expresses the intensity with which he feels his solution—because these "beauteous forms" will continue to serve not only as vehicles of vision but even more crucially as the means of resolving the haunting perplexities of that immanent vision. In fact, of course, Wordsworth's "religion of nature" is a means of providing symbolic form to the underworld, darker and more chaotic than "lowest Erebus," which is opened by reflexive self-awareness. And his "Therefore" emerges from the practical reason, not the theoretical. For his solution is to be almost exclusively experiential, derived from the "language of the sense." But at least in one respect his "religion of nature" will be Pauline: his "God," like Paul's, is a hidden God, that is to say, hidden from the discursive eye of speculative reason.

NOTES

1. Louis Martz, *The Poetry of Meditation*, rev. ed. (New Haven, 1962), p. 329.

2. Albert S. Gérard, "Dark Passages: Exploring *Tintern Abbey*," *SIR*, III (1963), 22. David Ferry, in his *The Limits of Mortality* (Middletown, Conn., 1959), observes of the poem that it is "hard not to mistake for a confusion of feeling what may be a complexity of feeling, a contemplated and contained ambivalence" (pp. 110–111). Others who have proved helpful to me in preparing this reading are: Harold Bloom, *The Visionary Company: A Reading of English Romantic Poetry* (New York, 1963), pp. 149-159; Roger N. Murray, *Wordsworth's Style* (Lincoln, Neb., 1967), pp. 25–32; Christopher Salvesen, *The Landscape of Memory* (Lincoln, Neb., 1965), pp. 38–39; Carl Woodring, *Wordsworth* (Boston, 1965), pp. 59–64; and especially Geoffrey Hartman *Wordsworth's Poetry, 1787–1814* (New Haven, 1964), pp. 26–30, 175–176, *passim*.

3. I use the word "immanent" in two slightly different senses throughout this essay: (1) to indicate "being within," as in "mind is immanent in nature"; (2) to indicate "have a 'within' or interior," as in "nature made immanent," i.e., made to have mind inside it. This second usage (far less frequent than the first) is prompted by Wordsworth's habit of obscuring the distinction between container and contained, indeed of reversing the roles without warning. Which of the two senses is intended should be clear from the context. In my analysis of what I later call Wordsworth's "language of immanence" I have been especially helped by C. C. Clarke's *Romantic Paradox* (New York, 1963), pp. 44–53.

4. "The Drunken Boat: The Revolutionary Element in Romanticism," *Romanticism Reconsidered*, ed. Northrop Frye (New York, 1963), p. 16.

5. Rudolf Otto, *The Idea of the Holy*, trans. John W. Harvey, 2d ed. (London, 1950). I introduce Otto's term for the sake of corroborating my connection between Wordsworth's act of visionary introspection (Frye's journey downward and inward) and the experience of awe and dread. According to Otto's

phenomenology of religious consciousness, one of the essential
characteristics of an encounter with a "numinous object" is the
experience of "*mysterium tremendum*." See Otto's analysis of
"The Element of Awfulness," pp. 13–19. Wordsworth himself
corroborates this connection in *The Recluse* lines cited in the text.
The experience of "*mysterium tremendum*" is closely related to the
feeling of a special kind of fear that many commentators have
observed is a characteristic of the experience of the sublime, a
relationship Otto himself notes (p. 42).

6. G. W. Knight, *The Starlit Dome* (London, 1959), p. 11. Knight's
   study of "The Wordsworthian Profundity," pp. 1–82, is a
   brilliantly suggestive treatment of the poet's fascination with
   depths, dwelling places, and, in his later poems, architectural
   structures of all kinds; and in this respect corroborates the point
   of view taken in this chapter, i.e., regarding "Tintern Abbey" as
   a poem about interiors.

7. *Poetical Works*, V, 4, II. 35–41.

8. For a discussion of Locke's metaphors of the mind, see *The
   Mirror and the Lamp*, pp. 57–58. Also see Ernest Lee Tuveson,
   The Imagination as a Means of Grace (Berkeley, 1960), p. 19.

9. *The Prelude*, XIV, 194–196. All references to *The Prelude* are,
   unless otherwise indicated, to the 1850 version (book and line),
   ed. Ernest de Selincourt, 2d ed. rev. Helen Darbishire (Oxford,
   1959).

10. *The Prelude* (1805), XIII, 56, 62–65, 69. In the 1850 version
    (Book XIV) the explicit connection between imagination and
    the blue chasm disappears; the Snowdon scene is

    > All meek and silent, save that through a rift—
    > Not distant from the shore whereon we stood,
    > A fixed, abysmal, gloomy, breathing-place—
    > Mounted the roar of waters, torrents, streams
    > Innumerable, roaring with one voice!
    > Heard over earth and sea, and, in that hour,
    > For so it seemed, felt by the starry heavens.
    > [Ll. 56–62]

11. *Ibid.* (1850), VI, 592–596. See Hartman's analysis of this
    episode, *Wordsworth's Poetry*, pp. 45–48.

12. *The Prelude*, VI, 600–601.

13. *Poetical Works*, V, 4, l. 57. This paragraph is especially indebted to Hartman's central thesis that Wordsworth, throughout his major poetry, exhibits a fear of what Hartman calls "apocalypse," i.e., the "death of nature."

14. *The Prelude*, V, 45–49.

15. Hartman, *Wordsworth's Poetry*, p. 173.

16. Gaston Bachelard, in his *The Poetics of Space*, trans. Maria Jolas (New York, 1964), analyzes what he calls the "phenomenological reverberation" of the image of the hermit's hut as it is used in poetry. He offers a suggestive corroboration of the visionary implications I have been arguing attach to Wordsworth's image of the Hermit's cave: "The hermit's hut is an engraving that would suffer from any exaggeration of picturesqueness. Its truth must derive from the intensity of its essence, which is the essence of the verb 'to inhabit': The hut immediately becomes centralized solitude, for in the land of legend, there exists no adjoining hut. . . . The image leads us on towards extreme solitude. The hermit is *alone* before God. His hut, therefore, is just the opposite of the monastery. And there radiates about this centralized solitude a universe of meditation and prayer, a universe outside the universe" (p. 32). In Wordsworth, of course, the "universe outside" is a "universe inside," and "centralized solitude" is the condition of the mind's encountering its own powers.

17. Wordsworth's sense of, and language of, space is not confined to his own practice but seems to be one of the commonplaces of the Romantic Period. Thomas De Quincey, for example, offers what could almost be taken as a paradigm for the kind of reading I am pursuing: "Great is the mystery of Space, greater is the mystery of Time. Either mystery grows upon man as man himself grows; and either seems to be a function of the godlike which is in man. In reality, the depths and the heights which are in man, the depths by which he searches, the heights by which he aspires, are but projected and made objective externally in the three dimensions of space which are outside of him. He trembles at the abyss into which his bodily eyes look down, or look up; not knowing that abyss to be, not always consciously suspecting it to be, but by an instinct written in his

prophetic heart feeling it to be, boding it to be, fearing it to be, and sometimes hoping it to be, the mirror to a mightier abyss that will one day be expanded in himself" (*Collected Writings*, ed. David Masson, 14 vols. [London, 1896, 1897], VIII, 15).

18. *Poetical Works*, II, 517. I use the term "antistrophe" (Gk. *antistrephein*, to turn against or opposite) in somewhat of a Romantic way: to refer to a movement of the mind rather than to a stanza in the traditional "sublime ode." The usage is suggested by Wordsworth's note.

19. The introspective act described by Wordsworth in the second verse paragraph is, in certain respects, similar to one of the ways in which a man might pursue, in Addisonian terms, the "pleasures of the imagination." Addison writes in *The Spectator*, no. 411, how by "this Faculty a Man in a Dungeon is capable of entertaining himself with Scenes and Landskips more beautiful than any that can be found in the whole Compass of Nature." Addison of course would probably disallow Wordsworth's claim that in his city dungeon he saw into the "life of things": the imagination, to be sure, can give great pleasure, but to say that it is capable of such metaphysical insight is to allow the pursuit of imagination's pleasures to turn into a dangerous form of enthusiasm. Is Wordsworth here vaguely troubled by the possible charge of enthusiasm? In any case, Wordsworth's "antistrophe" is related to what Robert Langbaum, in "Romanticism as a Modern Tradition," *A Grammar of Literary Criticism*, ed. Lawrence Sargent Hall (New York, 1965), has said is a recurring problem of many Romantic moments of "illumination": "As an experience, the illumination is undeniably valid. But once the perception of value is abstracted from the immediate experience and formulated for application elsewhere, it becomes mere theory and therefore problematical (p. 255). For a recent study of the Romantic problem of experience vs. formulation, as this problem is worked out in a single poem, see Bernard J. Paris, "Coleridge's 'The Eolian Harp'," *PMASAL*, LI (1966), 571–582.

20. An anchor is also the traditional symbol of hope. Saint Paul establishes the equation in Hebrews 6: 19: "hope we have as an anchor of the soul, both sure and steadfast, and which entereth into that within the veil" (King James Version). In English

poetry examples of this traditional emblem can be found in George Herbert's "Hope" and in Spenser's portrait of Speranza in Book I, Canto X, xiv, *The Faerie Queene*. In "Tintern Abbey," just as Wordsworth meditates his way toward a pledge of continuing faith in nature, so also he is seeking grounds for a continuing sense of hope: he dares "to hope" in line 65. In terms of traditional symbolism to "anchor" one's "purest thoughts in nature and the language of the sense" is to posit a purely sensationalistic ground for hope—an extraordinary reversal of the Christian grounding of hope in the world beyond. Note also how Saint Paul's metaphor of hope as that "which entereth into that within the veil" suggests a movement into a transcendent interior (his vehicle, of course, is the veil of the Jewish temple). Likewise, in Herbert's poem personified Hope presents the poet with an "optick" or telescope, a means of penetrating otherwise hidden spaces. These associations become even more provocative if we regard Wordsworth's counting of the "gifts" he has received from nature as a secularized version of a traditional meditation recommended for those tempted by despair. Jeremy Taylor, for example, gives as his ninth "remedy" against despair the directive: "Gather together into your spirit and its treasure-house the memory, not only all the promises of God, but also the remembrances of experience and the former senses of the Divine favours, that from thence you may argue from times past to the present, and enlarge to the future and to greater blessings. For although the conjectures and expectations of hope are not like the conclusions of faith, yet they are a helmet against the scorching of despair in temporal things, and an anchor of the soul, sure and steadfast, against the fluctuations of the spirit in matters of the soul" (*The Rule and Exercises of Holy Living*, ed. Thomas S. Kepler [New York, 1956], p. 160). I am not suggesting "source" or "influence," but certainly Wordsworth's oblique echoing of these traditions suggests that an illuminating reading of the poem might be developed by regarding it as a meditation principally concerned with the problem of hope—a suggestion enforced when we recall that the longest poem published by Wordsworth during his lifetime, *The Excursion*, has as its central theme the correction of despondency or despair. Two final observations:

(1) the prevailing color of the landscape of Tintern Abbey is
green, another traditional emblem of hope; (2) in Book VI of
The Prelude, at the moment of Wordsworth's unmediated contact
with imagination rising from the mind's abyss, the poet claims
to see, among other things, that

>   our being's heart and home
> Is with infinitude, and only there;
> With hope it is, hope that can never die.
>   [Ll. 604–606]

The vision provided by his encounter with imagination, in
other words, reveals the grounds of hope. In "Tintern Abbey"
Wordsworth decides that "nature and the language of the
sense" will be his anchor immediately *after* his encounter with
the transcendent "something." It goes without saying that the
parallel is striking: in "Tintern Abbey" Wordsworth searches
through the dwelling-places of nature to a "sense sublime" of the
activity of his own consciousness, i.e., the act of imagination.

21. *The Prelude*, XII, 272–273, 277–280.
22. In sect. IV of this chapter I deliberately abandon the use
of the term "imagination." Up to this point I have been
employing the term freely because I have been attempting
to trace indications of certain features of what I have called
Wordsworth's "geography of introspection"; and from that point
of view it seemed necessary to say—led on by the example of
Wordsworth's own metaphors—that imagination is encountered
by the act of introspection in the depths of subjectivity. In the
concluding analysis of sect. IV, however, I try to shift my terms
away from metaphor toward greater precision. The reader is
asked to assume that I intend a rough equation between "the
act of reflexive self-awareness" and "the act of imagination."
The grounds of this equation [...] are exceedingly intricate
and cannot be faced now without muddling somewhat the
analysis of the poem. To avoid this muddle, I momentarily
suspend my use of the term "imagination," and ask my reader's
patience. Hartman occasionally uses the term "imagination" as
almost a synonym for "self-consciousness." He does not, in my
judgement, sufficiently distinguish between what I call in sect.
IV "thinking" about the self, i.e., constituting the subject as an
object for thought, and what I call "reflexive self-awareness" or

"apperception," i.e., becoming conscious of the activity of the subject's consciousness *without* the subject's constituting this activity as an object of consciousness. This distinction is related to one of the central questions of modem phenomenology: whether the subject can become aware of the subject *qua* subject without losing itself as an object of thought: See Pierre Thevenaz's discussion of this "Charybdis and Scylla" of introspection in *What is Phenomenology?*, esp. pp. 113–115.

23. *The Prelude* (1805), XIII, 108–111.

24. Cf. the implication of Donne's "Who sees God's face, that is self life, must die" ("Good Friday, 1613," I. 17).

25. *Poetical Works*, IV, 283, II. 130–131.

26. Kenneth Burke, *A Grammar of Motives and A Rhetoric of Motives* (New York, 1962), p. 24. From this Burkean point of view we might also suggest that the previously noticed complaint by Wordsworth about the inadequacy of the frail lodges of nature is, among other things, a complaint about the inadequacy of nature as a language whereby to express the reality of his mind. In Book V of *The Prelude* Wordsworth sees the language of poetry as a "mansion" (like the dwelling-places of nature?) which embodies "Visionary power" and "the host of shadowy things" (II. 595–600). We noted in the introductory chapter how words, according to Wordsworth, ideally should be an "incarnation" of thought. If nature is also to provide a "language," then of course it too ideally should be an "incarnation" of thought, i.e., of the visionary underworld.

THE POETRY OF ROBERT LOWELL

"Robert Lowell, Emerson, and the American Sublime"
by Henry Hart, in *ESQ: A Journal of the American Renaissance* (1993)

INTRODUCTION

In "Robert Lowell, Emerson, and the American Sublime," Henry Hart examines how Lowell was both influenced and repelled by Boston's "familiar hometown ghost," Ralph Waldo Emerson, and the tradition of sublime poetry. Though influenced by his close associations with modernist and neoclassicist writers who were openly hostile to Emerson's naïveté and the "ravenous free-enterprise capitalism" it allegedly allowed, Hart argues that Lowell's "ambivalence toward Emerson jibed with his ambivalence toward himself, America, and the sublime." Detailing Lowell's frequent critiques of America's quest for dominance over the natural and political world—and the Ahab-like attitude to the sublime that undergirds it—Hart concludes that Lowell and Emerson "hold central positions in American literature partly because of their enchantments with a particularly American sublime."

Hart, Henry. "Robert Lowell, Emerson, and the American Sublime." *ESQ: A Journal of the American Renaissance* 39.4 (1993): 279–307.

In his bid to embody the contradictions of the sublime and to become a quintessentially American poet in the process, Robert Lowell had to grapple with that familiar hometown ghost, Ralph Waldo Emerson, whose essays gave to traditional European conceptions of the sublime a local inflection. Toward this father of American sublimity Lowell expressed the sort of Oedipal combativeness that characterized his relations with his own father and with most father figures. His guns loaded with neoclassic ammunition provided by T.S. Eliot and New Critics such as Allen Tate, John Crowe Ransom, Robert Penn Warren, and Yvor Winters, Lowell fired the hackneyed salvo: Emerson was so caught up in transcendental illusions that he was blind to their nefarious consequences in the real world. If Emerson's celebration of sentiment, solitude, self-reliance, and a personal Over-soul amounted to yet another romantic regression to the egotistical sublime, for Lowell and his cohorts it also amounted to another endorsement or at least an encouragement of ravenous free-enterprise capitalism and all sorts of other modern ills. To a classicist steeped in Catholicism and Calvinism, Emerson's cheerful Unitarianism was dangerous in its naiveté. Endowed with original sin and constantly lapsing into moral turpitude, human nature needed to be bridled with conventional rituals and rules. As T.E. Hulme, one spokesman for the antiromantic modernist charge, put it: "Man is an extraordinarily fixed and limited animal whose nature is absolutely constant. It is only by tradition and organisation that anything decent can be got out of him."[1] In his New Critical phase, Lowell agreed.

Those southern and British mentors who guided the young Lowell's thought revered tradition while Emerson often blithely dismissed it. To them Emerson was too democratic, too radical, too Protestant, too American. While Emerson blasted aristocratic hierarchies and authoritarian ways, Lowell's neoclassicist teachers sought to resurrect them. "The root of all romanticism," Hulme maintained in his attack, is "that man, the individual, is an infinite reservoir of possibilities; and if you can so rearrange society by the destruction of oppressive order then these possibilities will have a chance and you will get Progress."[2] To the jaundiced eye of the neoclassicist, Emerson represented revolutionary "Progress," a repudiation of past orders with all their hallowed rules and a mindless plunge into the future. To this way of thinking, authoritarian regimes were necessary to prevent society from descending into anarchy.

For at least two of Lowell's early mentors, Tate and Winters, Emerson was an avatar of Lucifer determined to lead America to the madhouse, albeit unwittingly. Lowell's view of Emerson and his brand of sublimity was shaped by these New Critical biases. Like his attitude toward Lucifer, however, his attitude toward Emerson remained ambivalent. Although he often expressed a southern or British contempt for Emerson's revolutionary idealism, he just as often confessed to an enchantment with all revolutions. In many ways he was as anti-authoritarian as Emerson. If Lucifer symbolized the iconoclastic energy required to wrestle sublimity from traditional powers, Lowell and Emerson, like Blake's Milton, were of the devil's company without always admitting it. As Boston Brahmins, however, they never lost their ambiguous respect for tradition, no matter how much they pilloried it. If contemporary scholars such as Harold Bloom dismiss Lowell because of his supposed antipathy toward Emersonian romanticism and sublimity, they do so out of a misconception. Lowell and Emerson, in fact, share many of the same paradoxical attitudes toward the sublime. Lowell was drawn by the sort of transcendental idealism Emerson espoused, but because of his manic-depressive illness and his tragic sense of history, he obsessively exposed the destructive consequences of that idealism. A new look at Lowell's Emersonian roots is needed to clarify the complex relationship between these two elusive New England writers.

1

When Lowell confessed in a 1963 interview with A. Alvarez that his love affair with sublime power was embarrassingly American and Ahabian, he could have been declaring empathy for Emerson as well. "If I have an image of [an American]," he said, "it would be one taken from Melville's *Moby-Dick*: the fanatical idealist who brings the world down in ruins through some sort of simplicity of mind. I believe that's in our character and in my own personal character."[3] From Lowell's point of view, Emerson was also implicated in the tragic results of fanatical idealism. If Emerson kept his ideals in check, thereby avoiding tragedy, he nevertheless encouraged their fanatical eruptions in others. In another interview with Alvarez, Lowell elaborated on his earlier comments, this time dwelling on the American addiction to sublimity: "We leap for the sublime. You might almost say American literature and culture begins with *Paradise Lost*. I always think there are two great symbolic figures that stand behind American ambition and culture. One is Milton's Lucifer and the other is Captain Ahab: these two sublime ambitions that are doomed and ready, for their idealism, to face any amount of violence."[4] What Lowell means, and what he emphasizes repeatedly in his early poetry, is that the early Puritan settlers and their pioneering heirs ruined the American paradise the way Lucifer ruined Eden, and also that America's wars with tyrannical father figures, from King George to Mussolini, Hirohito, and Hitler, are comparable to Lucifer's apocalyptic battles with God or Ahab's with Moby Dick. A similar lofty idealism propelled America in its early quest for cultural independence and its later bid for superpower status; a feeling of sublime triumph crowned its achievements. Although Lowell's analogy is farfetched when logically extended (America is not always Luciferian or Ahabian, its enemies are not always gods or angels, it has not been defeated in most of its wars), he is repeating in coded form what Eliot and his southern apostles said about Emersonian idealism (and by extension about American sublimity): that the enchantment with ideals of self-reliant and self-aggrandizing power is dangerous and perverse.

When Emerson remarks with mischievous gusto at the end of "History" that "[t]he idiot, the Indian, the child, and unschooled farmer's boy, stand nearer to the light by which nature is to be read, than the dissector or the antiquary,"[5] he sets himself up for the kind of rebuke Lowell and his mentors hurled at his idealism. Why should the idiot and child be closer to the Over-soul and to nature's lessons of self-reliance and self-worth? Lowell would undoubtedly laugh at such unguarded romanticism. When Emerson asserts that any and every person should "know that he is greater than all the geography and all the government of the world" (*CW*, 2:6), Lowell would be correct in echoing Winters's caveat: this sort of self-aggrandizement is akin to madness. A victim of manic-depression, Lowell himself regularly suffered from such delusions of grandeur. To say Emerson is wholly oblivious to the psychological repercussions or corollaries of his grandiose ideas, however, would be false. One of his brothers, Edward, suffered from manic-depressive delusions similar to Lowell's and in fact was treated in the same hospital, McLeans outside of Boston. In other contexts Emerson refers to these delusions as products of "enthusiasm," a term traditionally used to describe Protestant fanaticism as well as mistaken feelings of sublimity. Lowell does the same. As Lowell's biographer Ian Hamilton points out, "'enthusiasm' is a word he regularly uses to describe his manic episodes (the term probably derives from his reading in theology)."[6] Emerson also harks back to the longstanding theological controversy over enthusiasm; he could hardly help being aware of it since his father named one of his brothers after Harvard's most vociferous anti-enthusiast, Charles Chauncey, the scourge of Jonathan Edwards and all those who followed his brand of enthusiastic evangelism. Lowell dwells on the same debate in his auto-biographical prose and poetry; he considers enthusiasm in its religious, pathological, and aesthetic contexts as a dubious boon whose sublime uplift always pitches one toward a disastrous fall.

Like theorists of the sublime from Longinus to Burke and Kant, both Emerson and Lowell describe enthusiasm (from *entheos*, the god within) as a highly charged but also a dangerous form of sublimity. Both realize its potential for personal and mass hysteria, and value a religion based on reason rather than on unbridled emotion. Still, they find a place for enthusiasm in their worldviews. Their private debates with enthusiasm and sublimity take much of their impetus from Kant, whose aesthetics echo in Emerson's essays and Lowell's poems. While Emerson absorbed Kant's doctrines from Coleridge and friends like James Elliot Cabot, Lowell studied them in an aesthetics course taught by Ransom at Kenyon College. An excerpt from Kant's *Critique of Judgement* that discusses the sublime was included in E.F. Carritt's *Philosophies of Beauty*, the textbook used in Ransom's class. Determined to differentiate the sublime's rational, moral, and divine attributes from their false appearances in religious frenzy, Kant proclaims: "The idea of the good to which affection is superadded is enthusiasm. This state of mind appears to be sublime: so much so that there is a common saying that nothing great can be achieved without it." Although it casts reason to the winds, Kant believes that "from an aesthetic point of view, enthusiasm is sublime, because it is an effort of one's powers called forth by ideas which give to the mind an impetus of far stronger and more enduring efficacy than the stimulus afforded by sensible representations."[7] In a passage from his essay "Circles" that Lowell must have read, Emerson repeats Kant's claim that "[n]othing great was ever achieved without enthusiasm," and then adds with his characteristic high spirits: "The way of life is wonderful: it is by abandonment. The great moments of history are the facilities of performance through the strength of ideas, as the works of genius and religion" (*CW*, 2:190). The strength of ideas could propel even the healthiest mind, however, toward delusions of transcendence, and for this reason Kant stipulates: "If enthusiasm is comparable to *delirium*, fanaticism may be compared to *mania*. Of these the latter is least of all compatible with the sublime, for it is *profoundly* ridiculous. In enthusiasm, as an affection, the imagination is unbridled"; in fanaticism, however, the mind is afflicted by "an undermining disease."[8]

In Emerson, Lowell found a Kantian enthusiast disguised as a rationalist, a homespun philosopher who because of his cool, well-mannered temperament could endorse sublimity and even flirt with fanaticism while still remaining sober and sane. But to Lowell's overheated psyche, Emerson's sublimity and enthusiasm, as Winters insisted, was always potentially pathological. Reading in "The Over-Soul" that "[t]he simplest person, who in his integrity worships God, becomes God," yet that "forever and ever the influx of this better and universal self is new and unsearchable" (*CW*, 2:173), Lowell could have discovered a description of the "fanatical idealist" whose "simplicity of mind" mirrored his own. Indeed, his diagnosis of the American psyche to which he felt so attached may have derived from Emerson's discussion of enthusiasm and sublimity in "The Over-Soul." Out of the heart of nature, Emerson avers, God's spirit descends to inspire and unify all in democratic harmony:

> We distinguish the announcements of the soul, its manifestations of its own nature, by the term *Revelation*. These are always attended by the emotion of the sublime. For this communication is an influx of the Divine mind into our mind.... By the necessity of our constitution, a certain enthusiasm attends the individual's consciousness of that divine presence. The character and duration of this enthusiasm varies with the state of the individual, from an extasy and trance and prophetic inspiration ... to the faintest glow of virtuous emotion.... A certain tendency to insanity has always attended the opening of the religious sense in men, as if they had been "blasted with excess of light." (*CW*, 2:166–67)

Lowell knew all too well what it was like to be "blasted with excess of light" and to have the light of Lucifer and his various historical avatars illuminating his mind rather than the faint glow of a benign divinity. He was regularly hospitalized when pathological enthusiasms convinced him that he was possessed by gods and devils.

Strikingly, then, this passage from Emerson contains in germinal form an ambivalence like Lowell's toward the American sublime and its often unsavory cousin, enthusiasm. Although Emerson seems to have condoned or abetted enthusiastic responses to the sublime, his attitude was divided. His debate with himself paralleled his debate with his father's sister, the eccentric, well-informed, and very devout Aunt Mary who influenced many of his ideas. "She was an enthusiast," one of Emerson's biographers points out.[9] What Emerson's Uncle William said about her would be said about Emerson by detractors years later: "She was full of vagaries and misshapen by religious enthusiasm, capable of producing 'sublime epistles,' but too 'elevated' above mortal concerns to appreciate the just and simple truths of existence."[10] In his mocking "Homage to Emerson, on Night Flight to New York," Robert Penn Warren similarly criticizes Emerson for his blindness to the worldly facts he has transcended. According to Warren, Emerson believed 'There is / No sin. Not even error." Therefore, only "At 38,000 feet Emerson / Is dead right."[11] At lower altitudes, Warren implies, his sublime perceptions are dead wrong.

Lowell questions and counters this charge in an essay on Emerson: "Can we honestly accuse him of ignoring Original Sin? He was unable to do so."[12] Emerson actually expressed some of the same reservations about sublime attitudes and altitudes as Warren. Although Emerson liked to quote his aunt's aphorisms ("Sublimity of motive must precede sublimity of style" and "Sublimity of character must proceed from sublimity of motive"),[13] in the end he could not agree wholeheartedly with her high-flying sentiments. Commenting on a journal entry for 1827, Evelyn Barish observes, "[A]lready ... he had understood that enthusiasm was not enough, that inner conviction of the light was not all-sufficient, that 'the great multitude of the best men who have lived and left a name [were] what the enthusiast calls 'cold and prudent Christians.'"[14] With this in mind Emerson's Aunt Mary accused him of "Kantism." Emerson *was* Kantian, but only in those moods when he believed the sublime originated in reason's divine and moral powers. In other moods, he at least pretended to be a guileless romantic, enthusiastically advocating religious and political assaults on the establishment and its sacred traditions. To say he was blind to American evils while addicted to the sublime altitudes of jet airplanes is a simplification. His comment inspired by the Fugitive Slave Law, a law passed a decade before the Civil War to appease disgruntled Southerners, exemplifies his ambiguous position: "My own quarrel with America, of course, was, that the geography is sublime, but the men are not."[15] Like Lowell, Emerson combined idealistic and realistic views.

2

It took Lowell a long time to recognize the complexity of Emerson's attitudes toward America, religious enthusiasm, and sublime idealism, and to realize that Emerson's ambivalence reflected his own. In his early poetry Lowell generally expressed the same sort of sardonic contempt for his precursor found in Warren's poem—understandably, since Warren was one of his early teachers. His other like-minded teacher, Tate, was even more contemptuous of Emerson. Tate's harsh appraisal no doubt appealed to a young Lowell determined to put his Boston heritage behind him. In a discussion of the breakup of Puritanism in New England, which he implicitly compares to heaven, Tate lambasts Emerson as a befuddled, starry-eyed devil: "At this juncture Emerson came upon the scene: the Lucifer of Concord, he had better be called hereafter, for he was the light-bearer who could see nothing but light, and was fearfully blind. He looked around and saw the uniformity of life, and called it the routine of tradition, the tyranny of the theological idea." Rapidly switching epic analogies, Tate compares Emerson to a Greek destroying Troy (Northerners were usually Greeks in his imagination, the South being another Troy for them to burn). By rebutting Puritan theology and tradition, "Emerson unwittingly became the prophet of a piratical industrialism, a consequence of his own transcendental individualism that he could not foresee."[16] Lowell was similarly piratical, individualistic, and iconoclastic. In his reminiscence "Visiting the Tates," he describes how on his way to study with his mentor in 1937 he "crashed the civilization of the South" by smashing Tate's mailbox, casting himself in the role of a piratical Lucifer with "sublime ambition." "My head was full of Miltonic, vaguely piratical ambitions," he says.[17] He might as well have said his head was full of piratical Emersonian ambitions, and that like one of his Northern Civil War heroes he planned once again to invade and overthrow the aristocratic powers of the South.

Two years after his southern venture, Lowell went to Kenyon College, where he studied aesthetics under Ransom. Ransom's preference for Kant's sublime—a contemplative elation kindled by the mind's perception of its own divine reason subduing the natural world to manageable concepts, and distinguished from religious and political enthusiasm—must have spurred Lowell's skepticism of Emerson's more mystical version. Eliot's anti-Emersonian bias, reinforced by the similar stance taken by Lowell's Harvard teacher Irving Babbitt and his mentor Winters, drew the poet even further from his New England forebear. While at Kenyon he reviewed Winters's *Maule's Curse*, a book that excoriated Emerson with a ferocity almost equal to Tate's. Although Winters agreed with some of Emerson's moral pronouncements, he argued otherwise in a statement that Lowell quotes: "[H]is central doctrine is that of submission to emotion."[18] This romantic sentiment, according to the curmudgeonly rationalist and moralist Winters, invalidated all Emerson's moral claims; in fact it precluded the possibility of moral claims. Emerson was therefore a "limb of the Devil," another piratical Lucifer, a rabid enthusiast whose sublime pursuits were doomed to failure. In Winter's view, although Emerson was protected from madness by his ethical training, he incited madness in others with his transcendental proposals. The mad poet Jones Very, for example, is the tragic victim of Emerson's inflammatory idealism according to Winters's laudatory explication of Very's work. The critic declares: "It is worthy of repetition in this connection, that had Emerson accomplished the particular surrender which as a pantheist, he directly or indirectly recommended, he would have been mad, that is, an automaton guided by instinct." In an earlier chapter on Melville, Winters compares the epic ambitions documented in *Paradise Lost* and *Moby-Dick*, claiming that although the latter contains "a sublimity and terror probably never surpassed in literature," its main character is an automaton whose submission to passion leads to madness: "Ahab ... obeys the traditional law of tragedy, and destroys himself through allowing himself to be dominated by an heroic vice."[19] Winters would continue to harangue all writers he suspected of Emersonian romanticism for the rest of his career.

Early in his own career, Lowell echoed the harangue but later qualified it with empathy as he grew more aware that Emersonian romanticism influenced his own Luciferian and Ahabian quests for the sublime. Lowell incorporates what Winters says about Ahab,

Lucifer, and Emerson not only in his comments on the sublime to Alvarez but also in his short essay on Emerson, which was written at about the same time, in the mid-sixties, and included in "New England and Further." Ahab, Winters asserts, "is Promethean, in that he defies the gods; but he goes beyond Prometheus in his fury, for he seeks to destroy a god. He represents, essentially, the ultimate distillation of the Calvinistic temperament."[20] He is an inverted Lucifer; he wants to kill the god of evil represented by Moby Dick rather than the God of virtue. Lowell views Emerson similarly; he calls him "our fire-bringer Prometheus without the menace of Zeus" (CP, 187), implying that he lacks Zeus's oratorical thunderbolts (the "sublime crash of fireworks," as Lowell calls Zeus's powers in his adaptation of *Prometheus Bound* [PB, 54]) and also that he is not menaced or tortured by Zeus or any other angry, jealous god. He is not a tormented Calvinist fire-breather like Edwards. To the question, What sort of fire did he steal from the European gods to kindle a native American sublime? Lowell answers cryptically: "A new mythical or imaginary America harmoniously comes into being with Emerson. It arrived during Europe's high age of function, power, and every variety of intellectual and artistic genius ... the blindness that still lights our days. It was then that inquiring minds first clearly saw our heritage as something to exploit and evade" (CP, 186). This is obviously a reworking of Tate's contention that Emerson was so dazzled by mystical lights and mythical ideals that he was blind to tragic socioeconomic facts.

Lowell, however, is no parrot of Tate's and Winters's prejudices. In his review of *Maule's Curse*, he points out that Winters's rigorous moralizing is an offshoot of the Protestant ideology he seeks to uproot: "For he is himself a late beneficiary and victim of the Calvinism whose manifestations in literature [he] has so well analyzed."[21] To Tate's contention that Emerson believed man, "being ... the Over-Soul, is innately perfect,"[22] thus precluding tragedy and much southern litera-ture, Lowell responds that Emerson may have wanted to ignore evil but "was unable to do so" (CP, 186). While Lowell agrees with his mentors in viewing Emerson as an exemplary proponent of America's revolutionary idealism—one who could be blind to the adverse social and psychological effects of transcendental doctrines—he disagrees with their way of stereotyping Emerson as a blissfully insouciant bard. Like most of the powerful historical figures Lowell contemplates and dramatizes, Emerson becomes an alter ego onto which he projects his most pressing compulsions. To his sympathetic imagination, Emerson is both ally and enemy. Another of Lowell's multifaceted personae with iconoclastic ideals (like Lucifer and Ahab), Emerson exemplifies the vices and virtues of the American sublime.

3

For Emerson as well as for Lowell and other theorists of the sublime, the ancient aesthetic term has multifarious significance. Emerson scholars, however, tend to focus on one or two of his many references to the sublime, and usually cite as the quintessential instance of sublimity in his work the famous passage at the beginning of "Nature": "I become a transparent eyeball. I am nothing. I see all. The currents of the Universal Being circulate through me; I am part or particle of God" (*CW*, 1:10). The lines resonate with Wordsworth's similar description in "Tintern Abbey" of "a sense sublime":

> A motion and a spirit, that impels
> All thinking things, all objects of all thought,
> And rolls through all things.[23]

For Emerson the sublime influx depends on a contemplative *askesis*, a sensory deprivation common to most mystical exercises that prepares the way for communion with the divine. Claiming that "[t]he mind of Emerson is the mind of America," Bloom dwells on Emerson's experience while crossing the bare common as a sublime confrontation between the self-reliant ego and the fertile abyss:

> Emersonian transparency is ... a sublime crossing of the gulf of solipsism, but *not* into a communion with others.... A second-century Gnostic would have understood Emerson's "I am nothing; I see all" as the mode of negation through which the knower again could stand in the Abyss, the place of original fullness, *before* the Creation.... A transparent eyeball is the emblem of the Primal Abyss regarding itself.[24]

In his essay "Whitman and the American Sublime," Joseph Kronick more convincingly traces Emerson's use of the term "abyss" to Jacob Boehme. Kronick quotes from a November 1845 journal entry in which Emerson explains the term's importance: "There must be the Abyss, Nox, & Chaos out of which all come, & they must never be far off. Cut off the connexion between any of our works & this dread origin & the work is shallow & unsatisfying."[25] The abyss is an original emptiness preceding any creation or communion, the transparent eyeball a consequence of the mystic's contemplative *askesis*. For Emerson there is a correspondence between mental abyss and cosmic abyss, and the point of his meditation is to align the two so that he can witness creation as if for the first time, or so that he can actually partake in creation. The mysterious abyss before the creation confers a traditional "sense sublime," a commingling of fear and awe, as does the experience of divine influx that culminates in the mind's conviction that it is partly divine, an incarnation of the Over-soul, a host to "the Universal Being," a creator in its own right.

Although some scholars differentiate the abyss in Emerson's passage from Kant's notion of the sublime, the concept bears many similarities to Kant's transcendentalism as expounded in *The Critique of Judgement*. Kant's experience of the sublime, like Emerson's, involves a number of stages; it begins with an overpowering natural phenomenon that voids human powers of understanding and imagination, and culminates with reason, which is "part or particle of God," producing a transcendent concept to explain it. Sublimity resides not in nature per se but in the calm, reflective mind that contemplates nature, reduces it to concepts and words, and proves reason's superiority over nature. For Kant nature is the cause or mediator of sublimity, human reason its ultimate destiny. He explains:

> Everything that provokes this feeling in us, including the *might* of nature which challenges our strength, is then, though improperly, called sublime, and it is only under presupposition of this idea within us, and in relation to it, that we are capable of attaining to the idea of the sublimity of that Being which inspires deep respect in us, not by the mere display of its might in nature, but more by the faculty which is planted in us of estimating that might without fear, and of regarding our estate as exalted above it.[26]

Although Kant picked up much of his transcendental philosophy secondhand, Emerson had great respect for him. Both regarded nature's infinite spaces, mysterious origins, and overwhelming events as the text of a supreme being whose greatest creation was the mind that could interpret it with sublime serenity rather than superstitious terror. Both shrugged off Calvinist bogeys and aspired to a higher reason.

Emerson's determination to shed his culture's Puritan past, and indeed to shed history and tradition altogether, has obvious political ramifications. In his provocative study of American Renaissance writers, Donald Pease ferrets out the paradox inherent in Emerson's political program: "Cultural legitimation becomes a problem when citizens base their personal identity as well as their nation's identity on a refusal to acknowledge the authority of institutions inherited from the nation's past. Without a past to inform their present lives, individuals have no basis for present history."[27] However, when Emerson declaims that "[o]ur age is retrospective," that it "builds the sepulchres of the fathers," and when he asks, "[W]hy should we grope among the dry bones of the past, or put the living generation into masquerade out of its faded wardrobe?" (*CW*, 1:7), he too is returning, albeit carefully camouflaged, to the revolutionary moment of the Founding Fathers in a history he supposedly wants to abolish. According to Pease, "At a time in which politicians compromised on founding principles for the sake of expediency, Emerson . . . returned to the scene of the nation's founding to recover integrity for the principles of liberty and equality and make them available as motives for the actions of all Americans."[28] Emerson's "visionary compact" images an America where all citizens could gather together in a spiritual democracy. With a self-reliant revolutionary vision, they could realize their freedom from the hierarchical burdens of Europe. Cast the hoary scales of tradition from your eyes; experience the transcendental sublime in unmediated communion with nature and God, he seems to exhort. "The foregoing generations beheld God and nature face to face; we, through their eyes. Why should not we also enjoy an original relation to the universe?" Emerson asks (*CW*, 1:7). But he is obviously romanticizing the past, dressing it up with his own "faded wardrobe" of noble savages and mystical naturalists even while consigning all such mythical wardrobes to the dump.

Emerson's belief in a divine light that nature dispenses like grace to every human without the intermediary help of priest, ritual, symbol, or tradition, a light that convinces each soul of its transcendent origin prior to and superior to nature, has obvious precedents in Protestant ideology. For Bloom, Emerson's exhortation to get beyond tradition and nature derives from a compulsion to repress everything that Emerson calls "the NOT ME" (*CW*, 1:8). Such an all-encompassing repression recuperates the primordial abyss in the self. "The glory of repression," Bloom remarks, "is that memory and desire, driven down, have no place to go in language except up onto the heights of sublimity, the ego's exultation in its own operations."[29] Emerson's solitary ego exults because it has managed to repress its precursors and through its revolutionary iconoclasm hollow out an abyss in which it can entertain the sublime illusion of originality. The rebellious son has abandoned "the sepulchres of the fathers" and in Oedipal fashion usurped their engendering powers to become, in turn, his own father—the author of a countersublime founded on democratic as opposed to aristocratic principles.

In his essay "Sublime Politics," Pease reveals the social impact of this transcendental repression of nature and culture in American history and offers a critique of Emersonian self-reliance that is surprisingly close to Lowell's and his neoclassic cohorts. Like Tate and Winters, Pease argues that "Emerson does not condone or corroborate these ideological uses of the sublime" to justify ecological despoliation and cultural provincialism.[30] Nevertheless, he underwrites them willy-nilly. According to Pease, Emerson's belief that the soul should fly beyond nature and enjoy a sublime sense of transcendence got mistranslated into a doctrine of human superiority over nature, a repudiation of nature, and was finally turned to ecological plunder for industrial gain. Western expansionism and the simultaneous destruction of indigenous cultures and their natural habitats were the unintended political consequences of Emerson's high-flown ideals:

> Through the subtle turns of the American sublime, the liberal in taking axe and hammer to the virgin land could, with childlike innocence, proclaim that only through destruction of Nature's bounty could he feel by doing what nature commanded as if he were truly in touch with nature's will.
>
> Put simply, the sublime enabled the nineteenth-century American to create a second scene, a veritable world elsewhere where he could rewrite and reread national policies of commercialism and expansionism in quite ideal terms.[31]

As if to clear a space in the wilderness for the Over-soul or bulldoze the American continent into Emerson's primordial abyss, self-reliant entrepreneurs cut and plowed and mined and built until nature withered. Sublimating American resources into capitalist gold, they left a wasteland in their wake, a grotesque parody of Emerson's mystical "bare ground" (*CW*, 1:10).

4

Although it is obviously unfair to blame Emerson for America's ecological depredations, this is the gist of Lowell's critique of Emersonian and American sublimity. For Lowell, American history testifies to the tragic results of revolutionary onslaughts on tradition and nature, exposing the ruin instigated by the individualist's will to dominate. His diagnosis targets the sublime ideals that support that domination. Many of his early poems grapple with Emerson specifically and the tragic consequences of his idealism generally. The early poem "Concord" collected in *Land of Unlikeness*, for example, recalls Emerson's title "Concord Hymn" and launches a diatribe against Emersonian sublimities, even though Lowell implies that he is himself deeply implicated in the ideology he attacks. With Wallace Stevens he would no doubt agree that

> the [American] sublime comes down
> To the spirit itself,
>
> The spirit and space,
> The empty spirit
> In vacant space.[32]

Leaping for the sublime in the sociopolitical domain, these poets aver, produces hollow men who can only gaze in rapt bewilderment at wastelands and vacant spaces of their own making.

Lowell begins "Concord" with a favorite trope, his Bostonian home ground as hell, and implies that Emersonian Lucifers working side by side with avaricious capitalists are responsible for transforming what was once natural paradise into industrial pandemonium. Mammon, the gold-grubber in Milton's Pandemonium, could be another Henry

Ford stockpiling gold from his inventions (the later version in *Lord Weary's Castle* begins, "Ten thousand Fords are idle here in search / of a tradition" [*LWC*, 33]), while proclaiming (with Emerson and Ford) that "History is bunk." Among the ruins of Revolutionary battles and transcendentalist experiments, Lowell's search for history becomes a search for the crucified Christ. The search parallels Eliot's anthropological quest for "the Hanged Man" in *The Waste Land*,[33] and promises to redeem paradise lost by offering an explanatory emblem ("the Hanging Jesus") for the way sublime idealism gets misunderstood and crucified in the real world.

The poem begins with stasis, with idling machines (perhaps gold-colored cars) and with idle capitalist gold usuriously accumulating wealth (*contra naturam* as Lowell-the-Catholic would stipulate):

> Gold idles here in its inventor's search
> For history, for over city ricks,
> The Minute Man, the Irish Catholics,
> The ruined Bridge and Walden's fished-out perch,
> The belfry of the Unitarian Church
> Rings out the Hanging Jesus.
>
> (*LU*, 17)

With his Calvinist and Catholic perspectives twinned à la Eliot, Lowell punningly attacks Unitarian bell ringers for "wringing out" the flesh-and-blood Jesus, for making him otherworldly, overly spiritual, all Over-soul and no body. The last five lines reaffirm his earlier animadversions:

> This church is Concord, where the Emersons
> Washed out the blood-dots on my Master's robe
> And then forgot the fathers' flintlock gun,
> And the renown of that embattled scream
> Whose echo girdled the imperfect globe.
>
> (*LU*, 16)

Scrutinizing the Second Church where both Emerson and his father preached, Lowell repeats his charge that these high-minded Unitarians washed out the bloodiness and bodiliness of Christianity and history (in 1832, Emerson actually preached a sermon in the Second

Church against the ritual of Communion, and he later resigned because church officials would not accede to his request of abolishing the sacrament that commemorated Christ's blood and body).

According to Lowell, Emerson's Christ is a powerless, disembodied spirit, who in his transcendental preoccupations creates the vacuum or abyss for powerful capitalists to fill with their destructive gadgets and usurious practices. He may be inside the Second Church when he asks rhetorically:

> Crucifix
> How can your whited spindling arms transfix
> Mammon's unbridled industry, the lurch
> For forms to harness Heraclitus' stream.
>
> (LU, 16)

Lowell's complaint combines Catholic and Marxist injunctions against rampant industrialism and implies that a strong authoritarian master (a Pope or Stalin or Mussolini?—he identified with all three at one time or another) is needed rather than a wrung-out Jesus if modern evils are to be defeated. Lowell also implies, self-reflexively, that he is one of the devil's company. He does this more blatantly in later confessional poems like "Beyond the Alps," where, speaking of Mussolini, he admits, "He was one of us / only, pure prose" (*LS*, 3). In "Skunk Hour," alluding to Satan's acknowledgment of his psychological hell in *Paradise Lost*, he confesses, "I myself am hell" (*LS*, 90); he might as well say, "I myself am Satan." A powerful and at times anarchic formalist, Lowell is close kin to unbridled Mammon lurching for forms to channel his mind's Heraclitean stream. If he leaps for the sublime, he simultaneously struggles to find ritualistic patterns to harness and civilize those furious energies that the sublime unleashes.

This requires a repression of insurrectionary energy (what Lowell in his interview with Alvarez called "sublime ambition") that both Lowell and Emerson associate with the American Revolution. While Lowell shuns Emerson, he tacitly shares his ambiguous view of history. If Emerson attempts to repress history, he also bears witness to its uncanny way of returning. History's never-ending Oedipal rebellions against "the sepulchres of the fathers" do not vanish, as both writers might hope; they haunt their careers from beginning to end.

Lowell would also like to forget "the fathers' flintlock gun" because he was periodically tempted to turn it against all father figures. His poem "Rebellion" illustrates his paradoxical way of resurrecting revolutionary fathers in order to use their weapons against them. He seeks to limit the pain of guilty rebellion while glorying in the subliminal power it confers upon him. He acknowledges at the end:

> And I have sealed
> An everlasting pact
> With Dives to contract
> The world that spreads in pain;
> But the world spread
> When the clubbed flintlock broke my father's brain.
>
> (*LWC*, 35)

Dives, the rich man in the parable of Lazarus, is another Mammon. Lowell has signed a contract with this devil to stop devilish energies from spreading through the world. But revolutionary energies have been released in his country, family, and self, and like Emerson, he is as much their radical instigator as he is their conservative suppressor.

Although their iconoclastic rebellions take different forms and intensities, both Emerson and Lowell can play American Lucifers bent on wresting power from traditional authorities just as easily as they can play the authorities bent on bridling those Lucifers. They are radical and conservative by turn. With one hand they erect monuments to the past; with the other they defile them. In "Concord Hymn, Sung at the Completion of the Battle Monument, July 4,1837," for instance, Emerson advocates traditional ways of paying homage to the "sepulchres of the fathers" that at other times he renounces. The poem is dedicated to monuments that preserve the past. Emerson surveys time's ruins ("the ruined bridge has swept / Down the dark stream"), but now prays for historical longevity: "Bid Time and Nature gently spare / The shaft we raise to them and thee." In "Nature" he scoffed at this sort of genuflection to the dead. Now he praises the ground on which the dead once walked and fought: "Here once the embattled farmers stood / And fired the shot heard round the world."[34] Both Lowell and Emerson, in the end, vacillate dialectically in their celebrations and renunciations of tradition. Both stand up for revolutionary iconoclasts while thematically and stylistically paying homage to traditional forms.

As Lowell's career progressed his attacks on Emerson subsided, no doubt because he realized that his ambivalent attitudes toward the past were just as paradoxical as his precursor's. Tradition for Emerson and for Lowell, as for most writers, was a hairshirt that goaded them into spectacular attempts to wriggle free. They realized the necessity of history but spent much of their time damning and sublimating it. In their similarly antagonistic stances toward the hallowed past, they ritually repeated its revolutionary or modernist moments of transformation. Rob Wilson's *American Sublime: The Genealogy of a Poetic Genre* provides an incisive analysis of Emerson's contradictory quest for revolutionary origins of power as well as Lowell's despairing critique of that quest's results. Scrutinizing Emerson's peculiarly American obsessions with self-reliance and its various abysses, Wilson argues:

> [T] he will to American sublimity is read as the ego-quest to inaugurate origins of sublime power, which is to say to evacuate some self-authenticating ground out of which the wildness/newness of power can emerge. Such a struggle for strong selfhood must take place, as the Emersonian scenario mandates, whether this I-threatening "abyss" is imagined to comprise some ahistorical vacancy or gnostic nothingness; some natural immensity in which the entrepreneurial ego can lose and find itself as in an ocean or prairie; or, nowadays, the vast intertextuality of language which codes any lyric of self-intuition with traces of otherness.[35]

If an influx of sublime power depends on a mystical or pathological breakdown of the ego, a purgatorial clearing away of natural impediments to industrial progress, or a radical sloughing off of burdensome intertextual influences and historical forefathers, then Emerson differs from Lowell in mood rather than maneuver. Both are particularly American in their endorsements of iconoclastic power, although Emerson tends to assault the gods of tradition with a blithe indifference to the aftereffects, so confident is he in the moral underpinnings of those self-reliant Americans who will fill the void with their new creations. Coming later, Lowell is more wary. He knows that America's addiction to grandeur and novelty, like his own self-aggrandizing tendencies, is ultimately destructive. Emerson, however, can also be wary and downright contemptuous, as his many protests against politicians responsible for atrocities against Native Americans, the Fugitive Slave Law, secession, and the Civil War attest.

According to Wilson's argument that the "will to the *American* sublime becomes a way of doing battle in the nineteenth century with the hegemonic British tradition [and] . . . an attempt to wrest a cultural and social priority corresponding to the transformations of the American Revolution,"[36] Emerson would seem more blissfully revolutionary than Lowell and Lowell more agonizingly divided between American free-spiritedness and English traditionalism. Another poem collected in *Land of Unlikeness*, "Concord Cemetery after the Tornado," again suggests that the crux of Lowell's argument with Emersonian sublimity centers on the issue of the abyss that revolutions engender. Such power vacuums, as any student of revolutions knows, attract all sorts of terrors. Once again Lowell's depiction of Emerson as an abyss, a grave or void that lacks the strength or intelligence to combat the destructive storms that it incites, is also a caustic self-portrait, an attack on his own pacifist idealism that caused him to become a conscientious objector during the Second World War. According to Lowell's meteorological allegory:

> Buzzard's Bay had spun
> Back the tidal wave
> In its almighty tide;
> But Concord, by the grave
> Of Waldo Emerson,
> Rumbles from side to side
> Taunting the typhoon's groan
> And then turns down her thumb;
> There like Drake's drum,
> Wind's wings beat on stone.
>
> (*LV*, 13)

For Lowell, natural sublimities—tidal waves, mighty tides, typhoons—are comparable to political sublimities, and he interprets them as Darwin might, as struggles for survival in which the powerful triumph.

Another poem, "The Quaker Graveyard in Nantucket," develops these notions on a larger scale. The earlier poem echoes in its lines:

> The winds' wings beat upon the stones,
> Cousin, and scream for you and the claws rush

At the sea's throat and wring it in the slush
Of this old Quaker graveyard.

(*LWC*, 15)

In this elegy occasioned by the death of his cousin Warren Winslow in a freak torpedo accident on a naval ship, Lowell allegorically aligns numerous forms of military, religious, and ecological violence. Here Ahab, Lowell's prototypical American and tragic idealist whose sublime leaps pitch him toward doom, is a kind of Emersonian transcendentalist gone berserk. His revolutionary combativeness *contra naturam* has paradoxically created the vacuum that the violently breaking sea (which represents, in part, the violence of World War 2) rushes in to fill. In this grand argument with himself and his country, Lowell intimates that Quaker idealism and Emersonian transcendentalism beget their opposites: very real, bloody conflicts. "The heel-headed dogfish barks its nose / On Ahab's void," he writes, and the drowned Quaker sailors "are powerless / To sand-bag this Atlantic bulwark, faced / By the earth-shaker" (*LWC*, 14). When Ahab loses his battle with the White Whale, the sea (the Homeric "earth-shaker") unleashes its Poseidon-like fury. The balance of power collapses. Any intimation of a sublime triumph disappears and a Darwinian or Hobbesian state of brutal conflict resumes. In this complex dialectic, the quest for the American sublime by the supposedly pacifist Quakers begets tragic violence that, when abolished, allows even greater violence to prevail.

In "Concord Cemetery after the Tornado," Emerson's grave becomes a synecdoche for the vacuum at the heart of Concord as well as America, a vacuum that makes way for omnipresent violence. According to Lowell, Emerson's sublime produces revolutionary energies only to be destroyed by them, creating another abyss that then "taunts" other combatants (as Henry Newbolt's propagandistic poem "Drake's Drum" taunted Englishmen to fight in World War 1). Out of the void created by the First World War, the Second World War grew. To Lowell's jaded eye, America's Emersonian idealism is responsible not so much for an ahistorical transcendentalism as a history of escalating violence and ever more powerful ways of dispensing that violence. In this Emersonian wasteland, Lowell echoes Eliot:

What does this rubble say,
O Woman out in the rain?

"Concord, you loved the heart
Without a body."

(LU, 13)

Lowell's version of Madame Sosostris diagnoses current debacles as arising from Emersonian sentiment, a religion of the heart that repudiated or repressed the body and therefore could not cope with the all-too-bodily world when it had to. Implicit in his attack on Emerson's otherworldly idealism, however, is Lowell's attack on himself. His conscientious objection to the Second World War, for which he served a jail sentence, is the sort of pacifist idealism or appeasement that abets violence by creating a vacuum where it can rage unchecked. His leaps for the sublime, as much as Emerson's, are implicated in the oppressive realities they seek to transcend.

Lowell airs this traditional criticism of Emerson only to retract it partially at the end of his poem. Here Emerson appears as the Lucifer of Concord again, the Promethean light bringer, more lionhearted than angel-hearted, more fearsome revolutionary scaring off traditional spirits than otherworldly Christian unable to repel the real world's evil. In fact he resembles the young, apocalyptic Lowell himself, conducting a last judgment of dead townspeople with Jehovah-like ferocity:

In the dry winds of noon,
Ralph Waldo Emerson,
Judging the peaceful dead
Of Concord, takes the sun
From every gravestone. Soon
Angels will fear to tread
On that dead Lion's bones,
In their huge, unhewn hide.

(*LU*, 14)

Presumably the dead lion is Emerson, the angels Emerson's admirers who fear to tread on his grave out of sanctimonious respect. Or they could be those squeamish traditionalists that Emerson, and Lowell, too, in his anarchistic moods, rebuked or offended.

Lowell's ambivalence toward Emerson jibed with his ambivalence toward himself, America, and the sublime. During his last decade he again condemned the American sublime for threatening to turn not just consciousness and continent but the entire world into a void. The obsessive grasping for more and more powerful forms of domination, in politics as well as other fields, provoked Lowell to tell Alvarez, "[W]hat everyone finds wrong with American culture is the monotony of the sublime."[37] His trope of the earth as a hollow volcanic cone in "Waking Early Sunday Morning" transforms a stock image of sublimity into something even more frightening. As the environmental and cultural devastation wreaked on Vietnam by America reminds Lowell of the more harrowing devastation of nuclear Armageddon, he envisions a future planet reduced to "a ghost / orbiting forever lost / in our monotonous sublime" (NO, 24). An earlier draft of the final stanza harks back to that tragic pursuer of sublimity, Ahab, one whose Emersonian self-reliance is all the more dangerous for its ubiquity in America:

> say we fought and trusted in
> ourselves to free the earth from sin,
> were glad like Ahab to go down
> in pride of righteousness, and drown,
> that we were faithful to this boast,
> our appetite for which we lost
> the world, though free of other crime,
> in the monotonous sublime.[38]

In this version Lowell portrays himself as a volcano whose manic, fire-breathing energies, while dormant for the moment, unite him with figures like Ahab and Emerson, both in his lofty jeremiads and in his hollow victories.

One of Lowell's last grapplings with Emerson comes in *History*, his long sequence in which "the autobiographical sublime," as he calls it in the draft of one sonnet,[39] resembles his precursor's aggrandizement of the self. He may have recalled the adjuration in Emerson's own "History": "[A]ll public facts are to be individualized, all private facts are to be generalized. Then at once History becomes fluid and true, and Biography deep and sublime" (*CW*, 2:12). According to Emerson's logic, history is essentially autobiographical and, when universalized, sublime. Lowell conceives of history in a similar way, as a reflection of his autobiographical quest for sublime power. Emerson begins his essay with the neoplatonic apothegm 'There is one mind common to all individual men," and adds, "Of the works of this mind history is the record" (*CW*, 2:3). If "the whole of history is in one man, it is all to be explained from individual experience" (*CW*, 2:3), he says, as if forecasting Lowell's method of projecting his personal experience onto a large cast of historical personae. Mulling over the great lives of history, Lowell consistently punctures their affectations, wittily juxtaposing the sublime and the ridiculous. In his own way he is as dismissive of grandiosity as Emerson. Just as Emerson democratizes history, contending for instance that "[a]ll that Shakespeare says of the king, yonder slip of a boy that reads in the corner, feels to be true of himself," and that everyman "must sit solidly at home, and not suffer himself to be bullied by kings or empires, but know that he is greater than all the geography and all the government of the world" (*CW*, 2:5, 6), Lowell satirizes history, deconstructing the hierarchical values that support it.

Lowell's brief sketch of Emerson in *History* deploys Emersonian strategies of deflation to prick his charismatic bubble. The ordinary Puritan lies beneath the great rebel's mask. To show that Emerson's flights toward sublimity depend on a wearisome rejection of common pleasures, Lowell organizes his life study around images of coldness, winter, ice, and poison, asserting:

> Emerson is New England's Montaigne or Goethe,
> cold ginger, poison to Don Giovanni—
> see him on winter lecture-tours with Thoreau,
> red flannels, one bowl of broken ice for shaving;
> few lives contained such humdrum renunciations.
>
> (*H*, 85)

The image of Emerson shaving in his red flannel pajamas is a bathetic riposte to the first line in which he appears among European luminaries. It is the sort of double exposure, ridiculousness superimposed on sublimity, that Lowell practices most noticeably in *Life Studies* but in all his other volumes as well.

For Lowell, Emerson could be a cold, prudent, prudish Christian as well as a Promethean or Luciferian revolutionary who stole fire from European gods to kindle a native sublime. Like Prometheus bound to his crag, Emerson could also suffer second thoughts about his zealotry. If Lowell attacked Emerson as his mentors did, he also identified with his vacillations. That Lowell's vacillations intensified into manic-depressive outbursts proves a difference in their personalities rather than in their positions. As Bostonians at odds with their Puritan pasts, both understood the virtues and vices of revolutionary upheavals. Political and psychological breakdowns or breakaways attracted but also repelled them. If nature led them to contemplate a primordial abyss and Over-soul from which the creation mysteriously burgeoned, they found the transcendence of nature on behalf of the Over-soul both a boon and a danger. Both summoned reason to suppress their revolutionary enthusiasms; both recognized the destructiveness of personal and social mania; both could be adamantly traditional. In their onslaughts on tradition, however, they could also be radical enthusiasts. They embraced romantic ideals of free-spirited individualism as well as classical ideals of social restraint.

While the extremism of Lowell's bifurcated commitments to traditional rituals and symbols and the insurrectionary energies that demolish them distanced him from Emerson, both writers hold central positions in American literature partly because of their enchantments with a particularly American sublime. Their contradictory responses to the sublime parallel a contradiction in America's revolutionary past, arising, as Pease has remarked, "[w]hen citizens base their personal identity as well as their nation's identity on a refusal to acknowledge the authority of institutions inherited from the nation's past" even while realizing that "[w]ithout a past to inform their present lives, individuals have no basis for present identity."[40] Such a crisis, as Eliot pointed out long ago in "Tradition and the Individual Talent," confronts all artists who want to be original. Absorbing tradition in order to overhaul it, they appear to reject their precursors while actually incorporating and extending them. In their iconoclastic forays against tradition and their transcendental flights from nature, Emerson and Lowell engaged in traditional and natural attempts to resuscitate those "sublime ambitions" with which, as Lowell told Alvarez, "American literature and culture begins."[41]

NOTES

1. T. E. Hulme, *Speculations: Essays on Humanism and the Philosophy of Art* (London: Routledge and Kegan Paul, 1924), 116.
2. Hulme, *Speculations*, 116.

3. Qtd. in A. Alvarez, "Robert Lowell in Conversation," *Observer*, 21 July 1963, 19.

4. Qtd. in A. Alvarez, "A Talk with Robert Lowell," *Encounter* 24 (February 1965): 42.

5. *The Collected Works of Ralph Waldo Emerson*, ed. Alfred R. Ferguson and Joseph Slater et al., 4 vols. to date (Cambridge: Harvard Univ. Press, Belknap Press, 1971-), 2:23; here after cited in the text as *CW*, with volume and page numbers.

6. Ian Hamilton, *Robert Lowell: A Biography* (London: Faber, 1982), 226.

7. Immanuel Kant, *The Critique of Judgement*, trans. James Creed Meredith (Oxford: Clarendon Press, 1952), 124.

8. Kant, *Critique of Judgement*, 128.

9. Evelyn Barish, *Emerson: The Roots of Prophecy* (Princeton: Princeton Univ. Press, 1989), 36.

10. Barish, *Emerson*, 42; quoting an 1809 letter from William Emerson to Mary Moody Emerson, in the Ralph Waldo Emerson Memorial Association Archives, Houghton Library, Harvard University.

11. Robert Penn Warren, *Selected Poems, 1923–1975* (London: Seeker and Warburg, 1976), 153.

12. Robert Lowell, *Collected Prose*, ed. Robert Giroux (New York: Farrar, Straus and Giroux, 1987), 186; hereafter cited in the text as *CP*. The other abbreviations of Robert Lowell's books are as follows:

    H   *History* (New York: Farrar, Straus and Giroux, 1973).

    LS   *Life Studies* (New York: Farrar, Straus, and Cudahy, 1959).

    LU   *Land of Unlikeness* (Cummington: Cummington Press, 1944).

    LWC *Lord Weary's Castle* (New York: Harcourt, Brace and World, 1951).

    NO   *Near the Ocean* (New York: Farrar, Straus and Giroux, 1967).

    PB   *Prometheus Bound* (New York: Farrar, Straus and Giroux, 1967).

13. Qtd. in Barish, *Emerson*, 109, 165. In the latter case, Barish quotes from *The Journals and Miscellaneous Notebooks of Ralph Waldo Emerson*, ed. William H. Gilman and Ralph H. Orth et al., 16 vols. (Cambridge: Harvard Univ. Press, Belknap Press, 1960–82), 3:26; hereafter cited as *JMN*.

14. Barish, *Emerson*, 209; quoting from *Journals of Ralph Waldo Emerson, 1820–1876*, ed. Edward Waldo Emerson and Waldo Emerson Forbes (Cambridge, MA: Houghton Mifflin, 1909), 2:220.

15. *JMN*, 11:284.

16. Allen Tate, *Essays of Four Decades* (Chicago: Swallow, 1968), 284.

17. Robert Lowell, "Visiting the Tates," *Sewanee Review* 67 (1959): 557.

18. Yvor Winters, *Maule's Curse* (Norfolk: New Directions, 1938); qtd. in Robert Lowell, review of *Maule's Curse*, *Hika* (April 1939): 19.

19. Winters, *Maule's Curse*, 131, 133, 74–75.

20. Winters, *Maule's Curse*, 68.

21. Lowell, review of *Maule's Curse*, 21.

22. Tate, *Essays of Four Decades*, 284–85.

23. William Wordsworth, "Lines Composed a Few Miles above Tintern Abbey, on Revisiting the Banks of the Wye During a Tour. July 13, 1798," in vol. 2 of *The Poetical Works of William Wordsworth*, ed. Ernest de Selincourt and Helen Darbishire, 2nd ed. (Oxford: Oxford Univ. Press, Clarendon Press, 1952), 262.

24. Harold Bloom, *Agon: Towards a Theory of Revisionism* (New York: Oxford Univ. Press, 1982), 145, 158.

25. See Joseph Kronick, "On the Borders of History: Whitman and the American Sublime," in *The American Sublime*, ed. Mary Arensberg (Albany: State Univ. of New York Press, 1986), 54; quoting *JMN*, 9:325.

26. Kant, *Critique of Judgement*, 114.

27. Donald Pease, *Visionary Compacts* (Madison: Univ. of Wisconsin Press, 1987), 7.

28. Pease, *Visionary Compacts*, 47.

29. Harold Bloom, *A Map of Misreading* (New York: Oxford Univ. Press, 1975), 100.

30. Donald Pease, "Sublime Politics," in *The American Sublime*, ed. Arensberg, 47.

31. Pease, "Sublime Politics," 46.

32. Wallace Stevens, "The American Sublime," in *The Collected Poems* (New York: Random House, 1982), 130.

33. T.S. Eliot, *The Waste Land and Other Poems* (New York: Harcourt, Brace and World, 1934), 31.

34. *The Complete Works of Ralph Waldo Emerson*, ed. Edward Waldo Emerson (Boston: Houghton Mifflin, 1911), 9:158–59.

35. Rob Wilson, *The American Sublime: The Genealogy of a Genre* (Madison: Univ. of Wisconsin Press, 1991), 8.

36. Wilson, *American Sublime*, 30.

37. Qtd. in Alvarez, "A Talk with Robert Lowell," 43.

38. Qtd. in Alan Williamson, "The Reshaping of 'Waking Early Sunday Morning,'" *Agenda* 18 (Autumn 1980): 62.

39. Robert Lowell, a draft of "For John Berryman," in folder no. 2701 of the Lowell archive at the Houghton Library, Harvard University.

40. Pease, *Visionary Compacts*, 7.

41. Qtd. in Alvarez, "A Talk with Robert Lowell," 42.

MOBY-DICK
(HERMAN MELVILLE)

"The Inscrutable Sublime and the Whiteness of *Moby-Dick*"
by John Becker, independent scholar

Moby-Dick—by virtue of its breadth, excess, and explicitly defined themes and conflicts—has all the trappings of an epic *theodicy* that stands in a long literary tradition. Works of theodicy, spanning from the Bible to Dante to Milton, are concerned with explaining the ways of God to man and of defending God's goodness despite the existence of evil. In relation to this genre, *Moby-Dick* can be characterized as a carefully orchestrated failure, a failure where the sublime—in all of its obscurity and inscrutability—is set in the place of divine revelation. As Richard S. Moore asserts in his exhaustive study of sublimity in *Moby-Dick*, the White Whale is the "quintessential sublime" object, a symbol of all that remains inaccessible to the human mind (136). The stories of Ishmael and Ahab point to the failure of the very theodicy the book enshrines: By the end of the novel, the cosmic order does not seem available to human reasoning, whether that reasoning be obsessively single-minded (Ahab's reduction of all the world's injustices—all that needs explaining—into one symbol made "practically assailable") or expansive (Ishmael's multifaceted, negative descriptions and "scientific" anatomies). Of course, from someone who is telling and interpreting the story, Ishmael's sentiments are not easily separable from the defiant proclamations of Ahab, as John Wenke has noted (Wenke 710). The narrative of *Moby-Dick* is driven by Ahab and Ishmael's "hunt" for the sublime. But, as Nancy Fredericks argues, two distinct plots can be discerned in the novel: Ahab's heretical quest for vengeance and Ishmael's quest to represent the whale through artistic representation (Fredericks 31). Ahab's quest is predominantly framed in the grand, sweeping, theological language, equal parts egotistical defiance (in the vein of Milton's Satan and Goethe's Faust) and Job-like protestations of woe. Conversely, the language of Ishmael's attempts to represent and understand the sublime—which employs multiple forms of discourse and plays with each of them—is never at ease with itself.

Herman Melville's *Moby-Dick* can be read as a prolonged meditation on the nature, representation, and pursuit of the sublime, a contentious and multifarious aesthetic term that has changed much since it was first described as a superlative attribute of good rhetoric by Longinus in his treatise, *On the Sublime* (first century c.e.). In his recent study of the sublime in the history of aesthetics, Philip Shaw offers a succinct definition that manages to encompass many disparate theories: "Sublimity, then, refers to the moment when the ability to apprehend, to know, and express a thought or sensation is defeated. Yet, through this very defeat, the mind gets a feeling for that which lies beyond thought and language" (3). Thus the importance of the sublime lies in its ability to disclose what cannot be explained rationally. A feeling that can be conjured by encountering natural grandeur or artistic works, the sublime inspired countless poets, painters, and musicians. For many Romantic poets, most notably Coleridge, the power of sublime poetry and art to produce transcendent moments of awareness points to the central role of the poetic imagination in human life, the "living power and prime agent of all human perception" (Coleridge 202).

One of the most famous and influential definitions of the sublime was proffered by Edmund Burke in his 1757 study, *A Philosophical Enquiry into the Origins of our Ideas of the Sublime and the Beautiful.* Melville was well acquainted with the ideas of Burke and owned a copy of the treatise (Sealts 70). Burke's analysis of the sublime hinges upon the importance of fear. For Burke, the simultaneous apprehension of overwhelming power and terror lies at the heart of the sublime. Thus, according to Burke, the sublime is a psychological reaction: When we encounter scenes that fill us with fearful awe—that somehow imply mortal harm and inhuman scale—we are temporarily transported into a transcendent state of awareness. Unlike the merely beautiful, which, according to Burke, only "induce[s] in us a sense of affection and tenderness" (Burke 51), the sublime draws its emotive power from painfully disconcerting images: the immense vistas of the Pacific, the unfathomable power of Niagara Falls, and the godlike stature of the inscrutable whale all evoke sublime feelings due to their large scale (which suggests infinity), their power, and their obscurity. To fully appreciate the place of the sublime in Melville's novel, however, the development of aesthetics after Burke must be taken into account. More importantly, the intricacies of Melville's narrative point to a more nuanced view of the sublime and the metaphysical struggle depicted in Ahab and Ishmael's descriptions of Moby Dick. Rather than simply conclude that Melville was critiquing the aesthetic dogma of his age, we must, as Ishmael prescribes, "subtilize" our thinking.

The German idealist philosopher Immanuel Kant, heavily indebted to Burke's analysis, discusses the sublime at length in his *Critique of Judgment* (1790). Many have noted the central position of the sublime in Kantian philosophy, as it constitutes a link between what Kant called the phenomenal (the empirical world of sense impressions) and the noumenal (the world of undifferentiated things-in-themselves). This picture of the cosmos is aptly described by Ahab's rousing speech in "The Quarter Deck" chapter when he tries to enlist Starbuck to aid him in his quest for vengeance:

> Hark ye yet again,—the little lower layer. All visible objects, man, are but as pasteboard masks. But in each event—in the living act, the undoubted deed—there, some unknown but still reasoning thing puts forth the mouldings of its features from behind the unreasoning mask. If man will strike, strike through the mask! How can the prisoner reach outside except by thrusting through the wall? To me, the white whale is that wall, shoved near to me. Sometimes I think there's naught beyond. But 'tis enough. (140)

Here Ahab speaks of Moby Dick in a manner that suggests Kant's conception of the sublime: For Ahab, the White Whale is compared to a "wall," a limit that bars his inquiring mind from knowledge of the mysteries that determine lived experience. It is during Ahab's explanation of his grievances to Starbuck that we become acquainted with the "little lower layer" of metaphysical speculations that drive the narratives of Ishmael and Ahab. Here Ahab famously equates the visible world with an unreasoning "pasteboard mask," a "wall" that encloses us, holding us prisoner in an existence devoid of meaning. Though Ahab speculates that there might be "naught beyond," the maiming he has suffered and the injustices he has witnessed convince him that there is an "inscrutable malice" working behind the seemingly impersonal and mechanistic world of appearances. Similarly, when Ishmael starts to relate the qualities and profound magnitude of the White Whale in expository prose—a task that occupies many chapters of the book—he begins to do so by emphasizing the obscurity of the monster, how "out-blown rumors" and "half-formed foetal suggestions" invest the creature with "new terrors unborrowed from anything that visibly appears" (153). Later, in a chapter that deals exclusively with the whiteness of Moby Dick, this quality of excess, of oversignification, is singled out as the most affecting attribute of the whale.

"The Whiteness of the Whale" is an indispensable chapter for coming to terms with Melville's particular use and evocation of the sublime. Whereas Ahab strives to master the White Whale, to avenge himself against the unseen reality that hides behind and determines lived experience, Ishmael—as both mature narrator and young participant—desires understanding. Though their goals are not dissimilar, and at times appear to be one and the same, Ishmael's discussion of whiteness seems to set them distinctly apart. Ishmael begins his analysis of whiteness, the most "appalling" and thus the most sublime of the monster's attributes, by making the task insurmountable: How can the "mystical" and "ineffable" be put into a "comprehensible form" (159)? Most of Ishmael's discussion of whiteness is a study in meaningful failure. As Moore has pointed out, Ishmael's discussion moves through different analytical strategies which are each, in turn, discarded (Moore 159–165). As the argument proceeds from association to association, Ishmael links whiteness with a varied catalogue of objects ranging from sacred white dogs to albino men. Through these associations Ishmael notes how whiteness "enhances beauty," signifies gladness, connotes the sacred, and marks the divine. Conversely, whiteness is linked to ferocious storms and the "pallor of the dead" (Melville 160–162). He appeals to religious, mythical, and historical authorities, all the while noting their insufficiency in helping him communicate what, when "stripped of all direct associations" (162), appalls him about the color white. Moby Dick's whiteness is terrifying to Ishmael for reasons he cannot fully disclose, but in his discussion of the question, what stands out is his assertion that whiteness is simultaneously the absence of any color whatsoever, as well as the aggregate of all colors. This "dumb blankness" prompts Ishmael to ask us:

> Is it that by its indefiniteness it shadows forth the heartless voids and immensities of the universe, and thus stabs us from behind with the thought of annihilation, when beholding the white depths of the milky way? (165)

He goes further, stating that whiteness, both "the very veil of the Christian's Deity" as well as the "colorless all-color of atheism," deceptively "paints" the world to cover its essential absence (165). In this chapter, the defining characteristic of Melville's symbol for the sublime, the most appalling attribute of its appearance, is distilled by Ishmael to the "elusive something" lurking in its "innermost idea" (160). But, as with his previous attempts to define this "elusive something" throughout the chapter, what appalls is framed in terms of what it is not. This morbid line of thought culminates in Ishmael's postulation, borrowed from the "natural philosophers," that color is only assigned by the mind of those who observe, with "colored and coloring glasses upon their eyes" (Melville 165). This analogy is taken up later: Just as Ishmael's "wretched infidels," forsaking the protective coloring of their glasses, are blinded while travelling through an unbearably white landscape, so is Ahab also blinded in his confrontation with Moby Dick after he has destroyed his quadrant, which also has a colored glass with which to gaze at the sun (378).

The dangers of taking off the "colored glasses" are raised by Ishmael in a previous chapter, "The Mast-Head," where he describes the meditative repose of a Transcendentalist observer gazing upon the infinite sea:

> [... Lulled] into such an opium-like listlessness of vacant, unconscious reverie is this absent-minded youth by the blending cadence of waves with thoughts, that at last he loses his identity; takes the mysterious ocean at his feet for the visible image of that deep, blue, bottomless soul, pervading mankind and nature; and every strange, half-seen, gliding, beautiful

> thing that eludes him; every dimly-discovered, uprising fin of
> some undiscernable form, seems to him the embodiment of
> those elusive thoughts that only people the soul by continually
> flitting through it. (136)

Not only does Ishmael describe the meditative state, the absorption in "sublime uneventfulness" caused by the infinite vistas of the
all-encompassing ocean, but he also warns of the dangers to which
this gives rise. Ishmael frames this description of sublime exaltation in terms of identity and transcendental awareness; taking "the
mysterious ocean at his feet for the visible image of that deep,
blue bottomless soul, pervading mankind and nature," the observer
temporarily loses his awareness of the boundaries between consciousness and nature (136). This "dream," during which the spirit seems
"diffused through time and space," effaces the perceiver's awareness
of his own mortality, of what Ishmael calls the "Descartesian vortices"
humans are suspended over (136). As Glenn notes, Ishmael's account
of sublime contemplation in this passage is negative: The dreaming
sailor, forgetful of his mortality, unwittingly falls "through the transparent air into the summer sea, no more to rise for ever" (Glenn 181).
Tracing the symbolic implications of the final scene of the novel,
Glenn concludes that Melville pronounces his "final judgment" on
the value of the "sublime quest" in the sinking of the Pequod (182).
But Melville seems to be engaged in a much more critical and self-
aware enterprise. As Nancy Fredricks convincingly argues, there are
two quests that structure the narrative of *Moby-Dick*: Ishmael's epic
effort to represent the sublime White Whale and Ahab's monomaniacal quest to destroy and see beyond it. Though Ishmael certainly
takes issue with the abstract meanderings of the philosopher/aesthete
in "The Mast-Head," his juxtaposition of sublimity and death seem to
suggest a different line of inquiry. Here the sublime, which is always
attended upon by mortality, is characterized as a temporal event, an
epiphany that, as Ishmael describes in "The Fountain," flits through
our minds as light plays upon mist to create rainbows. Ishmael does
seem to endorse questing for a certain kind of sublime experience,
one that does not lead to worldly detachment or denying mortality.
The first hint the Pequod's crew has of the White Whale's presence is
the nocturnal "silvery jet" that Ishmael describes in the "Spirit-Spout"
chapter. Later, in the chapter titled "The Fountain," Ishmael describes

these jets as both a cause of sublime thoughts as well as an analogy for the mind as it experiences such thoughts:

> And how nobly it raises our conceit of the mighty, misty monster, to behold him solemnly sailing through a calm tropical sea; his vast, mild head overhung by a canopy of vapor, engendered by his incommunicable contemplations, and that vapor—as you will sometimes see it—glorified by a rainbow, as if Heaven itself had put its seal upon his thoughts. For, d'ye see, rainbows do not visit the clear air; they only irradiate vapor. And so, through all the thick mists of the dim doubts in my mind, divine intuitions now and then shoot, enkindling my fog with a heavenly ray. And for this I thank God; for all have doubts; many deny; but doubts or denials, few along with them, have intuitions. Doubts of all things earthly, and intuitions of some things heavenly; this combination makes neither believer nor infidel, but makes a man who regards them both with equal eye. (293)

Here Ishmael speaks of a balanced disposition to the sublime, one that can perhaps hold whiteness as "the very veil of the Christian's Deity" as well as the "colorless all-color of atheism" (165). Ishmael does not evoke the sublime in the voice of a unitary consciousness overheard in the act of apprehending the divine in nature as Shelley does in "Mont Blanc" or Wordsworth in "Tintern Abbey." Phenomenal indistinctness, rather than impressions of the transcendent, is the source of Ishmael's representation of the sublime. The ephemeral, in this context, does not reside in some timeless continuum. Pip, after all, is transported during his encounter with the sublime to the heart of the sensuous and ever-changing sea, a world of infinite flux and opacity. Ishmael describes the working of fate as prone to circumstance and characterized by uncertainty, a "Loom of Time" where chance delivers "the last featuring blow":

> Aye, chance, free will, and necessity—no wise incompatible—all interweavingly working together. The straight warp of necessity, not to be swerved from its ultimate course—its every alternating vibration, indeed, only tending to that; free will still free to ply her shuttle between given threads; and

chance though restrained in its play within the right lines of
necessity, sideways in motions modified by free will, though
thus prescribed to by both, chance by turns rules either, and has
the last featuring blow at events. (179)

This process bears little resemblance to the static "netherworld" of
unchanging forms, or as it may be, "inscrutable malice" and ineluctable
"iron rails" alluded to by Ahab, and with him Burke, Kant, and their
ilk. For Ishmael, God is a weaver, not a tyrant.

> [... The] mighty idler seemed the cunning weaver; himself
> all woven over with the vines; every month assuming greener,
> fresher verdure; but himself a skeleton. Life folded Death;
> Death trellised Life; the grim god wived with youthful Life, and
> begat him curly-headed glories. (345)

Ishmael as narrator is an omniscient weaver of diverse narrative
strategies and types of knowledge. These metaphors betray a different
conception of the cosmos than the static and stately picture afforded
us by Burke, a space where meaning occurs from the midst of flux,
an obscure, indistinct and earthly sublime that does not engender
transcendence, but rather a profound sense of immanence, of being-
in-the-world. This sublime, which Ishmael constantly defines in self-
defeating, often humorous ways, suggests that the sublime itself is
self-defeating: What causes the sublime—our finite understanding
and our awareness of death—ultimately defeats it. At the end of the
novel, Ishmael is left afloat on an incongruous symbol that captures
this predicament—a coffin that has been converted into a life-buoy,
inscribed with indecipherable hieroglyphics copied from Queequeg's
body, "a complete theory of the heavens and earth, and a mystical
treatise on the art of attaining truth" (366). The knowledge Ahab
and Ishmael hoped to acquire by penetrating and representing the
sublime, respectively, is inscribed on an object that symbolizes the
birth and decay of the mutable world, an answer "destined in the end
to moulder away with the living parchment" of which it is a mere
semblance (367).

For Ishmael, temporality, incompleteness, and mutability are
what characterize the sublime and its representation in art. In such a
conception, the sublime is much like the talismanic doubloon Ahab

has nailed to the mast of the Pequod. And, just as the doubloon never does find an adequate interpreter on the decks of the Pequod, the sublimities of *Moby-Dick* are left unresolved after being interrogated from multiple perspectives. By making the classification system of Ishmael's cetology absurd—equating the different sizes of whales to the size and classification of books—Melville suggests that applying methodological thinking to interrogate the sublime is reductionist. The cetology chapters serve two purposes: they emphasize the grand and storied stature of the whale to increase its symbolic power; they are a satirical portrait of scientific and, occasionally, philosophic methods of speculation. The heterogeneity of expository, rhetorical, dramatic, and narrative forms in Melville's novel, punctuated by the frequently humorous, "tall" episodes, vulgarities, and absurd opinions he relates, characterize an author who values the fecund nature of play. The obscurity that Burke asserts is necessary for the evocation of the sublime is achieved by the heterogeneity of Melville's style and the undercutting nature of Ishmael's double-edged rhetoric and his playfully indirect way of approaching the artistic representation of Moby Dick. This logic of negation, of description through circumscription (another vortex), is most apparent in the chapter that deals with Moby Dick's most appalling quality: the Leviathan's whiteness. Those who take a simple moral message away with them after encountering the book fail to do justice to Melville's supreme ambivalence regarding the nature of the cosmos. Though it is hard to say of Melville what William Blake said of Milton, namely, that he was secretly part of the devil's party, it is even harder to conceive of Ahab as a character that deserves our unequivocal moral approbation. A tyrant in search of justice, a victim turned monomaniacal hunter, an educated man ready to punch through the "pasteboard mask" of reality, Ahab conjures sympathy from any reader who has questioned their place in a seemingly unjust universe. Whereas Kant and other philosophers of the sublime view it as a guarantor of truth, a link between the real and the ideal, Ishmael's theorizing and aborted descriptions suggest that, as literary critic Gerald Bruns opines, "experience is essentially satirical, a self-unmasking, as if reason could only discover the truth of things, and so of itself, when it sees that it is a fool" (Bruns 183). Such a view is also suggested by Pip, who not only assumes the role of fool on the Pequod after his encounter with the sublime but also grasps the multiplicity of contradictory interpretations that the doubloon occasions from his shipmates. Ishmael hints at such a view when he notes:

> There are certain queer times and occasions in this strange mixed affair we call life when a man takes this whole universe for a vast practical joke, though the wit thereof he but barely discerns, and more than suspects that the joke is at nobody's expense but his own. However, nothing dispirits, and nothing seems worthwhile disputing. He bolts down all events, all creeds, and beliefs, and persuasions, all hard things visible and invisible, never mind how knobby; as an ostrich of potent digestion gobbles down bullets and gun flints. . . . That odd sort of wayward mood I am speaking of, comes over a man only in some time of extreme tribulation; it comes in the very midst of his earnestness, so that what just before might have seemed to him a thing most momentous, now seems but a part of the general joke. There is nothing like the perils of whaling to breed this free and easy sort of genial, desperado philosophy; and with it I now regarded this whole voyage of the Pequod, and the great White Whale its object. (188)

WORKS CITED

Brodtkorb, Paul, Jr. *Ishmael's White World: A Phenomenological Reading of* Moby Dick. New Haven: Yale University Press, 1965.

Bruns, Gerald. *Hermeneutics: Ancient and Modern*. New Haven: Yale University Press, 1992.

Burke, Edmund. *A Philosophical Enquiry into the Origins of our Ideas of the Sublime and the Beautiful*. London: Routledge, 1958.

Coleridge, Samuel Taylor. *Biographia Literaria*. Vol. 1. Ed. J. Shawcross. Oxford: Clarendon Press, 1907.

Glenn, Barbara. "Melville and the Sublime in *Moby-Dick*." *American Literature* 48.2 (May 1976): 165–182.

Melville, Herman. *Moby-Dick*. Ed. Hershel Parker and Harrison Hayford. New York: Norton, 2002.

Moore, Richard S. *That Cunning Alphabet: Melville's Aesthetics of Nature*. Amsterdam: Rodopi, 1982.

Sealts, Merton M., Jr. *Melville's Reading*. Revised ed. Columbia, SC: University of South Carolina Press, 1988.

Shaw, Philip. *The Sublime*. London: Routledge, 2005.

Wenke, John. "Ahab and 'the Larger, Darker, Deeper Part.'" *Moby-Dick*. Ed. Hershel Parker and Harrison Hayford. New York: Norton, 2002. 702–712.

PARADISE LOST
(JOHN MILTON)

"Milton"
by Samuel Taylor Coleridge, in *The Literary Remains of Samuel Taylor Coleridge* (1836)

INTRODUCTION

A brilliant essayist and lecturer, Samuel Taylor Coleridge is perhaps the most influential theorizer of sublimity among the British Romantic poets. His lectures on literature were widely attended, drawing such luminaries as Lord Byron, Charles Lamb, and Thomas De Quincey. In his lecture on Milton, delivered in 1818, Coleridge praises *Paradise Lost*, asserting that "sublimity is [its] pre-eminent characteristic": "There is a greatness arising from images of effort and daring, and also from those of moral endurance; in Milton both are united." Coleridge singles out Milton's portrayal of Satan, with its "singularity of daring, [its] grandeur of sufferance, [and] ruined splendor," as a model of sublime writing. In the end, Coleridge claims that the revelation of Milton's mind "producing itself and evolving its own greatness" is *Paradise Lost*'s most sublime attribute.

Coleridge, Samuel Taylor. "Lecture X: Milton." *The Literary Remains of Samuel Taylor Coleridge* Vol. 1. Ed. Henry Nelson Coleridge. London: William Pickering, 1836. 166–178.

If we divide the period from the accession of Elizabeth to the Protectorate of Cromwell into two unequal portions, the first ending with the death of James I, the other comprehending the reign of Charles and the brief glories of the Republic, we are forcibly struck with a difference in the character of the illustrious actors, by whom each period is rendered severally memorable. Or rather, the difference in the characters of the great men in each period, leads us to make this division. Eminent as the intellectual powers were that were displayed in both; yet in the number of great men, in the various sorts of excellence, and not merely in the variety but almost diversity of talents united in the same individual, the age of Charles falls short of its predecessor; and the stars of the Parliament, keen as their radiance was, in fulness and richness of lustre, yield to the constellation at the court of Elizabeth;—which can only be paralleled by Greece in her brightest moment, when the titles of the poet, the philosopher, the historian, the statesman and the general not seldom formed a garland round the same head, as in the instances of our Sidneys and Raleighs. But then, on the other hand, there was a vehemence of will, an enthusiasm of principle, a depth and an earnestness of spirit, which the charms of individual fame and personal aggrandisement could not pacify,—an aspiration after reality, permanence, and general good,—in short, a moral grandeur in the latter period, with which the low intrigues, Machiavellic maxims, and selfish and servile ambition of the former, stand in painful contrast.

The causes of this it belongs not to the present occasion to detail at length; but a mere allusion to the quick succession of revolutions in religion, breeding a political indifference in the mass of men to religion itself, the enormous increase of the royal power in consequence of the humiliation of the nobility and the clergy—the transference of the papal authority to the crown,—the unfixed state of Elizabeth's own opinions, whose inclinations were as popish as her interests were protestant—the controversial extravagance and practical imbecility of her successor—will help to explain the former period; and the persecutions that had given a life and soul-interest to the disputes so imprudently fostered by James,—the ardour of a conscious increase of power in the commons, and the greater austerity of manners and maxims, the natural product and most formidable weapon of religious disputation, not merely in conjunction, but in closest combination, with newly awakened political and republican zeal, these perhaps account for the character of the latter aera.

In the close of the former period, and during the bloom of the latter, the poet Milton was educated and formed; and he survived the latter, and all the fond hopes and aspirations which had been its life; and so in evil days, standing as the representative of the combined excellence of both periods, he produced the *Paradise Lost* as by an after-throe of nature. "There are some persons (observes a divine, a contemporary of Milton's) of whom the grace of God takes early hold, and the good spirit inhabiting them, carries them on in an even constancy through innocence into virtue, their Christianity bearing equal date with their manhood, and reason and religion, like warp and woof, running together, make up one web of a wise and exemplary life. This (he adds) is a most happy case, wherever it happens; for, besides that there is no sweeter or more lovely thing on earth than the early buds of piety, which drew from our Saviour signal affection to the beloved disciple, it is better to have no wound than to experience the most sovereign balsam, which, if it work a cure, yet usually leaves a scar behind." Although it was and is my intention to defer the consideration of Milton's own character to the conclusion of this Lecture, yet I could not prevail on myself to approach the *Paradise Lost* without impressing on your minds the conditions under which such a work was in fact producible at all, the original genius having been assumed as the immediate agent and efficient cause; and these conditions I find in the character of the times and in his own character. The age in which the foundations of his mind were laid, was congenial to it as one golden era of profound erudition and individual genius;—that in which the superstructure was carried up, was no less favourable to it by a sternness of discipline and a show of self-control, highly flattering to the imaginative dignity of an heir of fame, and which won Milton over from the dear-loved delights of academic groves and cathedral aisles to the anti-prelatic party. It acted on him, too, no doubt, and modified his studies by a characteristic controversial spirit, (his presentation of God is tinted with it)—a spirit not less busy indeed in political than in theological and ecclesiastical dispute, but carrying on the former almost always, more or less, in the guise of the latter. And so far as Pope's censure[1] of our poet,—that he makes God the Father a school divine—is just, we must attribute it to the character of his age, from which the men of genius, who escaped, escaped by a worse disease, the licentious indifference of a Frenchified court.

Such was the *nidus* or soil, which constituted, in the strict sense of the word, the circumstances of Milton's mind. In his mind itself there were purity and piety absolute; an imagination to which neither the past nor the present were interesting, except as far as they called forth and enlivened the great ideal, in which and for which he lived; a keen love of truth, which, after many weary pursuits, found a harbour in a sublime listening to the still voice in his own spirit, and as keen a love of his country, which, after a disappointment still more depressive, expanded and soared into a love of man as a probationer of immortality. These were, these alone could be, the conditions under which such a work as the *Paradise Lost* could be conceived and accomplished. By a life-long study Milton had known—

> What was of use to know,
> What best to say could say, to do had done.
> His actions to his words agreed, his words
> To his large heart gave utterance due, his heart
> Contain'd of good, wise, fair, the perfect shape;

and he left the imperishable total, as a bequest to the ages coming, in the *Paradise Lost*.[2]

Difficult as I shall find it to turn over these leaves without catching some passage, which would tempt me to stop, I propose to consider, 1st, the general plan and arrangement of the work;—2ndly, the subject with its difficulties and advantages;—3rdly, the poet's object, the spirit in the letter, the ἐνθύμιον ἐν μύθῳ, the true school-divinity; and lastly, the characteristic excellencies of the poem, in what they consist, and by what means they were produced.

1. As to the plan and ordonnance of the Poem.

Compare it with the *Iliad*, many of the books of which might change places without any injury to the thread of the story. Indeed, I doubt the original existence of the *Iliad* as one poem; it seems more probable that it was put together about the time of the Pisistratidae. The *Iliad*—and, more or less, all epic poems, the subjects of which are taken from history—have no rounded conclusion; they remain, after all, but single chapters from the volume of history, although they are ornamental chapters. Consider the exquisite simplicity of the *Paradise Lost*. It and it alone really possesses a beginning, a middle, and an end;

it has the totality of the poem as distinguished from the *ab ovo* birth and parentage, or straight line, of history.

2. As to the subject.

In Homer, the supposed importance of the subject, as the first effort of confederated Greece, is an after-thought of the critics; and the interest, such as it is, derived from the events themselves, as distinguished from the manner of representing them, is very languid to all but Greeks. It is a Greek poem. The superiority of the *Paradise Lost* is obvious in this respect, that the interest transcends the limits of a nation. But we do not generally dwell on this excellence of the *Paradise Lost*, because it seems attributable to Christianity itself;—yet in fact the interest is wider than Christendom, and comprehends the Jewish and Mohammedan worlds;—nay, still further, inasmuch as it represents the origin of evil, and the combat of evil and good, it contains matter of deep interest to all mankind, as forming the basis of all religion, and the true occasion of all philosophy whatsoever.

The Fall of Man is the subject; Satan is the cause; man's blissful state the immediate object of his enmity and attack; man is warned by an angel who gives him an account of all that was requisite to be known, to make the warning at once intelligible and awful; then the temptation ensues, and the Fall; then the immediate sensible consequence; then the consolation, wherein an angel presents a vision of the history of men with the ultimate triumph of the Redeemer. Nothing is touched in this vision but what is of general interest in religion; any thing else would have been improper.

The inferiority of Klopstock's *Messiah* is inexpressible. I admit the prerogative of poetic feeling, and poetic faith; but I cannot suspend the judgment even for a moment. A poem may in one sense be a dream, but it must be a waking dream. In Milton you have a religious faith combined with the moral nature; it is an efflux; you go along with it. In Klopstock there is a wilfulness; he makes things so and so. The feigned speeches and events in the *Messiah* shock us like falsehoods; but nothing of that sort is felt in the *Paradise Lost*, in which no particulars, at least very few indeed, are touched which can come into collision or juxta-position with recorded matter.

But notwithstanding the advantages in Milton's subject, there were concomitant insuperable difficulties, and Milton has exhibited marvellous skill in keeping most of them out of sight. High poetry is the translation of reality into the ideal under the predicament of succession of time only. The poet is an historian, upon condition of moral power being the only force in the universe. The very grandeur of his subject ministered a difficulty to Milton. The statement of a being of high intellect, warring against the supreme Being, seems to contradict the idea of a supreme Being. Milton precludes our feeling this, as much as possible, by keeping the peculiar attributes of divinity less in sight, making them to a certain extent allegorical only. Again, poetry implies the language of excitement; yet how to reconcile such language with God? Hence Milton confines the poetic passion in God's speeches to the language of scripture; and once only allows the *passio vera*, or *quasi-humana* to appear, in the passage, where the Father contemplates his own likeness in the Son before the battle:—

> Go then, thou Mightiest, in thy Father's might,
> Ascend my chariot, guide the rapid wheels
> That shake Heaven's basis, bring forth all my war,
> My bow and thunder; my almighty arms
> Gird on, and sword upon thy puissant thigh;
> Pursue these sons of darkness, drive them out
> From all Heaven's bounds into the utter deep:
> There let them learn, as likes them, to despise
> God and Messiah his anointed king.
>
> B. VI. v. 710.

3. As to Milton's object:—

It was to justify the ways of God to man! The controversial spirit observable in many parts of the poem, especially in God's speeches, is immediately attributable to the great controversy of that age, the origination of evil. The Arminians considered it a mere calamity. The Calvinists took away all human will. Milton asserted the will, but declared for the enslavement of the will out of an act of the will itself. There are three powers in us, which distinguish us from the beasts that perish;—1, reason; 2, the power of viewing universal truth; and 3, the power of contracting universal truth into particulars. Religion is the will in the reason, and love in the will.

The character of Satan is pride and sensual indulgence, finding in self the sole motive of action. It is the character so often seen *in little* on the political stage. It exhibits all the restlessness, temerity, and cunning which have marked the mighty hunters of mankind from Nimrod to Napoleon. The common fascination of men is, that these great men, as they are called, must act from some great motive. Milton has carefully marked in his Satan the intense selfishness, the alcohol of egotism, which would rather reign in hell than serve in heaven. To place this lust of self in opposition to denial of self or duty, and to show what exertions it would make, and what pains endure to accomplish its end, is Milton's particular object in the character of Satan. But around this character he has thrown a singularity of daring, a grandeur of sufferance, and a ruined splendour, which constitute the very height of poetic sublimity.

Lastly, as to the execution:—

The language and versification of the *Paradise Lost* are peculiar in being so much more necessarily correspondent to each than those in any other poem or poet. The connexion of the sentences and the position of the words are exquisitely artificial; but the position is rather according to the logic of passion or universal logic, than to the logic of grammar. Milton attempted to make the English language obey the logic of passion as perfectly as the Greek and Latin. Hence the occasional harshness in the construction.

Sublimity is the pre-eminent characteristic of the *Paradise Lost*. It is not an arithmetical sublime like Klopstock's, whose rule always is to treat what we might think large as contemptibly small. Klopstock mistakes bigness for greatness. There is a greatness arising from images of effort and daring, and also from those of moral endurance; in Milton both are united. The fallen angels are human passions, invested with a dramatic reality.

The apostrophe to light at the commencement of the third book is particularly beautiful as an intermediate link between Hell and Heaven; and observe, how the second and third book support the subjective character of the poem. In all modern poetry in Christendom there is an under consciousness of a sinful nature, a fleeting away of external things, the mind or subject greater than the object, the reflective character predominant. In the *Paradise Lost* the sublimest parts are the revelations of Milton's own mind, producing itself and evolving its own greatness; and this is so truly so, that when that which is merely entertaining for its objective beauty is introduced, it at first seems a discord.

In the description of Paradise itself you have Milton's sunny side as a man; here his descriptive powers are exercised to the utmost, and he draws deep upon his Italian resources. In the description of Eve, and throughout this part of the poem, the poet is predominant over the theologian. Dress is the symbol of the Fall, but the mark of intellect; and the metaphysics of dress are, the hiding what is not symbolic and displaying by discrimination what is. The love of Adam and Eve in Paradise is of the highest merit—not phantomatic, and yet removed from every thing degrading. It is the sentiment of one rational being towards another made tender by a specific difference in that which is essentially the same in both; it is a union of opposites, a giving and receiving mutually of the permanent in either, a completion of each in the other.

Milton is not a picturesque, but a musical, poet; although he has this merit that the object chosen by him for any particular foreground always remains prominent to the end, enriched, but not incumbered, by the opulence of descriptive details furnished by an exhaustless imagination. I wish the *Paradise Lost* were more carefully read and studied than I can see any ground for believing it is, especially those parts which, from the habit of always looking for a story in poetry, are scarcely read at all,—as for example, Adam's vision of future events in the 11th and 12th books. No one can rise from the perusal of this immortal poem without a deep sense of the grandeur and the purity of Milton's soul, or without feeling how susceptible of domestic enjoyments he really was, notwithstanding the discomforts which actually resulted from an apparently unhappy choice in marriage. He was, as every truly great poet has ever been, a good man; but finding it impossible to realize his own aspirations, either in religion, or politics, or society, he gave up his heart to the living spirit and light within him, and avenged himself on the world by enriching it with this record of his own transcendent ideal.

Notes

1. *Table Talk*, vol. ii. p. 264.
2. Here Mr. C. notes: "Not perhaps here, but towards, or as, the conclusion, to chastise the fashionable notion that poetry is a relaxation or amusement, one of the superfluous toys and luxuries of the intellect! To contrast the permanence of poems with the transiency and fleeting moral effects of empires, and what are called, great events." *Ed.*

"ODE TO THE WEST WIND"
(PERCY BYSSHE SHELLEY)

"'Ode to the West Wind' and 'Mont Blanc':
Shelley and the Method of the Sublime"
by David Brendan Hopes,
University of North Carolina at Asheville

A full definition of the word "sublime" must encompass the simple physicality of "lifted up" or "above," a material orientation as well as a metaphysical phenomenon. It is an excellent word for the operations of poetry, expressing literally "under the lintel"—that is to say, a door, the opening of a passage from one place or state of being to another—while implying that a certain elevation of perception is required to achieve such a passage. The lintel marks the passage from the cozy room of preconception into the infinite dome of spiritual speculation.

The palpable "aboveness" of the concept of Sublimity has no more precise or pervading habitation than in the poetry of Percy Shelley. He is the wind's poet, and the mountain's, and when he is the wind's poet he is not satisfied with anything less than material identity with the wind; and when he is the mountain's poet his perspective is upon, or even above, where the secrets of the highest places may be discovered and revealed. When reading Shelley, it is easy to forget—because he is so convincing in his depiction—that no man had ever seen a mountain from above the mountain or a cloud from above the cloud.

Shelley is surely of all English poets the most consciously enamored with sublimity, in both the metaphysical and physical senses.

Merely allowing the eyes to glance over random passages of *Alastor*, for example, reveals "While daylight held / the sky, the Poet kept mute conference / With his soul," and "At midnight /the moon arose: and lo! The ethereal cliffs / of Caucasus, whose icy summits shone / Among the stars like sunlight," and innumerable birds and wafting winds. Habitual use of "sky" and "airy," his perpetually stratospheric subject matter—"The Cloud," "Mont Blanc," "Ode to the West Wind"—give the reader a crick in the neck from gazing almost unvaryingly up.

A brief comparison with his contemporary John Keats (time is almost all they have in common) reveals—for example in their avian rhapsodies, "Ode to a Nightingale" and "Ode to a Skylark"—Keats's remaining steadfastly on the ground, in the realm of the senses, and Shelley levitating almost instantly into a Platonic empyrean. Keats' nightingale abides in low thickets and shrubs, and when she finally disappears from the poet's ken, she does so by flitting from one copse and hedgerow to another, low, concealed, mysterious. The poet is ravished by the earthy joys of wine and the very earthy "comfort" of death. He rolls voluptuously in flowers at his feet. His experience with his bird is addressed through association and contemplation. The skylark normally attracts human attention by shooting straight off the ground into the air at morning, the very image of the aspiring soul. Shelley can't get past the third line without mentioning "heaven" nor past the second stanza without crying, "Higher still, and higher." His relationship with his skylark is associative but, beyond that, almost purely ecstatic.

Shelley's perspective is not just more "sublime" than Keats's; for Shelley, sublimity is the default of the perceptions. He does not accept the sublime as an incidental outpouring of the cosmos; he does not wistfully pursue it from the darkling mazes of everyday life; he wakes in the midst of it, and never leaves it fully behind. Part of his notorious obscurity and the difficulty he presents to students is that a vocabulary natural to the sublime seems elusive or obscure to those who do not dwell in sublimity. Taken in sum, Shelley's poetry is about the soul's pursuit of sublimity. And, unlike some poets who stall on their first beautiful perception, the direction of Shelley's work is to draw ever near to its first object, at last achieving identity with it.

In "Hymn to Intellectual Beauty" (1816)—a suitable introduction to Shelley's oeuvre, if not actually his first fully realized poem—he recounts the moment when the shadow of awful loveliness falls on him and assigns it credit for birthing him as a poet:

> Sudden, thy shadow fell on me:
> I shrieked, and clasped my hands in ecstasy!
>
> I vowed that I would dedicate my powers
> To thee and thine—have I not kept the vow?

We should take him at his word, that this passage marks both the beginning and the goal. Whereas other poets associated with sublimity, say Wordsworth or Coleridge, are content to accept the sublime moment when it comes, along the banks of the Wye or in the Vale of Chamouni at sunrise, Shelley seeks and courts it, is homesick when he is not immersed in it, is inconsolable when it tarries afar.

> Depart not—lest the grave should be
> Like life and fear, a dark reality.

When Shelley speaks of beauty or loveliness, he is speaking of the Sublime, for beauty and loveliness seem not to be qualities naturally possessed by the objects of Shelley's appreciation, but visitations, sudden infusions of the divine into the material world. The coat is not beautiful unless the sublime wearer is wearing it. Indeed, one might be bold to say that though there are innumerable things in Shelly's work, flowers and odors and forests and crags, none of these objects is necessarily sensual—as they would be for Keats, or for that matter nearly anybody else—but rather they are objects seized upon by the poet's eye because they momentarily gleam with the sublime indwelling.

Shelley writes "Mont Blanc" in the same year as "Hymn to Intellectual Beauty," as apparently a sort of companion to that poem, or an investigation of its principles. That year, 1816, saw also the premiere of Rossini's *The Barber of Seville*, worth citing as a calculating, sensual, wily, cultural bookend to the soaring sublimity of Shelley's poem and to show how far afield Shelley worked from the popular conceptions of his day. Shelley's ideas in "Mont Blanc" are not developed with technical precision. One looking to derive a systematic Shellyan philosophy from the poem will be frustrated. It is rather exploratory and speculative, and what it speculates on, basically, are the perilous qualities of the sublime. Approaching any deity is fraught with danger, and sublimity is no exception. Scarcely an image in the poem is not terrifying in some way. The terror of the sublime is payment for extended association with it, for one is at length sure to see that under every mountain is the fire of the underworld, and every soul-filling storm wreaks havoc elsewhere. The powers of the mountain are "Now dark—now glittering—now reflecting gloom—" and when there is finally a full-fledged personification it is "Power in likeness of the Arve" come down "From the ice gulfs that gird his secret throne."

Ruin, death, convulsion, and commotion are ubiquitous. Though not even Shelley could think of these things as lovely or desirable on their own, they become so because of the dwelling in them of the power which is governing and creating the awful splendor of the mountain. Like beauty, terror is fully transfigured when it becomes the garment of the sublime. In the first two verse paragraphs of the poem, the poet ransacks the shattered evidence of nature unleashed for proof of its spiritual component, for proof of a governing soul, and finally finds it at line 45:

> Seeking among the shadows that pass by,
> Ghosts of all things that are, some shade of thee,
> Some phantom, some faint image; till the breast
> From which they fled recalls them: thou art there!

The clear implication is that without the sublime, without the inhabiting spirit of beauty, the Alps would be what they seem, a terrifying, if picturesque, wilderness of death and futile expense of energy. In stanza three, Shelley is very direct:

> I look on high:
> Has some unknown omnipotence unfurled
> The veil of life and death? Or do I lie
> In dream, and does the mightier world of sleep
> Spread far around and inaccessibly
> Its circles? For the very spirit fails,
> Driven like a homeless cloud from steep to steep . . .

The final justification of the labor of cognition is the discovery, behind the apparent terrible chaos of things, of a transcendent spirit. The horror and dread of succeeding lines, the earthquake demons and the eagles with the hunters' bones in their claws, are mitigated by the hope that they are imperfectly understood attributes of the awful governing power, all of whose panoply resolves at last into beauty.

The existential qualities of this poem abound. Shelley knows that saying the mountain and river are full of transcendent spirit doesn't necessarily mean that they are. It is an act of faith, bordering on an act of desperation, and like the founders of all great religions, Shelley acknowledges the doubt, incorporates it as part of the articles of faith, and goes on.

Why doesn't Shelley simply call this power God? Repellent conceptions derived from the Christianity of the poet's own time are, of course, part of the answer, but not all. Shelley is an impersonal poet. Even a person whose name appears in the title of one of his poems, or to whom a poem is addressed, might feel herself rendered as a disembodied spirit, as an idea more than an individual. This is the cost of dwelling habitually in the sublime. The power upon Mont Blanc has nothing of the personal to it. It is not Jesus. Shelley's often awkward naming of this spirit reveals that it cannot properly be named, for it cannot fully be defined. It is not vague; rather, we are not empowered to apprehend it. It dwells in the objects of the earth but does so with indifference to our tutelage or admonishment. It does not come to save us, or come at all in any intentional sense. It may be approached—and the continuing valor of Shelley is to approach the awful conflagration of beauty again and again—but it is as likely to reward the acolyte with lonely death as it is with greeting. It does not reveal itself, except as the yearning eye sometimes captures the aspects of its own immensity and delight. Shelley certainly was no Christian. There is no covenant between man and Shelley's vast spirit, only the freedom of the human soul to approach the sublime if one is willing to risk annihilation:

> Thou hast a voice, great Mountain, to repeal
> Large codes of fraud and woe, not understood
> By all, but which the wise, and great, and good
> Interpret, or make felt, or deeply feel.

The conditionals in this passage do not, in the end, instill confidence. How does Shelley know that a ravine or a glacier is a moral presence? Shelley has already declared in "Hymn to Intellectual Beauty" that he has taken beauty as the test of right, and in that sense the revelations of "Mont Blanc" fall back on an unfolding and very personal orthodoxy.

Shelley calls the round of earthly time a "detested trance," a loathsome, mechanical repetition from which the sublime is set apart:

> Power dwells apart in tranquility,
> Remote, serene, and inaccessible.

One might wonder how much comfort there is in the inaccessible, but
Shelley means inaccessible to any approach other than the ecstasy of
the poet.

> The race
> Of man flies far in dread: his work and dwelling
> Vanish, like smoke before the tempest's stream,
> And their place is not known.

This biblical citation of human vanity is immediately contrasted to
the caverns through which rush the secret streams of the mountains,
which, if barren and ruinous, are at least spectacular. The weary cycles
of men come to dust and exhaustion, but the circles of the natural
world, so long as sublimity indwells, are vast climbing spirals, in the
invisible heights of which lies meaning, if the questing human imagination would but persevere. Some things are disgusting in violence;
other things are magnificent.

"Mont Blanc" possesses a curious resonance with that most un-
Shelleyan poem, Tennyson's "In Memoriam," for both allow, through
faith, a fullness of comfort not attested by the evidence. Tennyson
clings to God through a thousand demonstrations of his random
cruelty. Shelley clings to the sublime through awful implications of
the savage meaninglessness of material things. Why does he do so?
The concluding lines of the poem suggest a wistful longing and a faith
whose main support is imagination:

> The secret Strength of things,
> Which governs thought, and to the infinity dome
> Of heaven is a law, inhabits thee!
> And what were thou, and earth, and stars, and sea,
> If to the human mind's imaginings
> Silence and solitude were vacancy?

True emptiness amid the crags of Mont Blanc is a concept too horrible to be contemplated.

What bothers me as a reader of "Mont Blanc"—and what bothered the author, too, if we can judge by his later composition "Ode to the West Wind"—is the uncertainty of it all, the lack of specifics, the hopeful randomness of any approach to the sublime. We stand in the Vale of Chamouni, and the spirit might be there, or the day may be overcast and we apprehend nothing at all. An eagle might drop a dead hunter on our heads. What Shelley needs to develop is a method for the worship of the sublime. The method of the sublime is laid out pretty clearly in "Ode to the West Wind" (1819). If power does not change itself to come to us, as did Jehovah in the Incarnation, we must change ourselves to come to it. Even employment of Dante's *terza rima* implies a kind of discipline, a habit which, laborious at first, becomes fluid, even exultant, as one catches on and moves forward. The poem gives the effect of tempestuous ease while employing one of the most difficult verse forms to render into English.

Shelley often apostrophizes the spirit, without any apparent expectation of response, but in "West Wind" it is clear that he requires it to heed his words:

> Wild Spirit, which art moving everywhere:
> Destroyer and preserver: hear, O, hear!

Here we have a worshiper advancing in the faith. Here we have contemplation rendered into prayer, prayer which might move the hearer to remake the petitioner's life. Part of the new approach is Shelley's recognition of what aspects of his own personality are most like that of the sublime. Holy men of any faith seek more and more, as much as humanly possible, to resemble their God, and Shelley does the same. He recognizes that his impetuosity, his swift thought and yearning body are not unlike "the steep sky's commotion." He recognizes that the transmutation of flesh into spirit would render him a force of nature, a vessel of awful loveliness:

> If I were a dead leaf thou mightest bear;
> If I were a swift cloud to fly with thee;
> A wave to pant beneath thy power, and share

The impulse of thy strength, only less free
Than thou, O uncontrollable! If even
I were as in my boyhood, and could be

The comrade of the wandering over Heaven,
As then, when to outstrip thy skiey speed
Scarce seemed a vision; I would ne'er have striven

As thus with thee in prayer in my sore need.
O! Lift me as a wave, a leaf, a cloud!
I fall upon the thorns of life! I bleed!

A heavy weight of hours has chained and bowed
One too like thee: tameless, and swift, and proud.

One prayer recognized as righteous by all faiths is "Lord, make me as you are." Shelley accepts his redemption as a natural, cyclic process, which must begin with annihilation. The spirit will redeem him according to the customary operations of its own dispensation, so Shelley petitions to enter the processes of nature, to be a fallen leaf in autumn, to be a polyp under the shallow Mediterranean, to be a drowsy summer day wakened suddenly into apprehension by "the locks of the approaching storm." The same annihilation is present but understated in Christianity, where being again means first dying. Shelley has no problem with the midstage. He welcomes annihilation. He makes it beautiful. It is as if he suddenly recognized what all the peril and death and ruin upon Mont Blanc were *for*. The riven valleys and the earthquakes and the freezing winter storms are invitations, open doors, lintels to be passed under in pursuit of the sublime. Why am I exhausted and decaying? Because the west wind, which is the present body of the spirit is about to lift me up, about to shatter me as it does the forests, is about to sow me into the earth as the seeds of a fairer world. The sublime will take me into itself because I, by my own will and longing, have made myself almost indistinguishable from it.

It is unlikely that the famous, and famously unsatisfying, concluding couplet of this poem can be taken as purely rhetorical.

O Wind,
If Winter comes, can Spring be far behind?

We recall the wistful uncertainty of the conclusion of "Mont Blanc," the assertion not that the world brims with moral spirit but that it would be discouraging and unthinkable if it did not. All genuine mysticism carries with a sense of the experimental, the uncertain, and Shelley ends his great ode with a fervent wish, the factuality of which cannot be established except by experience.

Song of Myself
(Walt Whitman)

"The Sublime Self: Whitman's Sense of the Sublime in *Song of Myself*"
by David Brendan Hopes, University of North Carolina at Asheville

---

The critic may well feel hesitancy in broaching the subject of "The Sublime" in connection to an American poet. Sublimity is not an American quality. The sublime excludes in order to elevate. It is momentary and selective. It is very much a respecter of persons. It is a sensual connoisseurship. It is *elite*. American poets such as Hart Crane or Robinson Jeffers do occasionally court the sublime, but their efforts are descriptive rather than experiential. That is to say, sublime things, such as the "great unblinking eye of earth," the Pacific Ocean, are named, but their sublimity is not actually experienced or grown into, as are the sublime moments of Shelley or Coleridge. Ezra Pound, with his Dionysian theophanies and gods moving through crystal, invites the sublime, but such moments are fleeting, effete, and in any case have nothing to do with any primarily American experience. Eliot's rhetoric can be majestic, though even when he is talking about God he is not "sublime" in the sense I would use the term but rather the opposite, excruciatingly tender, intimate, inward.

Ginsberg is expansive, but expansiveness is to sublimity as a Hollywood war scene is to war. The Confessionals, as well as many more recent poets, may recognize their own experience as in some measure "sublime," but the quality does not communicate in pure form to the reader, who may identify pathos rather than sublimity. "Pathos," in fact, may be the accepted form of sublimity on our shores in this time.

There are outright enemies of the sublime—John Ashbery is the readiest example—who assume minuteness, mundaneness, peculiarity, and repetition to be the verifiable materials of the soul. Judging from a perusal of contemporary literary magazines, their number is surely legion.

Yet American architecture aims at, and often achieves, the sublime, and our geography would seem to cry out for it. Somehow our poets have not desired the vocabulary, or possessed the particular will, to communicate at a similar elevation. The sublime requires surrender, and the American idiom has always depended more on will—or, at the extreme, self-glorification—than on surrender. Most poetry this side of either ocean has sought genuineness or novelty and left sublimity to another people and another age. In a graduate poetry workshop, of which I was a member, at Syracuse University in the middle 1970s, American poet W.D. Snodgrass observed that "the effort at sublimity is a warning sign of fraudulence," a dictum which he illustrated with a reading of a very American, very down-to-earth, incontestably sincere passage out of Walt Whitman.

Such anti-sublimity prejudice can, perhaps, be laid at Whitman's door, but only if one takes Whitman's subject matter solely into account and then assumes that subject matter to remain untransfigured by the manner of its treatment. Whitman does remake the subject matter and image complex of poetry out of things derivable from vacant lots and veterans' hospitals, but it is the contention of this essay that he achieves something more remarkable still. Whitman transmutes the sublime into vessels no one before him would have imagined could contain it. He alters the locations and sources of the sublime in ways so radical that no poet, American or international, has yet fully followed his lead. All the Romantics—indeed, anyone I can think of in the history of poetry—found sublimity out there and up there, a communication from what was not only exterior but superior. Whitman finds it in his breastbone, in a blade of grass. Many poets acknowledge the near and "low," the homely and the mundane, but their doing so is usually a denial of the sublime, as class-bound or irrelevant, rather than a redefinition of it. Not so Walt Whitman. Every bit the democrat, he is unwilling to leave the aristocracy of the spirit behind. *Leaves of Grass* is a vast subsequent step in the radicalization of individual consciousness, the elevation of individual perception; Whitman opens up so willingly to the reader that we forget how smart he is. We fall into the trap of thinking him the jolly neighborhood bard with no more on his mind than the naming of things dear to his heart. Whitman presents to the critic the same identity crisis that he presents to the teacher: an unwonted uselessness based on the poet's painstaking elucidation of proof and extreme clarity of expression. Commentary is, if not quite unnecessary, fraught with the dangers of superfluity. Whitman goes as far out of his way to mention local, tactile, everyday things—"The caulking iron, the kettle of boiling vault-cement"—as his contemporaries do to draw in the ancient gods. A few personal obsessions and historical allusions passed, and the text unfolds to any intelligent reader.

One would expect, therefore, the democratization of the sublime in *Leaves of Grass*, certainly in *Song of Myself*, where the announced subject is, one first supposes, limited to the body, emotions, experiences, and apprehensions of a single man. Greater directness, and a greater radicalization of traditional poetic tone, can scarcely be imagined than that found in the blunt opening lines, "I celebrate myself, and sing myself." In many definitions of the sublime, "commonness"—even commonness transfigured—can have no part at all, but a reader of Whitman is soon accustomed to his practice of refocusing the visionary mode, wherein the small is made the courtyard of the vast and the squalid is the guise that the holy puts on to enter squalid environs. Blake does this as well but is hugely more selective in the objects and situations that may be counted on to ignite the visionary mode.

Because of his directness, Whitman's intellect is often underappreciated. His task, throughout *Leaves of Grass*, is to revise the locus of the sublime, as Christ revised the locus of the law. We note in the great English and German Romantics the growing ability to find sublimity in things without ostensible theological connections—in birds and waterfalls and riven ravines. The separation of sublimity from religion is among their triumphs. The separation of sublimity from the big and impressive is among Whitman's. Whitman takes the further step and finds sublimity in the barnyard and the slave market. This might seem equally an expressive innovation and a breach of decorum were the way not prepared by Emerson, whose transparent eyeball traversing Harvard Yard is empowered to take in all sights, great and small, and indeed may not be empowered to omit any sight of its own will at all. Perception has taken the place of discrimination, in an exchange that has not, I believe, been reversed, or even modified, in poetry to this day. The contemporary poet feels empowered to write about just anything at all. It was not always thus, and its being thus may be laid at Whitman's door, though it must be understood that at his best Whitman transfigures the mundane and at his worst puts it in the way of transfiguration. When Whitman references "The sniff of green leaves and dry leaves, and of the shore, and dark color'd sea-rocks, and of hay in the barn" (2),[1] he is not merely naming pleasant objects or sights but setting them within range of transfiguring power. In the same section of the great poem come the subsequent lines, "Stop this day and night with me and you shall possess the origin of all poems," to be discussed at greater length later. This resonant passage acknowledges the power of the poet to choose what will be elevated by the workings of the poem. It is very clear that the poet perceives and the poet elevates, and if something is to be sublime, it is not because it has descended from heaven but because it has been lifted to heaven from the streets of Manhattan.

If Whitman still feels tempted to look for the footsteps of God under some principle of discrimination, he does not seem to choose to indulge that temptation very often. He records the instances of revelation as they arise. Alive to the sudden resonance between the present and the transcendent, which we normally think of as "sublimity," Whitman lights upon it, in section 14:

> The litter of the grunting sow as they tug at her teats,
> The brood of the turkey-hen and she with her half-spread wings,
> I see in them and in myself the same old law.

I don't know whether Whitman is deliberately taking on Shelley's Mount Blanc or Wordsworth's Simplon Pass—I suspect he's not—but the contrast between the spark necessary to ignite the great English Romantics and that necessary to ignite Whitman is unmistakable. For some to see God it takes an uplifted continent; for some it takes a broody turkey hen. It is a gift to America to be able to accept the vector of revelation without preconceptions, or it would be if Whitman had his complete will. Whitman is deliberate in his relocation of the sublime. Hierarchies are here in abeyance. A mountain and a prairie flower named in the same line are not merely elements of a catalog but an implied equation, a discovery about the nature of significance, like Mrs. Turpin's vision at the end of Flannery O'Connor's short story "Revelation," where the zanies and the white trash enter heaven side by side with the saints and society ladies. The circumstances of the world do not define symbolic status: That is defined by the visionary moment, and Whitman withholds all judgment among high things and low things until the moment of transfiguration arrives.

Perhaps we should imagine a powerful flashlight and the dark interior of a church at night. Someone outside is training the flashlight on this or that image in the stained-glass windows, and we inside, if we know our business, do not worry about what the light *should* be illuminating but what it *does*. If it misses the face of an apostle and lingers over a little dog wagging its tail in the corner, we have our symbol, our image for contemplation. Appropriateness or inappropriateness is the business of the one with the light. The dog as well as the saint may be a door open to the next world, and if preconceptions prevent us from entering, we have only ourselves to blame. There are times when Whitman is the soul in the dark interior, watching, piecing together the impressions, and there are times when he is the mysterious wielder of the light, but in either case, he believes himself and his kind—which is to say, the poet—to be the best and proper guide:

> Stop this day and night with me and you shall possess the origin
>   of all poems,
> You shall possess the good of the earth and sun,
>   (there are millions of suns left,)
> You shall no longer take things at second or third hand,
>   nor look through the eyes of the dead,
>   nor feed on spectres in books (2)

Should we believe this is what Whitman really thinks? Should we accept it as part of our thought? When I teach, I studiously avoid suggesting that a poet's character is the measure of the truth of his poetry, but this seems to be what Whitman asserts. Is sublimity conferred when the poet turns his attention upon an object or event? Or is it only *this* poet, a special niche Whitman is carving out for himself? In "Song of Myself," other poets are not mentioned, and if they are referenced, I have missed the reference. One may assume that Whitman was underread, or one may assume that he is remaking the vocation of the poet, to include only those relations with the universe that are new, fresh, unprecedented, particular. What if John Keats had been free of the burden of Spenser and Milton? Would he have remained mute, or would he have been still more blindingly brilliant and many times more original? And, if Whitman means only himself, why shouldn't he? In this new definition of the poet, each poet must reference, at least in the heat of perception, only himself, or else the visionary sinks by slow degrees into the derivative.

When a poet is going full blast, who knows for sure what is merely part of the great structure of rhetoric and what is the revelation of central thought? But Whitman mentions often enough the identity, or at least the contiguousness, of the mundane and the sublime that we may be bold to investigate it as a lasting conviction. When he writes in section 31:

> I believe a leaf of grass is no less than the journey-work of the
>   stars,
> And the pismire is equally perfect, and a grain of sand,
>   and the egg of a wren,
> And the tree-toad is a chef-d'oeuvre for the highest,
> And the running blackberry would adorn the parlors of heaven,
> And the narrowest hinge in my hand puts to scorn all machinery,
> And the cow munching with depress'd head surpasses any statue,
> And a mouse is miracle enough to stagger sextillions of infidels.

part may be put down to the democratic exultation of things not normally exalted in European poetry, but part surely is immediate and inspired investigation of the locus of sublimity. Why do we look up and out for God when we might as well look down and in? Looking down and in is exactly what is found in the still-sensational opening passages of *Song of Myself*, in which Whitman declares the cosmos to be found in his own body, his own breath, his own sex-play. Surely these lines could not have been thoroughly understood in Whitman's own day, for they represent an assault on the traditional spiritual hierarchies at least as radical as that of Darwin. "Nature without check with original energy" (1) is still a radical principle, unrealized except in these ringing lines and certain lives that, one must admit, did not end happily.

In what way is "a mouse miracle enough to stagger sextillions of infidels" (31)? It is part of the power of poetry that we are inclined to believe such declarations without investigating them very much, but what if we were of a quibbling and literal-minded turn? On a normal day in a normally Whitmanesque associative mood, the mouse reminds us that the gigantic operation of the constellations is duplicated, if writ very small, in the person of the mouse, and the very smallness of the apparatus is part of the miracle. In moments of mystic apprehension, the mouse, the hand-hinge, the cow, are open doors onto a vista of their Maker, "a scented gift and remembrancer designedly dropt / Bearing the owner's name someway in the corners, that we may see and remark and say Whose?" (6). The meanest remembrancer may lead to the loftiest lender of remembrance. Other poets—Swift, Shakespeare—reference handkerchiefs, but they are never more than their original selves. Decorum does rather go out the door along with the democratization of the sublime, but some might find that an endurable loss.

When we see a violet or a lumberjack, do we think of God? Perhaps, but if not, it is because we lack the poet to direct and augment our senses. Whitman is offering to be that poet, not for every thing at every moment, but surely for every thing in its own proper time. *A Child asks What is the junebug . . . a Child asks What is the Holocaust?* The expansion is potentially infinite, and the poet would answer them all if there were time.

Whitman lacks Shelley's desire for a secular sublimity, for transcendence not governed by some plotting Jehovah dangling moments of radiance to draw us along toward conclusions he desires us to make. Shelley mistrusts God and therefore must remake him. Whitman's God requires no such bother. Whitman's God is casual, friendly, less the divine mystery than the great and affectionate Camerado. From section 48:

> Why should I wish to see God better than this day?
> I see something of God each hour of the twenty four . . .
> In the faces of men and women I see God, and in my
>   own face in the glass.

But it is difficult to conceive of God in any way without admitting, somewhere along the line, that he is dangerous. Indeed, there are hints in *Song of Myself* that seeking the transcendent in the mundane is a safety precaution as well as spiritual liberation. From section 25:

> Dazzling and tremendous, how quick the sun-rise would kill me
> If I could not now and always send the sun-rise out of me.

If I were not the source of the power and the majesty of the universe, the power and the majesty of the universe might destroy me. Shelley contemplates being annihilated by the frozen crags of Mount Blanc, by the blast of the West Wind. Whitman wants a peaceful sleep with his comrade's arm over his chest. I don't know why Whitman gained a reputation for arrogance and bombast. It seems the opposite to me.

Most definitions of the attitude of sublimity include refinement and distillation, but at the end of section 14, Whitman writes:

> What is commonest, cheapest, nearest, easiest, is Me,
> Me going for my chance, spending for vast returns,
> Adorning myself to bestow myself on the first that will take me,
> Not asking the sky to come down to my good will,
> Scattering it freely forever.

The sky comes down to the visionary Romantic—whether by his will or its own—but Whitman asks less than that. The sky may sit where it is and the probing imagination of the poet reads its signs and accepts its gifts with as much necessity and alacrity as it does the barnyard animals'. Even the beast of Annunciation is distinct, homely, and wholly American, not a nightingale or a skylark, but a wild gander:

> The wild gander leads his flock through the cool night,
> Ya-honk he says to, and it sounds to me like an invitation.
> The pert may suppose it meaningless, but I listening close,
> Find its purpose and place up there toward the wintry sky.
> (14)

Even a fair ornithologist knows that the goose flies highest of all the airy migrants, his Ya-honk sounding from where not even the emblematic eagle dares.

Whitman, of course, produces one of the great examples of the macrocosmic sublime in "Out of the Cradle Endlessly Rocking," whose interplay of the oceanic and celestial, the deep cradle of the waters and the empty heavens knit together by the sagging yellow moon, is the equal in magnificence and profundity of any poem in our experience. But in *Song of Myself*, Whitman consistently explores a democratic redefinition of sublimity, the world in a grain of sand rather than the coruscating face of the enormous. Section 6 of "Song of Myself" presents almost as a thought-problem on the sublime. "A child said What is the grass?" The rest of the section, the answer, shows as well as any other piece of writing in the tradition the process of poetic thought. It is not a process of blinding revelation, but of gradual, intensely personal discovery. Sublimity is achieved and not received. Questions of the grass lead, for Whitman, to questions of death, and there is no high road to the sublime higher than contemplations of mortality. Near the end of the section, we hear Whitman rephrasing the question, almost as if he were asking God, but if he is, he does not wait for the answer but supplies it himself:

> What do you think has become of the young and old men?
> And what do you think has become of the women and
>   children?
>
> They are alive and well somewhere,
> The smallest sprout shows there is really no death,
> And if ever there were it led forward life, and does not wait
>   at the end to arrest it,
> And ceas'd the moment life appear'd.
>
> All goes onward and outward, nothing collapses,
> And to die is different from what any one supposed, and luckier.

The fact is that the smallest sprout really does *not* show there is no death; Whitman does. In the face of the sublime, the poet has ceased to be the passive receptor and become the guide. Or—and the idea is yet so daring that I almost declined to say it—the poet is not even the guide but the creator, the one who lifts up any damn thing that strikes his fancy and makes it the milestone of the soul.

NOTE

1. All quotations from *Song of Myself* are cited by section number.

THE POETRY OF WILLIAM BUTLER YEATS

"Yeats: Tragic Joy and the Sublime"
by Jahan R. Ramazani, in *PMLA* (1989)

INTRODUCTION

In his revaluation of Yeats's poems and their place in the post-Romantic tradition of poetry, Jahan Ramazani focuses on their evocation of "tragic joy": "their affective movement from terror to joy (the psychological sublime) as well as their characteristically violent figures and fragmentary images (the rhetorical sublime)." Observing the sublime's long-held association with literary figurations of death, Ramazani asserts that the attempt to evoke sublimity is a kind of curse for Yeats and his Romantic predecessors, a self-destructive effort to "[integrate] with the final form of reality."

It is a violence from within that protects us from a violence without. It is the imagination pressing back against the pressure of reality. It seems, in the last analysis, to have something to do with our self-preservation; and that, no doubt, is why the expression of it, the sound of its words, helps us to live our lives.

Wallace Stevens

Ramazani, R. Jahan. "Yeats: Tragic Joy and the Sublime." *PMLA* 104.2 (March 1989): 163–177.

Do not go gentle into that good night,
Old age should burn and rave at close of day;
Rage, rage against the dying of the light.

Dylan Thomas

Like his modernist contemporaries Eliot and Hulme, Yeats rarely uses the word *sublime*. His critics have been all too willing to adopt his aversion to the term, even though his prophetic and apocalyptic lyrics of tragic joy descend from the Romantic sublime of Blake and Shelley and even though his primary aesthetic categories—ecstasy, passion, terror, *sprezzatura*, joy—descend from the vocabulary of writers on the sublime from Longinus to Schopenhauer.[1] Yeats continually draws on this rhetoric—for example, when he defines the poet's "ecstasy" as arising "from the contemplation of things vaster than the individual and imperfectly seen," or when he recommends symbols in art as a means "to escape the barrenness and shallowness of a too conscious arrangement," or, perhaps less obviously, when he mythologizes life and history as a turning between antithetical terms (*Autobiography* 319; *Essays* 87). Theories of the sublime can help us interpret the family resemblances among Yeats's controversial lyrics affirming death and destruction: late poems such as "The Gyres" and "Lapis Lazuli," middle poems such as "The Second Coming" and "The Fascination of What's Difficult," and even an early poem, "The Valley of the Black Pig." By reading these poems synchronically in the light of the poetics of the Romantic sublime, we can better understand the structure and genealogy of their affective movement from terror to joy (the psychological sublime) as well as their characteristically violent figures and fragmentary images (the rhetorical sublime). More generally, this approach can also reveal the interrelations between the sublime and such related modes as prophecy and the curse. Although the sublime is not a unitary concept, I hope to show, with Yeats's help, that death is its ultimate occasion.[2]

[...]

In my view, death precipitates the emotional turning called the sublime, although theorists of the sublime often refer to death by other names, or by what Kenneth Burke terms "deflections": nothingness, castration, physical destruction, semiotic collapse, defeat by a precursor, and annihilation of the ego.[3] Death is the recurrent obsession for these theorists, from Longinus to Heidegger and Bloom. Longinus offers various concepts of the sublime, but his examples make it clear that death is his organizing trope—witness Sappho's broken-tongued gasp, "I seem near to dying," and Homer's terrified sailors, "carried away from under death, but only just" (473). The sublime strife between heroes and gods, aspirants and masters, is good for mortals, but only if the mortals survive the threatened annihilation (476). For Edmund Burke, too, "ideas of pain, and above all of death," occasion the sublime (65). One of his most prominent examples is Death itself, in Milton's allegory (59). Kant amends Burke's emphasis on terror by arguing that we must be secure as we picture to ourselves danger and destruction, but even then, the imaginary threat is so great that we know "all resistance would be altogether vain" (100). It is our apparent security that allows our fundamental insecurity to come into view. His notion of the first step in the sublime as a defeat of the imagination, a momentary checking, is a kind of momentary death, the equivalent of Yeats's "Black out" in "Lapis Lazuli" and Wordsworth's "when the light of sense / Goes out" in *The Prelude* (1805, 6.534–35). For Freud, this is the moment of anxiety over castration in the oedipal struggle; for Heidegger, the sudden call of conscience that discloses Dasein's guilt and nullity—a call that "comes *from* me and yet *from beyond* me" (320). For my interpretation of the sublime as a staged confrontation with death, I draw on the psychoanalytic accounts of Hertz and Weiskel, supplementing them with a Heideggerian emphasis on the ecstatic encounter with death. But it is in Yeats that the sublime is explicitly a *staged* confrontation with death: his tragic heroes convey in their final utterances "the sudden enlargement of their vision, their ecstasy at the approach of death" (*Essays* 522–23).

In the temporal structure of the sublime, the anticipation of death gives rise to a counterassertion of life. Having torn out his eyes in horror, Yeats's antithetical Oedipus reasserts himself with a rage that "seemed to contain all life" (*Vision* 28). In psychological terms, the hero and the poet surmount the threat of the destructive father through identification with him.[4] This oedipal dynamic is clear and pervasive in Yeats's personal history, even though *Reveries over Childhood and Youth* displaces the figure of aggression onto his grandfather Pollexfen, a man whom Yeats confused with God and Lear, prayed to for punishment, and emulated as a model of courage (*Autobiography* 3, 4, 22).

This psychoanalytic model of the sublime can help us interpret the overarching affective movement of Yeats's poems of tragic joy.

In brief, these poems introject the violent, paternal threat, thereby permitting the conversion of defensive and pathetic energy into joy. In the psychic economy of these lyrics the energy released by the escape from the father—or from death, the final form of authority—often manifests itself as laughter. Fighting blindly the poet-hero suddenly "laughs aloud" (326; see also 159, 250, 293). The Shakespearean actors in "Lapis Lazuli" do not "weep. / They know that Hamlet and Lear are gay" (294). In generic terms, the unexpected joy of the sublime arises from the relinquishment of elegiac pathos. Indeed, the poems of tragic joy might be thought of as a countergenre to elegy. If mourning is the psychic correlative of elegy, as Sacks maintains (1–37), mania corresponds to the sublime; and mania, writes Freud, is the overcoming of mourning:

> In mania, the ego must have got over the loss of the object (or its mourning over the loss, or perhaps the object itself), and thereupon the whole quota of anticathexis which the painful suffering of melancholia had drawn to itself from the ego and "bound" will have become available. ("Mourning" 255)

The transition from elegiac mourning to affirmation marks the middle movement of many poems of tragic joy. In the pivotal line of "Meru," gaiety supervenes when the poet releases lost civilizations from the grip of mourning: "Egypt and Greece good-bye, and good-bye, Rome!" (289). In the middle stanza of "The Gyres," the youthful, elegiac poet who wept and "sighed" is overridden by the Nietzschean command "Rejoice" (293). Having faced his own death, Yeats writes in a late letter, "How strange is the subconscious gaiety that leaps up before danger or difficulty. I have not had a moment of depression—that gaiety is outside one's control" (*Letters* 733). Terror is converted into joy, "gaiety transfiguring all that dread," as Yeats writes in his strongest contribution to the sublime ("Lapis Lazuli" 294).

But as Longinus reminds us, the joy of the sublime is ultimately based on an illusion: "It is our nature to be elevated by true sublimity. Filled with joy and pride, we come to believe we have created what we have only heard" (467). The sublime is the momentary illusion that translates hearer into orator, son into father, and the weeping elegist of "The Gyres" into the "Old Rocky Face." In Stevens's words, it allows the violence within to conquer the violence without as a matter of self-preservation. This illusion is sometimes dangerously complete in Yeats's lyrics of tragic joy, where the poet may seem to cast too cold an eye on death and to inure himself to violence. Incorporating the Other (annihilative violence, "numb nightmare," superego on the rampage), the speaker of "The Gyres," for example, discards the singular pronoun *I*—associated with the earlier, weeping self—and exults as a plural identity: "We that look on but laugh in tragic joy" (293). The lyric attempts to deliver the poetic self from the deathly victimage of passive spectatorship (the defeated hearer of Longinus) by converting audience into author, the Rocky Face willing the bloody spectacle it must observe.

The theory of the sublime, as we can already see, helps to explain the intersubjective drama of Yeats's visionary lyrics. Such poems enact the strengthening of the ego by introjection, and yet, in doing so, they admit an "*alien* voice," as Heidegger calls it, that seems to tear the boundaries of the ego, bringing it perilously close to annihilation (321). The poet says of Oedipus, much as Longinus does of the Pythian priestess, that Delphi "spoke through him" (*Vision* 27–28). Yeats's theory of the mask is a theory of self-transformation through imitation of the not-self, a theory cognate with the sublime in both privileging the subject and violating its integrity: "all joyous or creative energy is a re-birth as something not oneself, something which has no memory and is created in a moment and perpetually renewed" (*Autobiography* 340). The voice that emerges from the Rocky Face is "not oneself," though its message of reassurance would seem intended to rouse the self to its fullest strength. If "The Second Coming" similarly rehearses death, putting on the power of the repressed father it represents as rough beast, then it risks destabilizing the self while trying to achieve stability. Appropriating the violence of the rough beast for its own aural action and impact, the poem enacts, in Hertz's phrase, a "transfer of power" typical of the sublime; but the transfer potentially endangers the integrity of the poetic self (Hertz, "Reading" 7). The "vast image" starts into the poet's mind out of a mind not his own:

> Surely some revelation is at hand;
> Surely the Second Coming is at hand.
> The Second Coming! Hardly are those words out
> When a vast image out of *Spiritus Mundi*
> Troubles my sight. . . . (187)

The Other of the Yeatsian sublime is that mind beyond our minds, *Anima Mundi*, the Daimon, the Mask, what we might also call (as Yeats occasionally does) the sub- or unconscious, labeled the Reason by Kant, the divine possessor by Longinus. In Yeats's sublime poems, words and images seem to have an "independent reality," invading the mind from beyond it, each like an "emblem" that "sails into the sight" (*Mythologies* 284; *Poems* 244).

Nevertheless, interpretations of the sublime that overemphasize this threat to the identity of the subject risk turning the sublime into mysticism, dressed up in Lacanian garb.[5] The sublime poet and the mystic share the conviction that, as Yeats puts it, "the borders of our mind are ever shifting," but whereas for the mystic the energy flows in one direction, from Other into self, the sublime poet also reverses the direction, in a reaction-formation, believing that the self has produced what it has heard (*Essays* 28). However hard Yeats tries to be a mystic, the lyric self in his poems is rarely the passive vessel of the Daimon. Self asserts its prerogatives over mystic Soul in many more lyrics than "A Dialogue of Self and Soul," and poetic identity is generated by their agon. Even Soul does not speak consistently in the rhetoric of self-abnegation but instead opens the dialogue with a favorite Yeatsian command, "I summon," much as the seemingly mystic speaker of "All Souls' Night" repeatedly asserts his provenance with the phrase "I call" (234; 228–29). In a declamatory poem that summons past and future, "To Ireland in the Coming Times," *materia poetica* is said to come "from unmeasured mind," but the paradox is that the poet's imposed "measure" gives access to the measureless Other (50). Without such heroic self-assertion, the poet would remain, like Sappho in Longinus's treatise, broken-tongued, in the same condition as Soul in "A Dialogue of Self and Soul," whose "tongue's a stone" (235), or as Soul in "Vacillation," "[s]truck dumb in the simplicity of fire!" (252). In the dialectic of the sublime, the poet must rise from this momentary death, the tongue recover from its muteness. By analyzing the formal strategies of Yeats's sublime lyrics we can concretize this general understanding of the poems' to-and-fro between psychic annihilation and assertion, terror and joy.[6]

II. STRUCTURE, IMAGERY, SOUND, AND RHETORIC

Because the Yeatsian sublime often compresses the moments of its dialectic, it does not always follow the clear Kantian stages of assertion of the Imagination, defeat or prosthetic death, and rescue by the Reason, or even the simpler but comparable steps in Burke of terror and joy, in Longinus of daimonic possession and expulsion. Even so, a structural similarity is perceptible in such poems as "The Valley of the Black Pig," "The Second Coming," and the lyrics composing the final movements of "Meditations in Time of Civil War" and "Nineteen Hundred and Nineteen." Each opens with a vision that shatters the sleepy complacency or boundedness of the poetic self, substitutes a more concentrated image for this confused and fragmented vision, and then, having enlarged the boundaries of the ego and totalized reality, drops a veil to separate self from Other.[7] Some of Yeats's sublime poems do not strictly conform to this temporal map. In "Nineteen Hundred and Nineteen," for example, the incubus Artisson—the equivalent of the black pig and the rough beast "lurches past" only after, and not before, the distancing moment of dropping wind and settling dust (210). Nor do the sublime lyrics easily separate into Kant's categories: the mathematical sublime, incremental and repetitive, and the dynamical sublime, singular and abrupt. Nevertheless, "Leda and the Swan" and "The Cold Heaven" exemplify, with their astonishingly violent openings, the sudden and single moment of rupture characteristic of the dynamical sublime:

> A sudden blow: the great wings beating still
> Above the staggering girl.... (214)

> Suddenly I saw the cold and rook-delighting heaven
> That seemed as though ice burned and was but the more
>   ice.... (125)

A Heideggerian call of conscience blasts through the speaker of "The Cold Heaven," as if it were a thunderbolt out of Longinus: "Until I cried and trembled and rocked to and fro, / Riddled with light." Other poems—for example, "The Magi" and part 6 of "Nineteen Hundred and Nineteen"—are exercises in the mathematical sublime, visionary encounters with an infinite repetition whose formal correlatives are iterative syntax ("With all their ... / And all their ... / And all their ..." [126]) and diction ("Violence ... violence," "round and round" [210]).[8]

"The Second Coming" conjoins the mathematical and the dynamical sublime. The initial stanza is a vision of anarchic repetition, a turning and turning without center, pounding in its first line with an insistent dactylic rhythm and, in its last lines, leaving the imagination exhausted by the effort to totalize:

> Turning and turning in the widening gyre
> The falcon cannot hear the falconer;
> Things fall apart; the centre cannot hold;
> Mere anarchy is loosed upon the world . . . (187)

But the terrifying beast that bursts into the mind in the second stanza seems more the violent father of the dynamical sublime, whom the poem attempts to introject in order to quell. This criss-crossing of the mathematical and the dynamical sublime should not surprise us, since even Kant does not distinguish between them with consistency. Similarly, "The Magi" is about an exhaustion through repetition of the quest:

> Now as at all times I can see in the mind's eye,
> In their stiff, painted clothes, the pale unsatisfied ones
> Appear and disappear in the blue depth of the sky
> With all their ancient faces like rain-beaten stones,
> And all their helms of silver hovering side by side,
> And all their eyes still fixed, hoping to find once more,
> Being by Calvary's turbulence unsatisfied,
> The uncontrollable mystery on the bestial floor. (126)

The repetition of the quest is duplicated within the poet's mind, the poet holding within "the mind's eye" the questers' "eyes still fixed." Out of the lyric's enactment of their rhythmical appearance and disappearance, which creates the mathematical sublime's texture of "on and on," erupts the last line's unpredictable and "uncontrollable mystery" (126).[9]

In a passage worthy of Longinus or Kant, Yeats describes this dynamic of the sublime:

> Does not all art come when a nature, that never ceases to judge itself, exhausts personal emotion in action or desire so completely that something impersonal, something that has nothing to do with action or desire, suddenly starts into

its place, something which is as unforeseen, as completely organised, even as unique, as the images that pass before the mind between sleeping and waking. (*Autobiography* 222)

The Imagination collapses and the Reason starts into place with its transcendental knowledge of the infinite. The rough beast and the uncontrollable mystery shatter the texture of the repetitive mental act of attempting to grasp reality. In generic terms, the Yeatsian sublime arises when one "exhausts . . . desire" in quest-romance or its temporal inverse, elegy. The mind can no longer strain toward libidinal objects:

> I think that we who are poets and artists, not being permitted to shoot beyond the tangible, must go from desire to weariness and so to desire again, and live but for the moment when vision comes to our weariness like terrible lightning. (*Mythologies* 340)[10]

A Longinian flash, the sublime rips unpredictably through Yeats's elegiac cycles of desire, the mind transported beyond its objects. The "insolent fiend" lurches into view at the end of "Nineteen Hundred and Nineteen" only after the mind has wearied itself in the effort to hold onto the horses' breaking circle of movement (210).

Whirling, gyring, spiring—the Yeatsian sublime often bolts out of such rhythmic and repetitive movement. In "The Wild Swans at Coole," the poet tries to count the swans, setting in motion the mental operation that Kant describes as the mathematical sublime:

> The nineteenth autumn has come upon me
> Since I first made my count;
> I saw, before I had well finished,
> All suddenly mount
> And scatter wheeling in great broken rings
> Upon their clamorous wings. (131)

The repetitive act of counting collapses as the swans mount above the poet, transporting his mind with an intimation of incalculable aggregates. These broken rings reappear as the widening gyre and reeling desert birds in "The Second Coming" and as the breaking equestrian courses in "Nineteen Hundred and Nineteen." The movement is sublime because it sets in motion the circle of Coleridgean formalism and breaks it apart.

For Yeats this figure is emblematic of eternal recurrence, a concept he shares with Nietzsche but modifies to allow for temporal variation. One of the most important historical links between Yeats and the sublime is, in my view, Nietzsche's *ewige Wiederkehr*.[11] Nietzsche generally avoids the term *sublime*, or *das Erhabene*, but he does occasionally use it to describe tragedy, as when he says that the sublime "subjugates terror by means of art" (*Birth* 52; *Werke* 49). Further, I would like to suggest that his notion of eternal recurrence is a covert version of the mathematical sublime, though he would never admit such a debt to Kant. For both Nietzsche and Kant, the intuition arrives suddenly; it comes from the failure to constellate reality into higher and higher aggregates; it is an intuition not subject to empirical tests; and it is a revelation of the infinite that is at once empowering and terrifying. Nietzsche and Yeats both take much pride in their ability to reconcile themselves to eternal recurrence, as Yeats announces in "A Dialogue of Self and Soul":

> I am content to live it all again
> And yet again, if it be life to pitch
> into the frog-spawn of a blind man's ditch,
> A blind man battering blind men.... (236)

Here the poet imagines eternal recurrence in a personal rather than a historical sense and arrives at a view of it that approximates Freud's repetition compulsion, another modern version of the mathematical sublime. The poet wills his endless return to the blindness of inorganic matter. But this affirmation of the eternal, autochthonous return is also compensatory. The kinship between eternal recurrence and the sublime should help us see that even though both Yeats and Nietzsche think that their belief in recurrence indicates their release from the spirit of revenge, or ill will toward time, it is in fact an illusion that allows them to think that they have transcended time, that they can live an infinite number of lives, and that they have therefore escaped the threatening scythe of the father beyond all fathers.

Because the sublime may be viewed as the attempt to identify with the father and thus overcome the threat of death—or of what psychoanalysis considers its unconscious correlative, symbolic castration—Yeats's images of the sublime are perhaps apotropaic representations of this threat. Many of his sublime lyrics have latent images of decapitation or castration. Heads without any clear connection with their bodies frequently appear in these poems. "The Magi" have "ancient faces like rain-beaten stones," out of which their eyes stare fixedly (126). Such a Rocky Face reappears in "The Gyres," where it is a totemic reminder of the paternal law of necessity, and thus also an apotropaic emblem of the Medusan fate. This mask and the general theory of the mask in Yeats—the severance of being from self-identity—may be in part meditations of castration anxiety. At the end of "Nineteen Hundred and Nineteen," the head of Robert Artisson also looks petrified, "his great eyes without thought / Under the shadow of stupid straw-pale locks," and it "lurches past" with the automatic movement of the rough beast in "The Second Coming" (210). Both incubus and beast have the same blank gaze and nightmarish dissociation of head from body. The late plays *A Full Moon in March* and *The King of the Great Clock Tower* feature castrative beheadings as their principal symbolic action. In "The Second Coming," the "head of a man" is fixed onto a "lion body" (187). The fetishistic image encodes simultaneously the aggressive, repressed father and the castration that has threatened the son. In rhetorical terms, it is a violation of decorum, for it has much in common with the examples that Horace considers at the beginning of the *Ars poetica*:

> If a painter should decide to join the neck of a horse to a human head, and to lay many-colored feathers upon limbs taken from here or there, so that what is a comely woman above ended as a dark, grotesque fish below, could you, my friends, if you were allowed to see it, keep from laughing? (51)

The sublime breaks through decorum and the wholeness of the beautiful. It is a rough beast that, as the seer of "The Second Coming" puts it, "troubles my sight."

It may also trouble the ear. The rhythms, phonemic patterns, and rhetorical figures of the Yeatsian sublime produce the impression of formlessness breaking through form or, in Yeats's terms, of Transfiguration occurring paradoxically within an aesthetic of Incarnation (*Letters* 402). Although Yeats uses the word *sublime* sparingly, he borrows Castiglione's notion of *sprezzatura*, or "recklessness," a

pre-eighteenth-century category for the nonrational in art that anticipates the concept of the sublime (Monk, "Grace"). The very strictness
of Yeats's tightly controlled aural patterns makes rhythmic variations
seem all the more reckless. His few comments on the subject accord
with the Longinian doctrine that insistently repetitive rhythms can
make the auditor ecstatic. But the sublimity of this mathematical
pounding accelerates when, at the end of his later iambic lyrics in this
mode, Yeats suddenly obtrudes into the speech rhythm a polysyllabic
word that contains a dactylic cadence, breaking apart the predictable
sequence: *punishment, turbulence, uncontrollable, terrible, Bethlehem,
indifferent, darkening, monuments, unfashionable, glittering.* This intrusion of rhythmic change often coincides with the sudden heightening
of alliterative resonances, especially the voiced stops *b, g,* and *d*: "beauty
is born," "Bethlehem to be born," "glittering eyes, are gay," and so on.[12]
These dark sounds heighten the effect of boundless power and mystery
thudding into existence:

> . . . and stricken
> *By* the injustice of the skies for *punishment?*
> ("The Cold Heaven" 125)

> *Being* by *Calvary's turbulence unsatisfied,*
> The *uncontrollable mystery on* the *bestial* floor.
> ("The Magi" 126)

> Are changed, changed *utterly*:
> A *terrible* beauty is born.
> ("Easter, 1916" 182)

> And what rough *b*east, its hour come round at last,
> Slouches towards *Bethlehem* to be born?
> ("The Second Coming" 187)

> We are *b*lest by everything,
> Everything we look upon is *b*lest.
> ("A Dialogue of Self and Soul" 236)

> *B*efore the in*different* beak could let her drop?
> ("Leda and the Swan" 215)

Where the swan *d*rifts upon a *darkening* flood.
("Coole Park and Ballylee, 1931" 245)

That *day* brings round the night, that *b*efore *d*awn
His glory and his *monuments* are gone.
("Meru" 289)

. . . and all things run
On that un*fashionable* gyre again.
("The Gyres" 293)

Their eyes mid many wrinkles, their eyes,
Their ancient *glittering* eyes, are gay.
("Lapis Lazuli" 295)

The endings of these lyrics also exemplify the many rhetorical figures that Longinus associates with the sublime: the rhetorical question emphasizing the momentary quality of emotion arising from the occasion, asyndeton hindering the reading while pressing it onward, anaphora combining with asyndeton to force meaning to leap ahead, and so forth. As Longinus says of Demosthenes, "His order becomes disorderly, his disorder in turn acquires a certain order" (483; 480–89). These formal strategies combine to hurry the mind out of form, reaching toward what Yeats calls, echoing Shelley's epithet for the west wind, the "uncontrollable."[13] In the early Yeats, in contrast, the poetic quest for "disembodied beauty" falls short of the sublime, lacking the complementary impulse in the later Yeats to "create form" and work through it (*Letters* 402).

III. The Curse

Yeats's later lyrics sometimes carry recklessness to the violent extreme of the curse. Exaggerating certain features of the sublime, the curse can help us analyze further the psychic and rhetorical structure of the Yeatsian sublime. In their eagerness to assume the voice of the aggressive father, poems like "The Gyres" and "Under Ben Bulben" seem to will the destruction they contemplate. Indeed, virtually all the poems of tragic joy draw on the curse modally. They reveal the destructive urge, or death drive, at work in the poetics of the sublime. We should keep this broad affinity in mind as we look at more direct manifestations of the curse in Yeats's prose and poetry. Both Allen Grossman and Hugh Kenner discuss "The Fish" as an instance of the Irish genre of the curse, but the curse surfaces in many other lyrics, essays, and stories (Grossman 162; Kenner 108–10). The older Yeats entitles a treatise *On the Boiler* out of fondness for a mad ship's carpenter who would denounce his neighbors and the wicked times. In another late self-portrait, Yeats calls the "cursing" Oedipus his "new divinity." As early as the story "The Crucifixion of the Outcast," Yeats celebrates the curse. Mistreated at a monastery, a gleeman sets a tub upside down under his window and mounts it to "sing a bard's curse on the abbot" (*Mythologies* 150). Lest the gleeman teach the curse to children and robbers, the abbot decides to crucify him. For the monks, the curse typifies poetic speech because of the way it violently and unpredictably transforms reality. If left alive, the gleeman would curse whenever "the mood to curse would come upon him," his soul, path, and purpose as unfixed as the wind (*Mythologies* 151, 153). But while the curse is a spontaneous and direct speech act, it is also, as Geoffrey Hartman observes, one of the oldest kinds of formalized speech (130). However sudden and unpredictable the urge to curse, the speakers seem possessed by a language and passion beyond themselves, as in the other modes of the sublime.

Yeats's first full-fledged curse in rhyme appears in the story "Red Hanrahan's Curse." A young girl who must marry an old man asks Red Hanrahan for help because she understands the curse to be the poet's version of the *lex talionis*: "when it is people of this earth that have harmed you, it is yourself knows well the way to put harm on them again" (*Mythologies* 240). Models of tragic gaiety for the older Yeats, Oedipus and King Lear wish on those who have hurt them an equivalent pain of thanklessness or destruction. The young girl in Yeats's story inadvertently wounds Red Hanrahan by telling him he is old, so that his curse seems partly an attempt to recover from this subversion of his potency. Like the aging Lear and Oedipus, Hanrahan curses to regain and dramatize this masculine potency and aggressivity. Seeing an old and gap-winged eagle and noting that it resembles him, Hanrahan goes on to curse ceremoniously not only his old, oedipal fathers but also himself:

> The poet, Owen Hanrahan, under a bush of may,
> Calls down a curse on his own head because it withers grey;

Then on the speckled eagle-cock of Ballygawley Hill
Because it is the oldest thing that knows of cark and ill....
    (243)

He curses the age, impotence, and death associated with the father,
but in doing so, he also assumes the voice of the father, so that the
curse becomes a self-curse too. Here as in the other modes of the
sublime, the relation of poet to father is simultaneously one of identification and aggression. As he curses, the poet comes dangerously
close to turning himself into the force of death to avoid becoming its
victim. But Hanrahan's curse backfires: his presumption in adopting
the father's voice brings down on him the fatherly "Old Men," as well
as "Old Age and Time and Weariness and Sickness" (245). The curse
redounds on the curser.

"The Fascination of What's Difficult" may be Yeats's most
powerful absorption of the curse into lyric, and it is also a paean to
the sublime (93). Like Hanrahan and Lear, the speaker of this poem
begins his denunciation in a moment of impotence, the blockage or
proleptic death that sets the sublime in motion:

> The fascination of what's difficult
> Has dried the sap out of my veins, and rent
> Spontaneous joy and natural content
> Out of my heart.

Sprezzatura has been lost, but even as the poet begins to describe his
deadness, he starts to recover from it, for the trope of rending is itself
a sublime figure of dislocation. It transforms the destructive power of
difficulty into the figurative violence of the poem:

> There's something ails our colt
> That must, as if it had not holy blood
> Nor on Olympus leaped from cloud to cloud,
> Shiver under the lash, strain, sweat and jolt
> As though it dragged road metal.

Yeats pictures Pegasus, his imaginative power, as trapped under the
weight of form and the everyday.[14] But instead of remaining underneath
oppressive forces of constraint, the poet is suddenly "on" top of them:

> My curse on plays
> That have to be set up in fifty ways,
> On the day's war with every knave and dolt,
> Theatre business, management of men.

The very act of uttering the curse restores the poet's power. By willing destruction on others, the poet defines himself, restores his sovereignty, and transcends the anonymity of the everyday. But his curse, like the protagonist's in *Prometheus Unbound*, is also a self-curse, for it falls partly on his own work. Although it ritually enumerates its intended objects, it also seems spontaneous and sudden, an influx of power after blockage. This impression is heightened by the asyndetons and unparallel objects of the curse. The poem ends with a full restoration of the poet's strength:

> I swear before the dawn comes round again
> I'll find the stable and pull out the bolt.

Counter to the repetitive revolutions of the sun, the poet asserts his own unpredictable and violent energy of self-disclosure.

The curse is a spontaneous overflow of powerful feelings, but the feelings discharged belong to Thanatos rather than to Eros. In the section of "Meditations in Time of Civil War" entitled "My Descendants," the poet curses, in an extraordinary act of anticipatory vengeance, the home of his offspring if they should degenerate:

> May this laborious stair and this stark tower
> Become a roofless ruin that the owl
> May build in the cracked masonry and cry
> Her desolation to the desolate sky. (203)

The passage offers a sublime image of fragmentation, but it purchases its sublimity with a symbolic act of self-destruction, displaced metonymically onto the descendants' tower. Like Lear, the poet defines his own potency by willing the ruin of his kin, but he attacks them by way of the totemic tower—the very emblem of the poet and of the book of poems to which this curse belongs. The object of aggression is thus a figure for the self, much as the uncanny sky is for the owl that cries to it.[15] Another of Yeats's birds with an uncanny shadow self leaps into the sky in "Nineteen Hundred and Nineteen," prefiguring apocalyptic completion and stirring the poet to curse his own work:

> That image can bring wildness, bring a rage
> To end all things, to end
> What my laborious life imagined, even
> The half-imagined, the half-written page.... (209)

Writing is a veil between the poet and integration with the final form of reality—death. The act of cursing his own work assimilates the poet to the destructive "winds of winter," winds that erase the word and the world (209). Attempting to evade death, the poet identifies with it. The transcendental impulse of the sublime is ultimately apocalyptic and self-destructive—a rage not only against order but also against the self and language.

IV. PROPHECY, APOCALYPSE, AND THE POLITICS OF THE SUBLIME

Another modality of the sublime, prophecy has long been thought to be related to the curse, and it too can help us interpret tragic joy in Yeats.[16] Twice in *Richard III*, for example, Shakespeare tellingly misremembers Queen Margaret's earlier "prophecies" as "curses" (3.4.15–18, 5.1.25–27). James Kugel remarks in his analysis of Hebraic prophecy: "the prophet's speech had always been *powerful*, effective; it could be said of him what was said of the soothsayer Balaam ben Be'or, 'those whom you bless are blessed, and those whom you curse are cursed' (Num. 22:6)" (81). As speech acts that simultaneously announce and transform the shape of reality, prophecy and the curse unite the word with divine authority, the transcendental signifier. But whereas the curse more obviously alters world and word by disfiguring them, the central difficulty about prophetic utterance, and about Yeats's prophetic lyrics, is the relation between passive witness and active transformation. In the tropes of Shelley's "Defense of Poetry," a document that Yeats quotes extensively and approvingly, is the prophetic poet "mirror" or "legislator"? In the imagery of the sublime, is he the defeated son or the violent father? The rhetoric of prophecy inevitably draws on both strands of figure, hoping to turn the interpreter of reality into its creator, just as the sublime converts the passive victim into the heroic orator. "Lapis Lazuli" and "The Gyres" prophetically envision a brutal and violent world; but they attempt to alter the prophet's relation to vision, changing elegiac submission into active celebration. We should be careful about equating Yeats with one pole of prophecy or the other: insofar as his prophetic lyrics of tragic joy are sublime and not fanatical, they inhabit the psychic and rhetorical space of both witness and legislator. The poetic activity of these poems is "the shooting of the gulf"—as Emerson defines "power"—between spectatorship and creation, which are both essential to prophecy (271). Without the defeated son there can be no father; without the witness, no legislator; and without the elegist, no Rocky Face.

Kant warns, however, that the sublime may become fanaticism if one goes "mad with reason" or, in the terms of Freud's *Group Psychology and the Analysis of the Ego*, if one allows the heroic father or politician to replace the superego (Kant 116). We have already seen that Yeats's lyric transformations of the curse approach such an extreme. Other late lyrics come dangerously close to celebrating the fanaticism of complete identification with the father and destructiveness, such as the canceled "Three Marching Songs." The apocalyptic impulse in Yeats sometimes approaches this extreme as well; it shares the alchemist's "consuming thirst for destruction" of the world and the "half-written page," the longing for a complete integration of self with "the desolation of reality" (*Mythologies* 269–70; *Poems* 289).

Another group of Yeats's visionary lyrics strays from the authentic dynamic of the sublime. If we think of apocalypse not as conflagration but as the disclosure and totalization of reality, Yeats writes many lyrics that assume an apocalyptic perspective toward history—the panoramic or god's eye view that Whitaker contrasts with the dramatic in Yeats's writing. Poems like "The Valley of the Black Pig" and "Two Songs from a Play" are in a mode of prophecy that so distances itself from the drama of history that it loses any sense of contingency and vulnerability—historical qualities allied with the sublime as against the aesthetic necessity of the beautiful. These poems illustrate what we might call Yeats's prophetic binarism, for they arrange history according to binary oppositions, much like the mythic mind in Lévi-Strauss ("Structural Study" 177–81). In the extraordinary early note to "The Valley of the Black Pig," Yeats sets up a series of paradigmatic opposites—light/dark, winter/summer, sterility/fruitfulness—a dualistic tendency reflected too in the poem's neat division into four lines of violence and four of recovery and prayer. The poem's reduction of the apocalyptic battle to "unknown" sounds heard at a distance suggests that the prophetic binarism has allowed the poet to control and miniaturize the violent scene all too well, helping him adopt the invulnerable perspective of the destructive "Master": "the clash of fallen horsemen and the cries / Of unknown perishing armies beat about my ears" (65). "Two Songs from a Play" also defeats the sublime terror of violent upheaval by condensing history into antithetical pairs: Virgo/Spica, Athena/Dionysus, Mary/Christ.[17] The prophetic binarism of these poems, like that of *A Vision*, muzzles the sublime, and one must ask whether such a poetics of miniaturization sometimes inures the poet to the ruptures of history. A similar tendency away from the sublime can be seen in the synchronistic aesthetic of Yeats's modernist contemporaries Eliot and Pound. Insofar as *A Vision* emphasizes violent upheavals, abrupt confluences of deity and man, dizzying rotations between eternally recurring antinomies, it is a sublime vision of history. But insofar as this work, like some of the prophetic lyrics, compresses history into the controlled binary patterns of a miniature, it may finally fit more properly into an aesthetic of the beautiful.[18]

What is the political form of the sublime in Yeats? As we have seen, the psychological structure of the sublime can lead to identification with the violent father and, ultimately, with the death drive; hence, it helps to explain the attraction that authoritarianism and eugenics held for the older Yeats. Even though the kinship between Yeats's later politics and the psycholinguistic structure of his sublime remains unremarked, Yeats's brief "flirtation" with the extreme right continues to generate a great deal of scholarship, supplementing the major statements by Elizabeth Cullingford and Conor Cruise O'Brien. But we may still have the lingering suspicion that Yeats's abhorrent authoritarian views are not the sole political potentiality of the Yeatsian sublime or of the sublime in general. Stephen Spender claims that Yeats's apocalyptic poems, such as "The Second Coming," were an important source of inspiration for the "intellectual Left" of his own generation (Spender 5–6, 13). How is that possible? Maybe we should look at the literary precedents of the Yeatsian sublime to find out more about its political parameters, asking whether its violence is part of a larger poetic impulse to use a violence within to counteract the violence without. If so, then much of what we condemn in these lyrics would logically entail a condemnation of the sublime as a whole. As pacifists we may well choose to reject the sublime altogether, but can we legitimately reject Yeats's sublime because of its violence, as Bloom does, and still praise the violence of earlier versions? To get at these questions, we might consider first the precedents for Yeats's disturbing exultation in war.[19] Many of Longinus's examples of the sublime describe combat or bloodshed, and Kant argues not only that we venerate the soldier because "his mind is unsubdued by danger" but also that "[w]ar itself . . . has something sublime in it" (102). Perhaps in this context the praise of war and the warrior in "Under Ben Bulben" is less astonishing, though for many (as for me) no less deplorable:

> You that Mitchel's prayer have heard,
> "Send war in our time, O Lord!"
> Know that when all words are said
> And a man is fighting mad,
> Something drops from eyes long blind,
> He completes his partial mind,
> For an instant stands at ease,
> Laughs aloud, his heart at peace. . . . (326)

The sublime is inextricable from the death drive, the hero's "partial mind" resembling the "half-written page" of "Nineteen Hundred and Nineteen"; both must be destroyed in the search for apocalyptic wholeness, a reunion, in Freud's reduction of the sublime, with inorganic matter (*Pleasure Principle* 36–39). If the mind is always partial because it is never complete until extinguished, and if writing is always half-written because it never absorbs what it signifies, then Yeats's apocalyptic sublime aggressively attempts to overcome the structure of deferral and desire inherent in every scene of thinking and writing (see Derrida 87).

Shelley and Blake in verse, no less than Longinus and Kant in prose, reveal the inevitable connection between the sublime and violence. In *Prometheus Unbound*, Shelley tries to transcend the attraction of poetic violence by decontextualizing the sublime curse and making it an echo, but the force of the work's Lear-like rhetoric arises in the first act from Prometheus's willing "endurance" of violence; similarly the Witch of Atlas, whom Yeats invokes at the beginning of "Under Ben Bulben," observes strife and suffering, yet "little did the sight disturb her soul ..." (Shelley, "The Witch of Atlas" 63.545).[20] In the prophetic poem *America*, Blake celebrates Orc's "fiery joy" in destruction (plate 8, line 3). And though we may regret that the Rocky Face knows only the word *Rejoice*, this word echoes throughout the end of *The Four Zoas* in response to total destruction. If we recall the "irrational streams of blood" in "The Gyres" that have un–nerved critics, and compare them with the streams of blood in "Night the Ninth," it seems hard to share Bloom's view of Yeats's tragic joy as uniquely "inhumane" (*Yeats* 434–39):

> Into the wine presses of Luvah howling fell the Clusters
> Of human families thro the deep, the wine presses were filld
> The blood of life flowd plentiful....

The poem appropriates the power of the scene's violence, sharing the apocalyptic joy of Luvah's sons and daughters, not the merely human dismay:

> How red the sons & daughters of Luvah how they tread the
>   Grapes
> Laughing and shouting drunk with odors many fall oerwearied
> . . . .
> But in the Wine Presses the Human Grapes Sing not nor dance
> They howl & writhe in shoals of torment in fierce flames
>   consuming ...
> . . . .
> The cruel joy of Luvahs daughters lacerating with knives
> And whip[s] their Victims & deadly sports of Luvahs sons
> (*Four Zoas* 135, lines 36–39; 136, lines 16–17, 21–27)

These "Victims" are sacrifices to the sublime, their pain essential to the joy assumed by the sons and daughters of Luvah and by the poem itself. In all versions of the sublime, not just Yeats's, the moment of gaiety presupposes the pain or death from which it rises.

Some recent works on literary apocalypses and prophecies assert that these sublime modes are inherently consistent with politically radical revolution (see, e.g., Hoagwood 57). Derrida remarks, "Nothing is less conservative than the apocalyptic genre" (89). Others, such as Gary Shapiro, have argued that the sublime has strong affinities with fascism (216). No doubt the political form of the sublime's tendency toward fanaticism is authoritarianism. No doubt, too, the sublime as a vision of history privileges violent ruptures of the sort we associate with revolution, despite Burke's contradictory dislike for the French Revolution. The sublime, in other words, is neither "left" nor "right," though it can be appropriated by either political rhetoric. The "Beautiful Necessity" Emerson praises at the end of the essay "Fate" and the similar "Power" Shelley invokes in "Mont Blanc" might be used for either fascist celebrations of force or radical visions of a force that can "repeal / Large codes of fraud and woe" (Emerson 967–68; Shelley, "Mont Blanc," lines 16, 80–81). The sublime does not easily accommodate centrist and pacifist politics, but it does not therefore belong to fascism.[21] Yeats's lyrics of tragic joy turn the sublime in a reactionary direction: in "The Gyres" the speaker celebrates destruction because it ushers in a feudal political order, and in "My Descendants" he curses the home of his children if they should marry into a lower class. But these political views have no exclusive relation to the Yeatsian sublime or to the sublime generally, any more than the Heideggerian sublime is intrinsically fascistic—even though fascism, partly by adopting the Romantic sublime for its own purposes, proved attractive to both Yeats and Heidegger. Because the sublime can rouse us from the blind and timid politics of the everyday and grant us the "courage," as Kant calls it, to face our own deaths with anticipatory resoluteness (Heidegger's *Entschlossenheit*), it is potentially an instrument of radicalism, even in Yeats.

Two plays illustrate how the Yeatsian sublime admits of a wider political appropriation than most critics have understood and how Spender's generation could therefore read the poems against the grain of Yeats's own authoritarian views. In *The King's Threshold*, Yeats explores the subversive potential of tragic joy. Having deprived the poet Seanchan of his traditional rights, the king compares his own institutional bonds to the anarchic sublimity of verse:

> But I that sit a throne,
> And take my measure from the needs of the State,
> Call his wild thought that overruns the measure,
> Making words more than deeds, and his proud will
> That would unsettle all, most mischievous,
> And he himself a most mischievous man.
>
> (*Variorum* 261–62)

Seanchan's poetic thought is measureless, breaking through all form, and thus dangerous to the hierarchies of state. His laughter is an energy that defies all boundaries, even the final boundary of death. He declares in his final taunt: "King! King! Dead faces laugh" (310). In the play Yeats also links the sublime to a repugnant racial theory of mastery by the "white-bodied" (310), but, again, it has no inherent and exclusive connection with such views. In *The Unicorn from the Stars*, the peasants interpret Martin's sublime vision of the apocalypse as a prophetic call for revolution and for the destruction of their oppressors—the English Law and enslaving Church (*Variorum* 684–85). The play turns against such an interpretation of the apocalypse, Martin thinking in the end that the destruction must be ethical and internal. Theorists now commonly distinguish between the conservatism of the internal apocalypse (associated with Augustine) and the revolutionary orientation of the external apocalypse (associated with Luther).[22] But in this play, Yeats shows that the tropes for the outer and inner apocalypse, as for the natural and psychological sublime, are easily translated into each other. If we regard death as the occasion of the sublime, the movement from inner to outer becomes intelligible, since death is neither one nor the other. And perhaps we should be more aware that Yeats's play conceives of radical action as a potential articulation of the sublime, if not the one it prefers. On the basis of such revisionary readings, Spender could go so far as to claim that the communist "apocalyptic vision" was compatible with Yeats's (13). Even though he and other poets of the thirties would ultimately reject Yeats's apocalypses, and even though Yeats will never be a hero of the left, the Yeatsian sublime may still be susceptible to the kind of transvaluation that Auden describes in his elegy for Yeats: "the words of a dead man / Are modified in the guts of the living" (197).[23]

NOTES

1. Harold Bloom alone invokes the sublime to interpret Yeats. But he restricts himself to the sublime of influence and, even while celebrating the transcendence of the human in earlier Romantics, condemns as inhumane the lyrics that seem to me to manifest the Yeatsian sublime. Compare his response to what he calls Yeats's "[in]humane nonsense" (*Yeats* 438) with his praise for Thomas Weiskel's assertion: "the essential claim of

the sublime is that man can, in feeling and in speech, transcend the human. . . . A humanistic sublime is an oxymoron" (Bloom, Foreword vii; Weiskel 3). In a later essay on Yeats, Bloom revises his negative view of the Yeatsian sublime but refers dismissively to the position I elaborate here: that the "daemonic or Sublime is thus merely another evasion of the unacceptable necessity of dying" (*Poetry* 209). Yeats's relationship with Blake and Shelley is the primary subject of Adams's *Blake and Yeats*, Bornstein's *Yeats and Shelley*, and Bloom's *Yeats*.

2. Much work has been done to synthesize the sublime, ranging from Monk's classic, *The Sublime*, to Weiskel 3–33. For the similarities between Longinus and Edmund Burke on the sublime, see Fry, *Reach* 60–61. In this essay I draw on Fry's discussion, which assimilates Kant's mathematical and dynamical sublime to Longinus's version; on Weiskel's synthesis; and on Hertz's interreading of Longinus, Burke, Kant, and Freud ("Notion").

3. Kenneth Burke's "thesaurus" of the necessary "deflections" of death differs from mine (cf. Burke 369). Nothing itself, death exemplifies and exaggerates the hidden metonymical structure of the sublime, and indeed of all naming, because death must inevitably undergo translation. A literal-minded reading of Yeats's myth of the afterlife would, of course, annul the importance of death in any of these forms, but it would also be incapable of explaining his lyrics' more ambivalent representation of death as an occasion for courage.

4. On the oedipal or preoedipal nature of the sublime, see Hertz, "Reading," and Weiskel 191–106. For my analysis of the interrelation between oedipal identification and aggression, I also borrow from Lacan (*Speech* 79; *Ecrits* 8–29).

5. Guerlac's version of Longinus sometimes approaches such a view, though her analysis is generally insightful. With the help of the later Heidegger, Guerlac argues against the affective theory of the sublime because "feeling" obscures the threat of the rhetorical sublime to the subject's self-identity. But Heidegger's analysis of the intersubjective basis of *Stimmung* 'mood,' and especially of *Mitbefindlichkeit* 'co-state-of-mind,' preserves the affective sublime without endorsing an ideological concept of the self.

6. Whitaker describes these two moments in the early apocalyptic romances as the psychic annihilation of "Rosa Alchemica" and the complementary inflation of "The Tables of the Law," the self-negating Christ and the self-asserting Lucifer (44).

7. As Brenda Webster argues of Yeats's bird and sword, the concentrated image may be thought of as a "talismanic object," a "defense against fears of nothingness and loss of individuality" (207). It may also be likened to Hertz's moment of "figurative reconstitution" in the sublime after the moment of "disintegration" ("Reading" 14).

8. Hillis Miller reads the figurative movement of "Nineteen Hundred and Nineteen" as a violent revolving without center (347).

9. Weiskel uses the phrase *on and on* to describe the mathematical sublime (22).

10. For an elaboration of Yeats's central aesthetic tenets on the basis of this passage, see Vendler 28.

11. See *Essays* 288. On eternal recurrence, or *ewige Wiederkehr*, in Yeats and Nietzsche, see Bohlmann 57–68. For another general discussion of Yeats's debt to Nietzsche, see Oppel.

12. Although the older Yeats was fond of such words and such sounds in general, they converge in a numerically higher quantity at the ends of his later sublime lyrics than they do elsewhere. They both intensify and surpass the general stylistic freedom of his verse in this period. The characteristic variations in meter—as in stanza and rhyme—have been amply described by critics from Gross (48–55) to Parkinson (182–91) and Dougherty and need not be rehearsed here.

13. Shelley addresses the wind with the apostrophe "O Uncontrollable!" in the "Ode to the West Wind," line 47.

14. Remaking himself, Yeats simultaneously converts two anti-sublime poets into precursors of his sublimity. In "An Essay on Criticism," Pope grudgingly allows for the waywardness of Pegasus and then suggests that there is a semisublimity or "*Grace beyond the Reach of Art*" (lines 150–55). Further, Yeats's verbal pileup echoes Ben Jonson's satiric "Ode to Himself": "Run on, and rage, sweat, censure, and condemn ... though thy nerves be shrunk, and blood be cold ... thy strain ..." (lines 9–10, 45, 49).

15. On the relation of uncanny doubling to the sublime, see Fry, "Possession" 196–201.

16. On Yeats and prophecy, see Stallworthy. Whitaker offers the best analysis of the apocalypse in Yeats, emphasizing its internal and alchemical nature (34–54).

17. For a discussion of the pairs in "Two Songs from a Play," see Ellmann 260–63; on miniaturization and binarism, see Lévi-Strauss, *The Savage Mind* 16–33.

18. White uses the regulative aesthetic categories of the sublime and the beautiful to analyze the discipline of history (125–37).

19. For an overview of Yeats's thought on war, see Farag. For Bloom's position on Yeats's violence, see, for example, the readings of "The Second Coming," "Lapis Lazuli," and "The Gyres" in *Yeats*.

20. Yeats suppresses this side of Shelley when he derides him for being "terrified of the Last Day like a Victorian child" (*Essays* 420).

21. I do not wish, however, to exaggerate the political flexibility of the sublime. The sexual politics of the sublime has traditionally been antifeminist, and we still need a full feminist review of the sublime as the violent agon of father and son or as a masculine war with danger. For these reasons, as well as for pacifist concerns, we may ultimately decide to reject the sublime altogether, as long as we do so consistently. But, in my view, we might also attempt to construct a version of the sublime that would be compatible with certain forms of revolutionary feminism.

22. See Lewis 184–235. Douglas Robinson criticizes Lewis's distinction but goes on to argue that the Augustinian, spiritual view is "suited to political conservatives" as against "implicitly revolutionary predictive interpretations"—an assertion that would seem to be contradicted by recent fundamentalism in the United States. See Robinson's helpful introductory analysis (17).

23. My thanks go to Richard Finneran, Paul Fry, Thomas Whitaker, and George Wright for their valuable comments on earlier drafts of this essay.

Works Cited

Adams, Hazard. *Blake and Yeats: The Contrary Vision*. 1955. New York: Russell, 1968.

Auden, W. H. *Collected Poems*. Ed. Edward Mendelson. New York: Random, 1976.

Blake, William. *The Complete Poetry and Prose of William Blake*. Ed. David V. Erdman. Rev. ed. New York: Anchor-Doubleday, 1982.

Bloom, Harold. Foreword. Weiskel vii–x.

———. *Poetry and Repression: Revisionism from Blake to Stevens*. New Haven: Yale UP, 1976.

———. *Yeats*. New York: Oxford UP, 1970.

Bohlmann, Otto. *Yeats and Nietzsche*. London: Macmillan, 1982.

Bornstein, George. *Transformations of Romanticism in Yeats, Eliot, and Stevens*. Chicago: U of Chicago P, 1976.

———. *Yeats and Shelley*. Chicago: U of Chicago P, 1970.

Burke, Edmund. *A Philosophical Inquiry into the Origin of Our Ideas of the Sublime and the Beautiful*. Ed. James T. Boulton. London: Routledge, 1958.

Burke, Kenneth. "Thanatopsis for Critics: A Brief Thesaurus of Deaths and Dyings." *Essays in Criticism* 2 (1952): 369–75.

Castiglione, Baldassare. *The Book of the Courtier*. Trans. Thomas Hoby. 1561. London: Dent, 1975.

Cullingford, Elizabeth. *Yeats, Ireland and Fascism*. New York: New York UP, 1981.

Derrida, Jacques. "Of an Apocalyptic Tone Recently Adopted in Philosophy." Trans. John P. Leavey, Jr. *Semeia* 23 (1982): 63–97.

Dougherty, Adelyn. *A Study of Rhythmic Structure in the Verse of William Butler Yeats*. The Hague: Mouton, 1973.

Ellmann, Richard. *The Identity of Yeats*. 2nd ed. New York: Oxford UP, 1964.

Emerson, Ralph Waldo. *Essays and Lectures*. New York: Library of America, 1983.

Engelberg, Edward. *The Vast Design: Patterns in W. B. Yeats's Aesthetic*. Toronto: U of Toronto P, 1963.

Farag, Fahmy. "Needless Horror or Terrible Beauty: Yeats's Ideas of Hatred, War, and Violence." *The Opposing Virtues*. Dublin: Dolmen, 1978. 7–19.

Fletcher, Angus. *Allegory: The Theory of a Symbolic Mode*. Ithaca: Cornell UP, 1964.

Fowler, Alastair. *Kinds of Literature: An Introduction to the Theory of Genres and Modes*. Cambridge: Harvard UP, 1982.

Freud, Sigmund. *Beyond the Pleasure Principle: Standard Edition* 18: 3–64.

———. *Group Psychology and the Analysis of the Ego. Standard Edition* 18: 65–143.

———. "Mourning and Melancholia." *Standard Edition* 14: 243–58.

———. *The Standard Edition of the Complete Psychological Works of Sigmund Freud*. 24 vols. Ed. James Strachey. London: Hogarth, 1953–74.

Fry, Paul H. "The Possession of the Sublime." *Studies in Romanticism* 26 (1987): 187–207.

———. *The Reach of Criticism*. New Haven: Yale UP, 1983.

Gross, Harvey. *Sound and Form in Modern Poetry: A Study of Prosody from Thomas Hardy to Robert Lowell*. Ann Arbor: U of Michigan P, 1964.

Grossman, Allen. *Poetic Knowledge in the Early Yeats: A Study of The Wind among the Reeds*. Charlottesville: UP of Virginia, 1969.

Guerlac, Suzanne. "Longinus and the Subject of the Sublime." *New Literary History* 16 (1985): 275–89.

Hartman, Geoffrey. *Saving the Text: Literature/Derrida/Philosophy*. Baltimore: Johns Hopkins UP, 1981.

Heidegger, Martin. *Being and Time*. Trans. John Macquarrie and Edward Robinson. Oxford: Blackwell, 1980.

Hertz, Neil. "The Notion of Blockage in the Literature of the Sublime." *Psychoanalysis and the Question of the Text*. Ed. Geoffrey Hartman. Baltimore: Johns Hopkins UP, 1978. 62–85.

———. "A Reading of Longinus." *The End of the Line: Essays on Psychoanalysis and the Sublime*. New York: Columbia UP, 1985. 1–20.

Hoagwood, Terence Allan. *Prophecy and the Philosophy of Mind: Traditions of Blake and Shelley*. University: U of Alabama P, 1985.

Horace. "The Art of Poetry." Trans. Walter Jackson Bate. *Criticism.: The Major Texts*. Ed. Bate. 2nd ed. New York: Harcourt, 1970. 51–58.

Jonson, Ben. *Ben Jonson: The Complete Poems*. Ed. George Parfitt. 1975. New Haven: Yale UP, 1982.

Kant, Emmanuel. *Critique of Judgment*. Trans. J. H. Bernard. London: Hafner-Macmillan, 1951.

Kenner, Hugh. *A Colder Eye*. New York: Penguin, 1983.

Kugel, James L. "Two Introductions to Midrash." *Midrash and Literature*. Ed. Geoffrey Hartman and Sanford Budick. New Haven: Yale UP, 1986. 77–103.

Lacan, Jacques. *Ecrits*. Trans. Alan Sheridan. New York: Norton, 1977.

———. *Speech and Language in Psychoanalysis*. Trans. Anthony Wilden. Baltimore: Johns Hopkins UP, 1968.

Lévi-Strauss, Claude. *The Savage Mind*. Trans. George Weidenfeld and Nicolson Ltd. London: Weidenfeld, 1966.

———. "The Structural Study of Myth." *The Structuralists: From Marx to Lévi-Strauss*. Ed. Richard DeGeorge and Fernande DeGeorge. New York: Anchor-Doubleday, 1970. 169–94.

Lewis, R. W. B. "Days of Wrath and Laughter." *Trials of the Word*. New Haven: Yale UP, 1965. 184–235.

Longinus. *On Sublimity.* Trans. D. A. Russell. *Ancient Literary Criticism: The Principal Texts in New Translations.* Ed. D. A. Russell and M. Winterbottom. Oxford: Clarendon, 1972. 460–503.

Miller, J. Hillis. *The Linguistic Moment.* Princeton: Princeton UP, 1985.

Modiano, Raimonda. "Humanism and the Comic Sublime: From Kant to Friedrich Theodor Vischer." *Studies in Romanticism* 26 (1987): 231–44.

Monk, Samuel Holt. "A Grace beyond the Reach of Art." *Journal of the History of Ideas* 5.2 (1944): 131–50.

———. *The Sublime: A Study of Critical Theories in Eighteenth-Century England.* 1935. Ann Arbor: U of Michigan P, 1960.

Murdoch, Iris. "The Sublime and the Beautiful Revisited." *Yale Review* 49 (1959–60): 247–71.

Nietzsche, Friedrich. *The Birth of Tragedy and The Genealogy of Morals.* Trans. Francis Golffing. New York: Anchor-Doubleday, 1956.

———. *Werke.* Ed. Karl Schlechta. Vol. 1. München: Hanser, 1954. 3 vols.

O'Brien, Conor Cruise. "Passion and Cunning: An Essay on the Politics of W. B. Yeats." *In Excited Reverie.* Ed. A. Norman Jeffares and K. G. W. Cross. New York: Macmillan, 1965. 207–78.

Oppel, Frances Nesbitt. *Mask and Tragedy: Yeats and Nietzsche, 1902–10.* Charlottesville: UP of Virginia, 1987.

Parkinson, Thomas. *W. B. Yeats: The Later Poetry.* Berkeley: U of California P, 1964.

Patrides, C. A. "'Gaiety Transfiguring All That Dread': The Case of Yeats." *Yeats* 5 (1987): 117–32.

Pope, Alexander. *The Poems of Alexander Pope.* Ed. John Butt. London: Methuen, 1963.

Reid, B. L. *William Butler Yeats: The Lyric of Tragedy.* Norman: U of Oklahoma P, 1961.

Robinson, Douglas. *American Apocalypses: The Image of the End of the World in American Literature.* Baltimore: Johns Hopkins UP, 1985.

Sacks, Peter. *The English Elegy: Studies in the Genre from Spenser to Yeats.* Baltimore: Johns Hopkins UP, 1985.

Schiller, Friedrich von. *Two Essays by Friedrich von Schiller: Naive and Sentimental Poetry and On the Sublime.* Trans. Julius A. Elias. New York: Ungar, 1966.

Schopenhauer, Arthur. *The World as Will and Representation.* Trans. E. F. J. Payne. 2 vols. New York: Dover, 1969.

Shapiro, Gary. "From the Sublime to the Political: Some Historical Notes." *New Literary History* 16 (1985): 213–35.

Shelley, Percy Bysshe. *Shelley's Poetry and Prose*. Ed. Donald H. Reiman and Sharon B. Powers. New York: Norton, 1977.

Spender, Stephen. *The Thirties and After: Poetry, Politics, People, 1933–1970*. New York: Random, 1978.

Stallworthy, Jon. "The Prophetic Voice." *Vision and Revision in Yeats's* Last Poems. Oxford: Oxford UP, 1969. 20–38.

Vendler, Helen. *Yeats's Vision and the Later Plays*. Cambridge: Harvard UP, 1963.

Webster, Brenda S. *Yeats: A Psychoanalytic Study*. Stanford: Stanford UP, 1973.

Weiskel, Thomas. *The Romantic Sublime*. 1976. Baltimore: Johns Hopkins UP, 1986.

Whitaker, Thomas. *Swan and Shadow: Yeats's Dialogue with History*. Chapel Hill: U of North Carolina P, 1964.

White, Hayden. "The Politics of Historical Interpretation: Discipline and De-sublimation." *Critical Inquiry* 9 (1982): 113–37.

Wordsworth, William. *The Prelude*: 1799, 1805, 1850. Ed. Jonathan Wordsworth, M. H. Abrams, and Stephen Gill. New York: Norton, 1979.

Yeats, William Butler. *The Autobiography of William Butler Yeats*. 1935. New York: Macmillan, 1965.

———. *Essays and Introductions*. London: Macmillan, 1961.

———. *The Letters of W. B. Yeats*. Ed. Alan Wade. London: Hart-Davis, 1954.

———. *Mythologies*. New York: Macmillan, 1959.

———. *The Poems of W. B. Yeats, a New Edition*. Ed. Richard J. Finneran. New York: Macmillan, 1983.

———. *The Variorum Edition of the Plays of W. B. Yeats*. Ed. Russell K. Alspach. New York: Macmillan, 1965.

———. *A Vision*. 1937. London: Macmillan, 1962.

❧ *Acknowledgments* ❧

Albrecht, W.P. "The Tragic Sublime of Hazlitt and Keats." *Studies in Romanticism* 20.2 (Summer 1981): 185–201. © 1981 by Boston University. Reprinted by permission.

Coleridge, Samuel Taylor. "Lecture X: Milton." *The Literary Remains of Samuel Taylor Coleridge* Vol. 1. Ed. Henry Nelson Coleridge. London: William Pickering, 1836. 166–178.

Dowden, Edward. "*Othello; MacBeth; Lear*" *Shakspere: A Critical Study of His Mind and Art.* New York: Harper Brothers, 1881.

Freeman, Barbara Claire. "*The Awakening*: Waking Up at the End of the Line." *The Feminine Sublime: Gender and Excess in Women's Fiction.* Berkeley, CA: U of California P, 1995. 13–39. © 1995 by The Regents of the University of California. Reprinted by permission.

Hart, Henry. "Robert Lowell, Emerson, and the American Sublime." *ESQ: A Journal of the American Renaissance* 39.4 (1993): 279–307. © 1993 by Washington State University. Reprinted by permission.

Longinus. Chapters 8–10. *On the Sublime; the Greek text edited after the Paris manuscript.* Ed. and trans. W. Rhys Roberts. Cambridge: Cambridge UP, 1899. 57–75.

MacWilliams, David C. "'Hurrying into the Shrubbery': The Sublime, Transcendence, and the Garden Scene in *Emma*." *Persuasions: The Jane Austen Journal*, Vol. 23 (2001): 133–138. © 2001 by *Persuasions*. Reprinted by permission.

Ramazani, R. Jahan. "Yeats: Tragic Joy and the Sublime." *PMLA* 104.2 (March 1989): 163–177. © 1989 by The Modern Language Association of America. Reprinted by permission.

Sherwin, Paul. '*Frankenstein*: Creation as Catastrophe.' *PMLA* 96.5 (October 1981): 883–903. © 1989 by The Modern Language Association of America. Reprinted by permission.

Wlecke, Albert O. "A Poem About Interiors." *Wordsworth and the Sublime.* Berkeley: University of California Press, 1973. 20–46. © 1973 by The Regents of the University of California. Reprinted by permission.

Index